Mutual Funds
M a g a z i n e

Billion Dollar Funds

The Investor's Guide To America's Most Successful Mutual Funds

Plus... All-Star Ratings For Over 2,000 Funds

Norman G. Fosback, Editor in Chief

BILLION DOLLAR FUNDS
1994

The author is Editor in Chief of
Mutual Funds Magazine

The author is also Editor of

Mutual Fund Forecaster
Mutual Fund Plus
Market Logic
Fund Watch
New Issues
The Insiders
Investor's Digest
Stock Market Weekly
Mutual Fund Weekly
Income Fund Outlook
The Professional Investor
Mutual Fund Buyer's Guide

Mutual Funds Magazine and these
advisory services are published by:
The Institute for Econometric Research
3471 N. Federal, Fort Lauderdale, FL 33306
800-442-9000

Mutual Funds
Magazine

Billion Dollar Funds

The Investor's Guide To America's Most Successful Mutual Funds

Plus... All-Star Ratings For Over 2,000 Funds

Norman G. Fosback, Editor in Chief

BILLION DOLLAR FUNDS – 1994 Edition

International Standard Book Number: 0-917604-47-4

Contents

Inside the
Billion Dollar Funds

We have created this volume especially for subscribers to *Mutual Funds Magazine.* We hope and trust it will prove to be a valuable and handy reference to America's most successful mutual funds. The funds featured here are the most widely-owned in America, and account for a large proportion of all the assets of all stock and bond mutual funds. In most cases, their popularity is a product of performance. Mutual fund investors are a nimble lot – when they see good performance, they go after it.

The Billion Dollar Funds have a significant performance advantage over their smaller brethren. Through economies of scale, their overall expense burden is much less than average. During the last 70 years, for example, common stocks have returned about 10% per annum. The average mutual fund has returned somewhat less than this because of their day-to-day managerial and operating expenses. The average stock fund has an annual expense ratio of 1½%, which is equal to fully 15% of the normal gross annual return, and directly reduces portfolio profits by that amount. The average expense ratio of the Billion Dollar Funds is only 1%. That gives these funds a performance advantage even before their portfolio managers start picking securities.

In Part II of this book, we present our All-Star Ratings for more than 2,000 funds. Each fund with at least two years of price history is awarded from one to five stars based upon their performance, adjusted for risk. The risk adjustment is important. It means that a fund with a relatively low total return can still deservedly achieve a large number of stars if its price volatility and risk of loss is also well below average. Ultimately, *risk-adjusted performance* is what every investor should monitor.

Here is a description of a few of the terms you will find featured in each Billion

Dollar Fund profile:

All-Star Ratings are based on funds' risk-adjusted relative returns over the last ten years, or such shorter periods (subject to a two-year minimum) for which they have been in existence, with the most recent years assigned the most weight. The top quintile of funds receive five stars; the next quintile receive four stars; the next, three stars; the next, two stars; and the lowest, one star. The relative performances of load funds include three-year amortizations of their sales and redemption charges, with closed-end funds assigned commission-equivalent loads of 2% to buy and 2% to sell.

Telephone Switching frequency limits and charges indicate the usefulness of a fund for frequent trading. Switching privileges may be subject to minimum share or dollar amounts, and in some cases may also incur sales and redemption fees.

Safety Ratings range from "0" (the least safe, most volatile funds) to "10" (the funds whose prices are most stable from week to week). They are based on the volatility of weekly total returns of each fund (with at least one year of price history) over the past five years, and on any demonstrated inferior performance. The Safety Ratings permit direct comparisons of the safety of dissimilar types of funds.

Up Market and Down Market Rankings range from "A" (best performance), to "E" (worst). Stock funds are graded according to their performance during all swings of 10% or more by the Standard & Poor's 500 Index since 1980. Bond funds are graded on their performance in all up and down swings of 5% or more in the Lehman Bros. Long Treasury Bond Index. Every fund is graded relative to the performance of all other funds in its category that have been in existence as long or longer. A fund must experience at least two up-market swings to receive an Up Market Ranking and at least two down-market swings to receive a Down Market Ranking.

Sales Loads are maximums, and are usually discounted for large investments, generally over $25,000. **Redemption Fees** are reduced by some funds on investments held for an extended period. **Distribution Fees** are maximum allowable annual charges, usually under "Rule 12b-1" plans and account service agreements. **Annual Expense Ratios** include management fees, distribution fees, and all operating costs except brokerage fees, margin-related interest expense, and annual account maintenance fees. Annual expense ratios below 0.5% are considered low, and ratios above 1.5% are high.

Average Portfolio Maturity is the average time to maturity of securities in a bond fund's portfolio.

Yield represents the current 30-day standardized yield as defined by the SEC for bond funds.

Correlations show the relationships between each stock fund with the S&P 500 Index and each bond fund with the Lehman Bros. Long Treasury Bond Index. A fund whose weekly total returns are perfectly correlated with an index has a correlation of 100%. If its weekly fluctuations are completely independent of the index, its correlation is 0%. If a fund tends to move in the opposite direction of the index, its correlation is negative.

Portfolio descriptions for each fund show the composition and other qualities of their investment portfolio. For example, for each equity fund we have computed the average price/earnings ratio (P/E ratio) of all of the stocks in its portfolio, with each stock weighted by its total dollar value in the fund. Similarly, the average price/book value ratio, average five-year earnings growth, and median market capitalization of each stock in the portfolio are also shown.

Market volatility (betas) indicates how much a portfolio fluctuates relative to the Standard & Poor's 500 Index. A volatility of 1.00 means the fund tends to move up and down in quite close relationship to the Index. Market volatility above 1.00 indicates the fund rises and falls faster than the S&P in any given market move, while volatilities of less than 1.00 mean the fund moves up and down less than the S&P. A market volatility of 0.00 would indicate that the fund's week-to-week price fluctuations are completely independent of the S&P.

The Superiority Rating is a fund's demonstrated historical superior or inferior return over the last five years relative to the Standard & Poor's 500 Index after removing whatever advantage or disadvantage the fund may have merely because it is more or less volatile than the S&P. The bar chart of industry diversification illustrates how the securities in the portfolio are distributed among twelve major industry sectors.

For bond funds, average bond quality can range from "AAA" (top investment grade) to "D" (lowest quality). Average maturity is the average maturity of all securities in the portfolio. Duration is the average maturity adjusted for the timing of the portfolio securities' coupon and principal cash flows. It is a better estimate of the interest-rate-sensitivity of the fund – the longer the duration, the more volatile the fund will be for any given change in interest rates. For all bond funds, we also show the distribution of the portfolio in each quality grade from "AAA" to "D." And for municipal bond funds, the distribution of portfolio securities among different types of municipal obligations shows how the fund focuses its portfolio in specific municipal sectors.

Inside the
Billion Dollar Funds

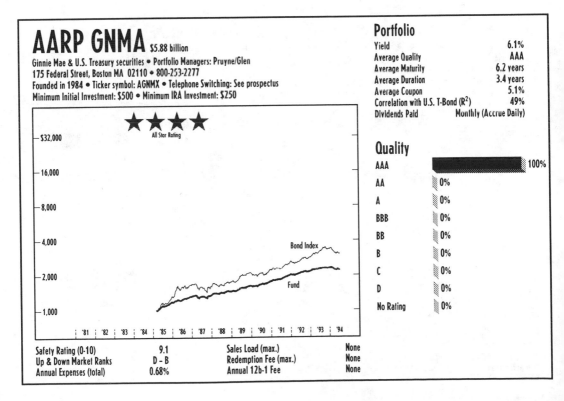

AARP GNMA $5.88 billion

Ginnie Mae & U.S. Treasury securities • Portfolio Managers: Pruyne/Glen
175 Federal Street, Boston MA 02110 • 800-253-2277
Founded in 1984 • Ticker symbol: AGNMX • Telephone Switching: See prospectus
Minimum Initial Investment: $500 • Minimum IRA Investment: $250

★★★★
All Star Rating

— $32,000

— 16,000

— 8,000

— 4,000   Bond Index

— 2,000   Fund

— 1,000

'81 '82 '83 '84 '85 '86 '87 '88 '89 '90 '91 '92 '93 '94

Safety Rating (0-10)	9.1	Sales Load (max.)	None
Up & Down Market Ranks	D – B	Redemption Fee (max.)	None
Annual Expenses (total)	0.68%	Annual 12b-1 Fee	None

Portfolio

Yield	6.1%
Average Quality	AAA
Average Maturity	6.2 years
Average Duration	3.4 years
Average Coupon	5.1%
Correlation with U.S. T-Bond (R^2)	49%
Dividends Paid	Monthly (Accrue Daily)

Quality

AAA	100%
AA	0%
A	0%
BBB	0%
BB	0%
B	0%
C	0%
D	0%
No Rating	0%

AARP Growth & Income $2.10 billion

Dividend-paying growth securities • Portfolio Managers: Hoffman/Millard
175 Federal Street, Boston MA 02110 • 800-253-2277
Founded in 1984 • Ticker symbol: AGIFX • Telephone Switching: See prospectus
Minimum Initial Investment: $500 • Minimum IRA Investment: $250

Portfolio

	Fund	S&P
Avg. P/E Ratio	27	20
Avg. Price/Book	3.0	3.1
Avg. 5-Year Earning Growth	–3.3%	5.2%
Median Mkt. Capitalization	$3.64 bil.	$3.60 bil.
Correlation v. S&P 500 (R^2)	74%	100%
Market Volatility (Beta)	0.72	1.00
Superiority Rating (Alpha)	+4%	0%

★ ★ ★ ★ ★
All Star Rating

Industry Diversification

Durables	4%
Energy	10%
Finance	25%
Industrial	28%
Non-Durables	3%
Retail	0%
Health	0%
Services	3%
Technology	18%
Utilities	9%
Precious Metals	0%
Other	0%

S&P 500
Fund

Safety Rating (0-10)	8.1	Sales Load (max.)	None
Up & Down Market Ranks	D – B	Redemption Fee (max.)	None
Annual Expenses (total)	0.83%	Annual 12b-1 Fee	None

AARP Insured Tax-Free Bond $2.00 billion

Tax-free; long maturity • Portfolio Managers: Donald Carlton/Condon
175 Federal Street, Boston MA 02110 • 800-253-2277
Founded in 1984 • Ticker symbol: AITGX • Telephone Switching: See prospectus
Minimum Initial Investment: $500 • Minimum IRA Investment: None

Portfolio

Yield	4.9%
Average Quality	AAA
Average Maturity	12 years
Average Duration	7.9 years
Average Coupon	6.7%
Correlation with U.S. T-Bond (R^2)	54%

★ ★ ★
All Star Rating

Quality

AAA	89%
AA	1%
A	2%
BBB	0%
BB & Below	0%
No Rating	8%

Sectors

General Oblig.	15%
Utility	36%
Health	18%
Housing	8%
Education	14%
Transportation	6%
Other	3%

Bond Index
Fund

Safety Rating (0-10)	8.8	Sales Load (max.)	None
Up & Down Market Ranks	A – E	Redemption Fee (max.)	None
Annual Expenses (total)	0.71%	Annual 12b-1 Fee	None

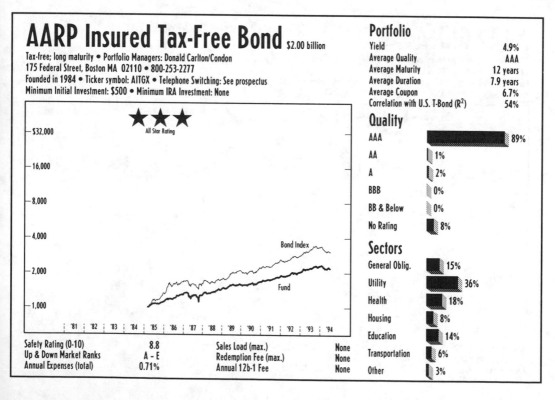

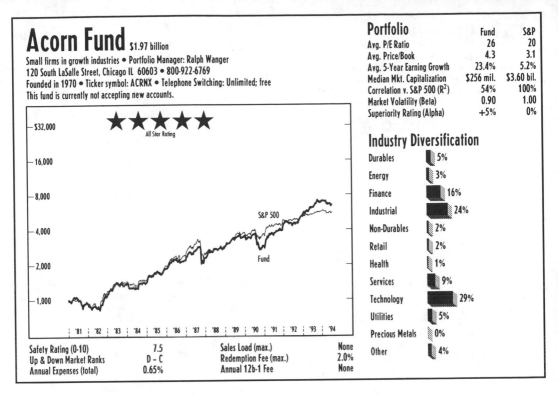

Acorn Fund $1.97 billion

Small firms in growth industries • Portfolio Manager: Ralph Wanger
120 South LaSalle Street, Chicago IL 60603 • 800-922-6769
Founded in 1970 • Ticker symbol: ACRNX • Telephone Switching: Unlimited; free
This fund is currently not accepting new accounts.

★★★★★
All Star Rating

Portfolio	Fund	S&P
Avg. P/E Ratio	26	20
Avg. Price/Book	4.3	3.1
Avg. 5-Year Earning Growth	23.4%	5.2%
Median Mkt. Capitalization	$256 mil.	$3.60 bil.
Correlation v. S&P 500 (R^2)	54%	100%
Market Volatility (Beta)	0.90	1.00
Superiority Rating (Alpha)	+5%	0%

Industry Diversification

Durables	5%
Energy	3%
Finance	16%
Industrial	24%
Non-Durables	2%
Retail	2%
Health	1%
Services	9%
Technology	29%
Utilities	5%
Precious Metals	0%
Other	4%

Safety Rating (0-10)	7.5	Sales Load (max.)	None
Up & Down Market Ranks	D – C	Redemption Fee (max.)	2.0%
Annual Expenses (total)	0.65%	Annual 12b-1 Fee	None

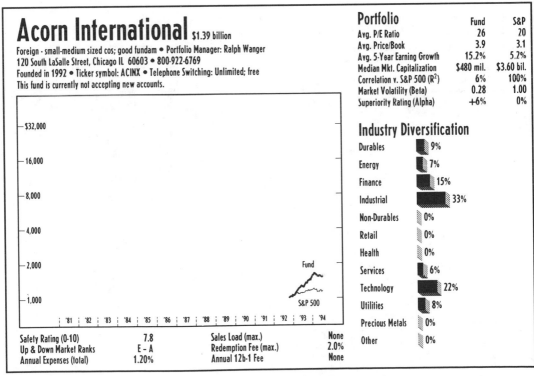

Acorn International $1.39 billion

Foreign - small-medium sized cos; good fundam • Portfolio Manager: Ralph Wanger
120 South LaSalle Street, Chicago IL 60603 • 800-922-6769
Founded in 1992 • Ticker symbol: ACINX • Telephone Switching: Unlimited; free
This fund is currently not accepting new accounts.

Portfolio	Fund	S&P
Avg. P/E Ratio	26	20
Avg. Price/Book	3.9	3.1
Avg. 5-Year Earning Growth	15.2%	5.2%
Median Mkt. Capitalization	$480 mil.	$3.60 bil.
Correlation v. S&P 500 (R^2)	6%	100%
Market Volatility (Beta)	0.28	1.00
Superiority Rating (Alpha)	+6%	0%

Industry Diversification

Durables	9%
Energy	7%
Finance	15%
Industrial	33%
Non-Durables	0%
Retail	0%
Health	0%
Services	6%
Technology	22%
Utilities	8%
Precious Metals	0%
Other	0%

Safety Rating (0-10)	7.8	Sales Load (max.)	None
Up & Down Market Ranks	E – A	Redemption Fee (max.)	2.0%
Annual Expenses (total)	1.20%	Annual 12b-1 Fee	None

Aim - Charter $1.57 billion

Dividend-paying growth stocks • Portfolio Managers: J.Lerner/L.Sachnowitz
One Financial Plaza, Springfield MA 01103 • 800-959-4246
Founded in 1968 • Ticker symbol: CHTRX • Telephone Switching: Unlimited; free
Minimum Initial Investment: $500 • Minimum IRA Investment: $500

Portfolio

	Fund	S&P
Avg. P/E Ratio	17	20
Avg. Price/Book	2.6	3.1
Avg. 5-Year Earning Growth	9.5%	5.2%
Median Mkt. Capitalization	$7.81 bil.	$3.60 bil.
Correlation v. S&P 500 (R^2)	81%	100%
Market Volatility (Beta)	0.82	1.00
Superiority Rating (Alpha)	+0%	0%

★ ★ ★ ★
All Star Rating

$32,000
16,000
8,000
4,000
2,000
1,000

S&P 500
Fund

'81 '82 '83 '84 '85 '86 '87 '88 '89 '90 '91 '92 '93 '94

Industry Diversification

Durables	2%
Energy	8%
Finance	35%
Industrial	20%
Non-Durables	2%
Retail	4%
Health	1%
Services	1%
Technology	24%
Utilities	3%
Precious Metals	0%
Other	0%

Safety Rating (0-10)	7.8	Sales Load (max.)	5.8%
Up & Down Market Ranks	C – C	Redemption Fee (max.)	None
Annual Expenses (total)	1.17%	Annual 12b-1 Fee	0.30%

Aim - Constellation $3.19 billion

Small-medium emerging growth stocks • Portfolio Managers: Schoolar/Barnard/Kippes
One Financial Plaza, Springfield MA 01103 • 800-959-4246
Founded in 1967 • Ticker symbol: CSTGX • Telephone Switching: Unlimited; free
Minimum Initial Investment: $500 • Minimum IRA Investment: $500

Portfolio

	Fund	S&P
Avg. P/E Ratio	23	20
Avg. Price/Book	4.4	3.1
Avg. 5-Year Earning Growth	36.7%	5.2%
Median Mkt. Capitalization	$1.00 bil.	$3.60 bil.
Correlation v. S&P 500 (R^2)	62%	100%
Market Volatility (Beta)	1.42	1.00
Superiority Rating (Alpha)	+3%	0%

★ ★ ★ ★ ★
All Star Rating

$16,000
8,000
4,000
2,000
1,000

S&P 500
Fund

'81 '82 '83 '84 '85 '86 '87 '88 '89 '90 '91 '92 '93 '94

Industry Diversification

Durables	5%
Energy	1%
Finance	13%
Industrial	11%
Non-Durables	4%
Retail	6%
Health	9%
Services	16%
Technology	33%
Utilities	1%
Precious Metals	1%
Other	0%

Safety Rating (0-10)	6.2	Sales Load (max.)	5.8%
Up & Down Market Ranks	A – E	Redemption Fee (max.)	None
Annual Expenses (total)	1.22%	Annual 12b-1 Fee	0.30%

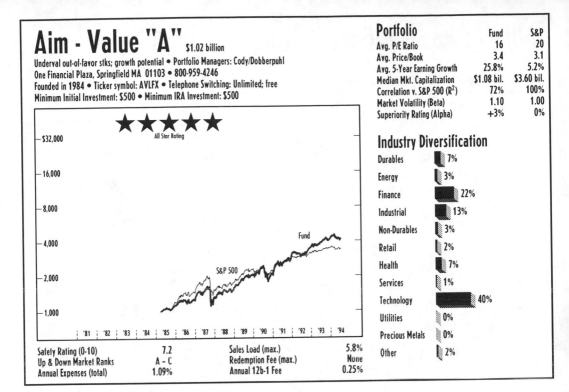

Aim - Value "A" $1.02 billion

Underval out-of-favor stks; growth potential • Portfolio Managers: Cody/Dobberpuhl
One Financial Plaza, Springfield MA 01103 • 800-959-4246
Founded in 1984 • Ticker symbol: AVLFX • Telephone Switching: Unlimited; free
Minimum Initial Investment: $500 • Minimum IRA Investment: $500

★★★★★
All Star Rating

Portfolio	Fund	S&P
Avg. P/E Ratio	16	20
Avg. Price/Book	3.4	3.1
Avg. 5-Year Earning Growth	25.8%	5.2%
Median Mkt. Capitalization	$1.08 bil.	$3.60 bil.
Correlation v. S&P 500 (R^2)	72%	100%
Market Volatility (Beta)	1.10	1.00
Superiority Rating (Alpha)	+3%	0%

Industry Diversification

Durables	7%
Energy	3%
Finance	22%
Industrial	13%
Non-Durables	3%
Retail	2%
Health	7%
Services	1%
Technology	40%
Utilities	0%
Precious Metals	0%
Other	2%

Safety Rating (0-10)	7.2	Sales Load (max.)	5.8%
Up & Down Market Ranks	A - C	Redemption Fee (max.)	None
Annual Expenses (total)	1.09%	Annual 12b-1 Fee	0.25%

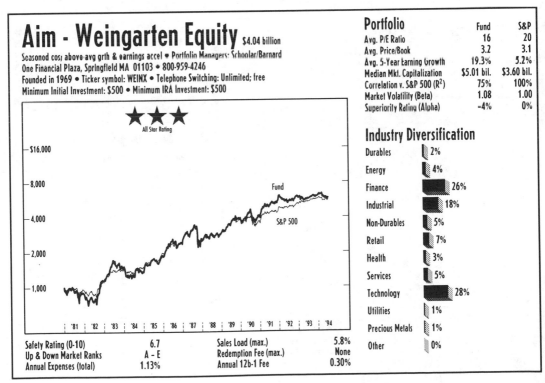

Aim - Weingarten Equity $4.04 billion

Seasoned cos; above-avg grth & earnings accel • Portfolio Managers: Schoolar/Barnard
One Financial Plaza, Springfield MA 01103 • 800-959-4246
Founded in 1969 • Ticker symbol: WEINX • Telephone Switching: Unlimited; free
Minimum Initial Investment: $500 • Minimum IRA Investment: $500

★★★
All Star Rating

Portfolio	Fund	S&P
Avg. P/E Ratio	16	20
Avg. Price/Book	3.2	3.1
Avg. 5-Year Earning Growth	19.3%	5.2%
Median Mkt. Capitalization	$5.01 bil.	$3.60 bil.
Correlation v. S&P 500 (R^2)	75%	100%
Market Volatility (Beta)	1.08	1.00
Superiority Rating (Alpha)	-4%	0%

Industry Diversification

Durables	2%
Energy	4%
Finance	26%
Industrial	18%
Non-Durables	5%
Retail	7%
Health	3%
Services	5%
Technology	28%
Utilities	1%
Precious Metals	1%
Other	0%

Safety Rating (0-10)	6.7	Sales Load (max.)	5.8%
Up & Down Market Ranks	A - E	Redemption Fee (max.)	None
Annual Expenses (total)	1.13%	Annual 12b-1 Fee	0.30%

Alliance No Amer Govt "B" $1.74 billion

BBB-rated & up US, Canada & Mexican govt bnds • Portfolio Manager: Wayne D. Lyski
500 Plaza Drive - 3rd Floor, Secaucus NJ 07094 • 800-221-5672
Founded in 1992 • Ticker symbol: ANABX • Telephone Switching: Unlimited; free
Minimum Initial Investment: $250 • Minimum IRA Investment: $250

Portfolio

Yield	9.8%
Average Quality	AA-
Average Maturity	5.9 years
Average Duration	3.8 years
Average Coupon	7.9%
Correlation with U.S. T-Bond (R^2)	14%
Dividends Paid	Monthly (Accrue Daily)

Quality

AAA	0%
AA	41%
A	33%
BBB	0%
BB	0%
B	0%
C	0%
D	0%
No Rating	26%

★ All Star Rating

Safety Rating (0-10)	8.5	Sales Load (max.)	None
Up & Down Market Ranks	E - D	Redemption Fee (max.)	3.1%
Annual Expenses (total)	2.31%	Annual 12b-1 Fee	1.00%

American - Amcap $2.93 billion

Fast growing companies • Portfolio Manager: Multiple Managers
333 South Hope Street, Los Angeles CA 90071 • 800-421-9900
Founded in 1967 • Ticker symbol: AMCPX • Telephone Switching: Unlimited; free
Minimum Initial Investment: $1,000 • Minimum IRA Investment: $250

Portfolio

	Fund	S&P
Avg. P/E Ratio	21	20
Avg. Price/Book	4.0	3.1
Avg. 5-Year Earning Growth	17.7%	5.2%
Median Mkt. Capitalization	$4.51 bil.	$3.60 bil.
Correlation v. S&P 500 (R^2)	78%	100%
Market Volatility (Beta)	1.06	1.00
Superiority Rating (Alpha)	-2%	0%

Industry Diversification

Durables	0%
Energy	1%
Finance	18%
Industrial	13%
Non-Durables	2%
Retail	2%
Health	4%
Services	16%
Technology	42%
Utilities	2%
Precious Metals	0%
Other	0%

★★★ All Star Rating

Safety Rating (0-10)	7.2	Sales Load (max.)	6.1%
Up & Down Market Ranks	C - C	Redemption Fee (max.)	None
Annual Expenses (total)	0.72%	Annual 12b-1 Fee	0.25%

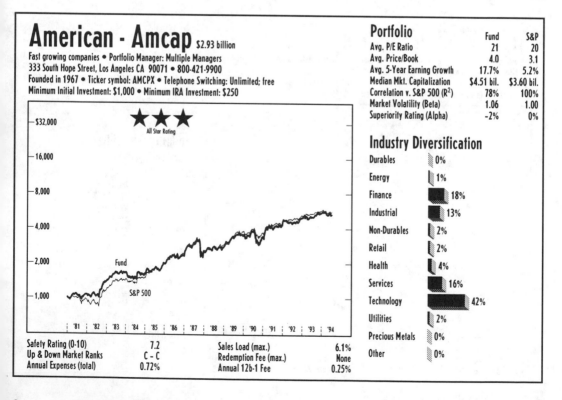

American - Balanced $1.83 billion

Long term earnings and dividend growth • Portfolio Manager: Multiple Managers
333 South Hope Street, Los Angeles CA 90071 • 800-421-9900
Founded in 1933 • Ticker symbol: ABALX • Telephone Switching: Unlimited; free
Minimum Initial Investment: $500 • Minimum IRA Investment: $250

Portfolio

	Fund	S&P
Avg. P/E Ratio	21	20
Avg. Price/Book	2.7	3.1
Avg. 5-Year Earning Growth	–1.7%	5.2%
Median Mkt. Capitalization	$9.51 bil.	$3.60 bil.
Correlation v. S&P 500 (R^2)	83%	100%
Market Volatility (Beta)	0.52	1.00
Superiority Rating (Alpha)	+4%	0%

★★★
All Star Rating

Fund

S&P 500

'81 '82 '83 '84 '85 '86 '87 '88 '89 '90 '91 '92 '93 '94

$32,000 / 16,000 / 8,000 / 4,000 / 2,000 / 1,000

Industry Diversification

Durables	6%
Energy	10%
Finance	19%
Industrial	32%
Non-Durables	9%
Retail	0%
Health	0%
Services	4%
Technology	12%
Utilities	8%
Precious Metals	0%
Other	0%

Safety Rating (0-10)	8.6	Sales Load (max.)	6.1%
Up & Down Market Ranks	E – A	Redemption Fee (max.)	None
Annual Expenses (total)	0.71%	Annual 12b-1 Fee	0.25%

American - Bond Fd of America $5.00 billion

60% A-rated and higher corporate bonds • Portfolio Manager: Multiple Managers
333 South Hope Street, Los Angeles CA 90071 • 800-421-9900
Founded in 1974 • Ticker symbol: ABNDX • Telephone Switching: Unlimited; free
Minimum Initial Investment: $1,000 • Minimum IRA Investment: $250

Portfolio

Yield	7.1%
Average Quality	BBB
Average Maturity	9.6 years
Average Duration	5.8 years
Average Coupon	8.6%
Correlation with U.S. T-Bond (R^2)	59%
Dividends Paid	Monthly (Accrue Daily)

★★★★★
All Star Rating

Bond Index

Fund

'81 '82 '83 '84 '85 '86 '87 '88 '89 '90 '91 '92 '93 '94

$32,000 / 16,000 / 8,000 / 4,000 / 2,000 / 1,000

Quality

AAA	11%
AA	10%
A	14%
BBB	25%
BB	19%
B	21%
C	0%
D	0%
No Rating	0%

Safety Rating (0-10)	9.2	Sales Load (max.)	5.0%
Up & Down Market Ranks	B – C	Redemption Fee (max.)	None
Annual Expenses (total)	0.71%	Annual 12b-1 Fee	0.25%

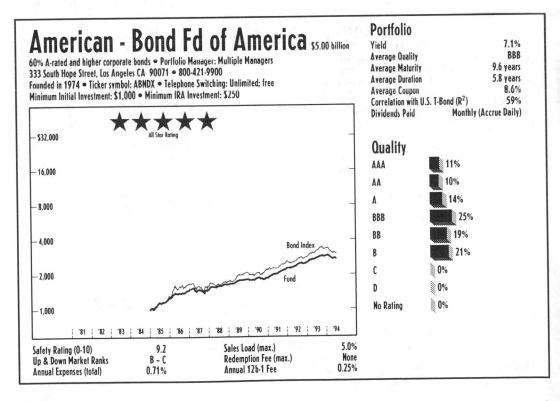

American - Capital Icm Builder $3.33 billion

Stocks with above-average yield ● Portfolio Manager: Multiple Managers
333 South Hope Street, Los Angeles CA 90071 ● 800-421-9900
Founded in 1987 ● Ticker symbol: CAIBX ● Telephone Switching: Unlimited; free
Minimum Initial Investment: $1,000 ● Minimum IRA Investment: $250

Portfolio

	Fund	S&P
Avg. P/E Ratio	18	20
Avg. Price/Book	2.6	3.1
Avg. 5-Year Earning Growth	2.0%	5.2%
Median Mkt. Capitalization	$5.10 bil.	$3.60 bil.
Correlation v. S&P 500 (R^2)	49%	100%
Market Volatility (Beta)	0.46	1.00
Superiority Rating (Alpha)	+6%	0%

★★★★
All Star Rating

Fund
S&P 500

$16,000
8,000
4,000
2,000
1,000

'81 '82 '83 '84 '85 '86 '87 '88 '89 '90 '91 '92 '93 '94

Industry Diversification

Durables	0%
Energy	7%
Finance	26%
Industrial	17%
Non-Durables	6%
Retail	0%
Health	0%
Services	3%
Technology	19%
Utilities	22%
Precious Metals	0%
Other	0%

Safety Rating (0-10)	8.6	Sales Load (max.)	6.1%
Up & Down Market Ranks	D – A	Redemption Fee (max.)	None
Annual Expenses (total)	0.72%	Annual 12b-1 Fee	0.30%

American - Capital World G & I $2.39 billion

Foreign & U.S. - stocks, bonds, money markets ● Portfolio Manager: Multiple Managers
333 South Hope Street, Los Angeles CA 90071 ● 800-421-9900
Founded in 1993 ● Ticker symbol: CWGIX ● Telephone Switching: Unlimited; free
Minimum Initial Investment: $1,000 ● Minimum IRA Investment: $250

Portfolio

	Fund	S&P
Avg. P/E Ratio	18	20
Avg. Price/Book	3.6	3.1
Avg. 5-Year Earning Growth	8.0%	5.2%
Median Mkt. Capitalization	$9.08 bil.	$3.60 bil.
Correlation v. S&P 500 (R^2)	18%	100%
Market Volatility (Beta)	0.45	1.00
Superiority Rating (Alpha)	+6%	0%

Fund
S&P 500

$32,000
16,000
8,000
4,000
2,000
1,000

'81 '82 '83 '84 '85 '86 '87 '88 '89 '90 '91 '92 '93 '94

Industry Diversification

Durables	3%
Energy	5%
Finance	13%
Industrial	29%
Non-Durables	6%
Retail	2%
Health	0%
Services	5%
Technology	32%
Utilities	5%
Precious Metals	0%
Other	0%

Safety Rating (0-10)	7.7	Sales Load (max.)	6.1%
Up & Down Market Ranks	E – B	Redemption Fee (max.)	None
Annual Expenses (total)	0.91%	Annual 12b-1 Fee	0.30%

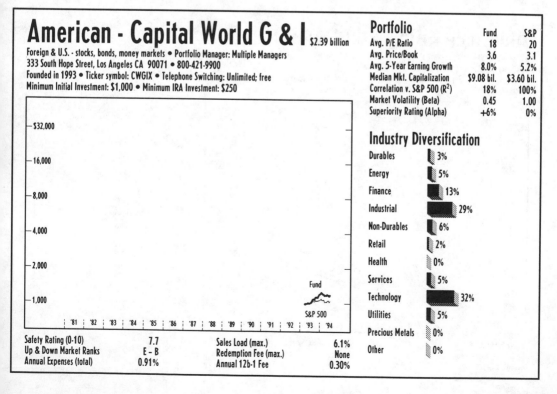

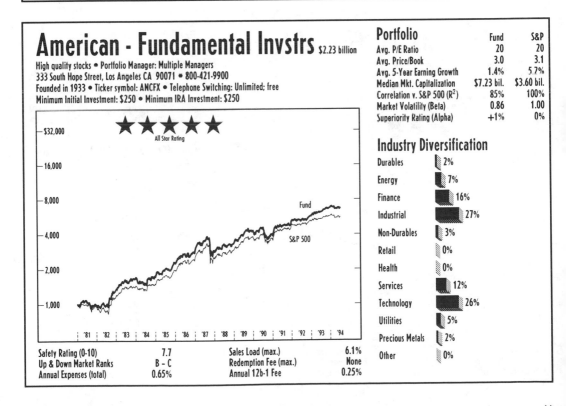

American - Europacific Growth $6.97 billion

Foreign - diversified stocks • Portfolio Manager: Multiple Managers
333 South Hope Street, Los Angeles CA 90071 • 800-421-9900
Founded in 1984 • Ticker symbol: AEPGX • Telephone Switching: Unlimited; free
Minimum Initial Investment: $250 • Minimum IRA Investment: $250

Portfolio	Fund	S&P
Avg. P/E Ratio	15	20
Avg. Price/Book	3.3	3.1
Avg. 5-Year Earning Growth	9.2%	5.2%
Median Mkt. Capitalization	$7.75 bil.	$3.60 bil.
Correlation v. S&P 500 (R^2)	19%	100%
Market Volatility (Beta)	0.45	1.00
Superiority Rating (Alpha)	+4%	0%

★★★★ All Star Rating

Fund
S&P 500

Industry Diversification

Durables	0%
Energy	6%
Finance	5%
Industrial	25%
Non-Durables	0%
Retail	0%
Health	0%
Services	10%
Technology	54%
Utilities	0%
Precious Metals	0%
Other	0%

Safety Rating (0-10)	7.9	Sales Load (max.)	6.1%
Up & Down Market Ranks	D – A	Redemption Fee (max.)	None
Annual Expenses (total)	0.99%	Annual 12b-1 Fee	0.25%

American - Fundamental Invstrs $2.23 billion

High quality stocks • Portfolio Manager: Multiple Managers
333 South Hope Street, Los Angeles CA 90071 • 800-421-9900
Founded in 1933 • Ticker symbol: ANCFX • Telephone Switching: Unlimited; free
Minimum Initial Investment: $250 • Minimum IRA Investment: $250

Portfolio	Fund	S&P
Avg. P/E Ratio	20	20
Avg. Price/Book	3.0	3.1
Avg. 5-Year Earning Growth	1.4%	5.7%
Median Mkt. Capitalization	$7.23 bil.	$3.60 bil.
Correlation v. S&P 500 (R^2)	85%	100%
Market Volatility (Beta)	0.86	1.00
Superiority Rating (Alpha)	+1%	0%

★★★★★ All Star Rating

Fund
S&P 500

Industry Diversification

Durables	2%
Energy	7%
Finance	16%
Industrial	27%
Non-Durables	3%
Retail	0%
Health	0%
Services	12%
Technology	26%
Utilities	5%
Precious Metals	2%
Other	0%

Safety Rating (0-10)	7.7	Sales Load (max.)	6.1%
Up & Down Market Ranks	B – C	Redemption Fee (max.)	None
Annual Expenses (total)	0.65%	Annual 12b-1 Fee	0.25%

American - Growth Fund of Amer $5.08 billion

High earnings growth stocks • Portfolio Manager: Multiple Managers
333 South Hope Street, Los Angeles CA 90071 • 800-421-9900
Founded in 1959 • Ticker symbol: AGTHX • Telephone Switching: Unlimited; free
Minimum Initial Investment: $1,000 • Minimum IRA Investment: $250

Portfolio

	Fund	S&P
Avg. P/E Ratio	20	20
Avg. Price/Book	3.7	3.1
Avg. 5-Year Earning Growth	20.7%	5.2%
Median Mkt. Capitalization	$3.15 bil.	$3.60 bil.
Correlation v. S&P 500 (R^2)	74%	100%
Market Volatility (Beta)	1.08	1.00
Superiority Rating (Alpha)	-1%	0%

★★★★
All Star Rating

Industry Diversification

Durables	0%
Energy	2%
Finance	9%
Industrial	18%
Non-Durables	1%
Retail	2%
Health	6%
Services	14%
Technology	46%
Utilities	1%
Precious Metals	0%
Other	1%

Safety Rating (0-10)	7.3	Sales Load (max.)	6.1%
Up & Down Market Ranks	B – D	Redemption Fee (max.)	None
Annual Expenses (total)	0.77%	Annual 12b-1 Fee	0.25%

American - Income Fund of Amer $10.4 billion

Diversified stocks and bonds • Portfolio Manager: Multiple Managers
333 South Hope Street, Los Angeles CA 90071 • 800-421-9900
Founded in 1971 • Ticker symbol: AMECX • Telephone Switching: Unlimited; free
Minimum Initial Investment: $1,000 • Minimum IRA Investment: None

Portfolio

	Fund	S&P
Avg. P/E Ratio	24	20
Avg. Price/Book	2.5	3.1
Avg. 5-Year Earning Growth	-2.5%	5.2%
Median Mkt. Capitalization	$5.19 bil.	$3.60 bil.
Correlation v. S&P 500 (R^2)	55%	100%
Market Volatility (Beta)	0.45	1.00
Superiority Rating (Alpha)	+4%	0%

★★
All Star Rating

Industry Diversification

Durables	1%
Energy	14%
Finance	24%
Industrial	25%
Non-Durables	9%
Retail	1%
Health	0%
Services	1%
Technology	12%
Utilities	11%
Precious Metals	2%
Other	0%

Safety Rating (0-10)	8.7	Sales Load (max.)	6.1%
Up & Down Market Ranks	E – A	Redemption Fee (max.)	None
Annual Expenses (total)	0.62%	Annual 12b-1 Fee	0.25%

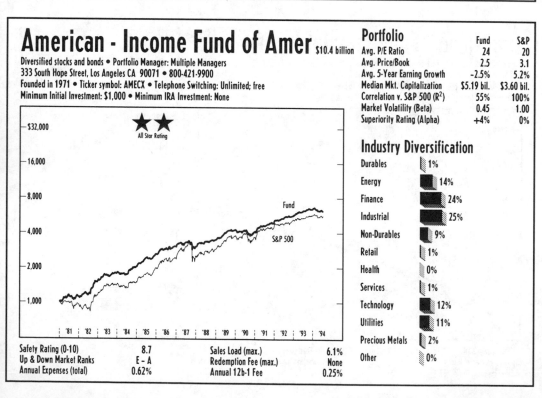

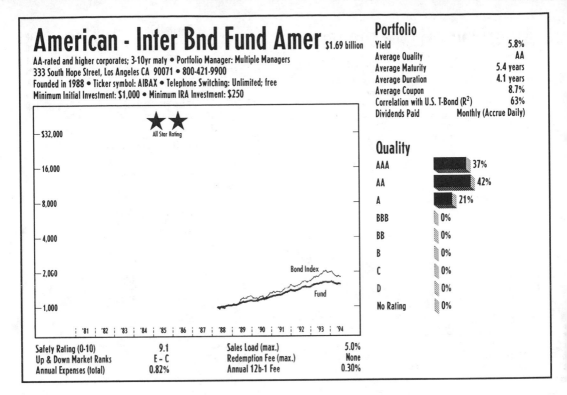

American - Inter Bnd Fund Amer $1.69 billion

AA-rated and higher corporates; 3-10yr maty • Portfolio Manager: Multiple Managers
333 South Hope Street, Los Angeles CA 90071 • 800-421-9900
Founded in 1988 • Ticker symbol: AIBAX • Telephone Switching: Unlimited; free
Minimum Initial Investment: $1,000 • Minimum IRA Investment: $250

Portfolio

Yield	5.8%
Average Quality	AA
Average Maturity	5.4 years
Average Duration	4.1 years
Average Coupon	8.7%
Correlation with U.S. T-Bond (R^2)	63%
Dividends Paid	Monthly (Accrue Daily)

Quality

AAA	37%
AA	42%
A	21%
BBB	0%
BB	0%
B	0%
C	0%
D	0%
No Rating	0%

★★ All Star Rating

Bond Index
Fund

Safety Rating (0-10)	9.1	Sales Load (max.)	5.0%
Up & Down Market Ranks	E – C	Redemption Fee (max.)	None
Annual Expenses (total)	0.82%	Annual 12b-1 Fee	0.30%

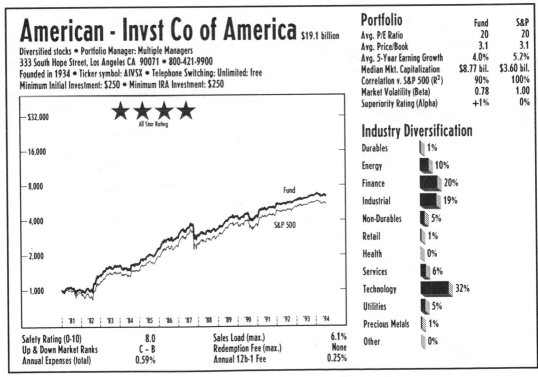

American - Invst Co of America $19.1 billion

Diversified stocks • Portfolio Manager: Multiple Managers
333 South Hope Street, Los Angeles CA 90071 • 800-421-9900
Founded in 1934 • Ticker symbol: AIVSX • Telephone Switching: Unlimited; free
Minimum Initial Investment: $250 • Minimum IRA Investment: $250

Portfolio

	Fund	S&P
Avg. P/E Ratio	20	20
Avg. Price/Book	3.1	3.1
Avg. 5-Year Earning Growth	4.0%	5.7%
Median Mkt. Capitalization	$8.77 bil.	$3.60 bil.
Correlation v. S&P 500 (R^2)	90%	100%
Market Volatility (Beta)	0.78	1.00
Superiority Rating (Alpha)	+1%	0%

Industry Diversification

Durables	1%
Energy	10%
Finance	20%
Industrial	19%
Non-Durables	5%
Retail	1%
Health	0%
Services	6%
Technology	32%
Utilities	5%
Precious Metals	1%
Other	0%

★★★★ All Star Rating

Fund
S&P 500

Safety Rating (0-10)	8.0	Sales Load (max.)	6.1%
Up & Down Market Ranks	C – B	Redemption Fee (max.)	None
Annual Expenses (total)	0.59%	Annual 12b-1 Fee	0.25%

American - New Economy $2.32 billion

Service and information companies • Portfolio Manager: Multiple Managers
333 South Hope Street, Los Angeles CA 90071 • 800-421-9900
Founded in 1983 • Ticker symbol: ANEFX • Telephone Switching: Unlimited; free
Minimum Initial Investment: $1,000 • Minimum IRA Investment: $250

Portfolio	Fund	S&P
Avg. P/E Ratio	20	20
Avg. Price/Book	3.8	3.1
Avg. 5-Year Earning Growth	20.1%	5.2%
Median Mkt. Capitalization	$2.63 bil.	$3.60 bil.
Correlation v. S&P 500 (R^2)	67%	100%
Market Volatility (Beta)	0.96	1.00
Superiority Rating (Alpha)	+2%	0%

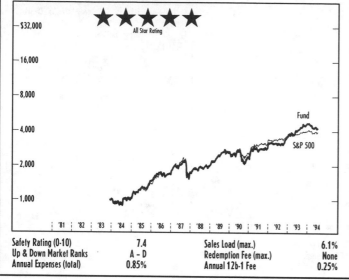

Industry Diversification

Durables	0%
Energy	2%
Finance	22%
Industrial	8%
Non-Durables	0%
Retail	10%
Health	1%
Services	14%
Technology	40%
Utilities	3%
Precious Metals	0%
Other	0%

Safety Rating (0-10)	7.4	Sales Load (max.)	6.1%
Up & Down Market Ranks	A – D	Redemption Fee (max.)	None
Annual Expenses (total)	0.85%	Annual 12b-1 Fee	0.25%

American - New Perspective $5.72 billion

Foreign & U.S. - 50% each • Portfolio Manager: Multiple Managers
333 South Hope Street, Los Angeles CA 90071 • 800-421-9900
Founded in 1973 • Ticker symbol: ANWPX • Telephone Switching: Unlimited; free
Minimum Initial Investment: $250 • Minimum IRA Investment: $250

Portfolio	Fund	S&P
Avg. P/E Ratio	21	20
Avg. Price/Book	3.9	3.1
Avg. 5-Year Earning Growth	11.8%	5.2%
Median Mkt. Capitalization	$11.8 bil.	$3.60 bil.
Correlation v. S&P 500 (R^2)	49%	100%
Market Volatility (Beta)	0.67	1.00
Superiority Rating (Alpha)	+2%	0%

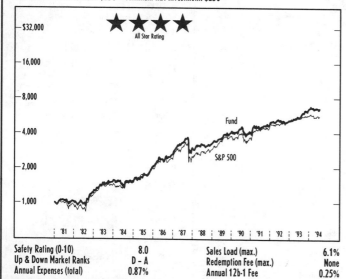

Industry Diversification

Durables	1%
Energy	8%
Finance	9%
Industrial	26%
Non-Durables	4%
Retail	0%
Health	0%
Services	9%
Technology	42%
Utilities	1%
Precious Metals	0%
Other	0%

Safety Rating (0-10)	8.0	Sales Load (max.)	6.1%
Up & Down Market Ranks	D – A	Redemption Fee (max.)	None
Annual Expenses (total)	0.87%	Annual 12b-1 Fee	0.25%

American - SmallCap World $3.14 billion

Foreign & U.S. - small cap stocks • Portfolio Manager: Multiple Managers
333 South Hope Street, Los Angeles CA 90071 • 800-421-9900
Founded in 1990 • Ticker symbol: SMCWX • Telephone Switching: Unlimited; free
Minimum Initial Investment: $1,000 • Minimum IRA Investment: $250

Portfolio	Fund	S&P
Avg. P/E Ratio	26	20
Avg. Price/Book	3.6	3.1
Avg. 5-Year Earning Growth	15.7%	5.2%
Median Mkt. Capitalization	$347 mil.	$3.60 bil.
Correlation v. S&P 500 (R^2)	59%	100%
Market Volatility (Beta)	0.80	1.00
Superiority Rating (Alpha)	+4%	0%

Industry Diversification

Durables	6%
Energy	1%
Finance	11%
Industrial	13%
Non-Durables	2%
Retail	13%
Health	1%
Services	11%
Technology	39%
Utilities	2%
Precious Metals	0%
Other	1%

★★★★ All Star Rating

Safety Rating (0-10)	7.8	Sales Load (max.)	6.1%
Up & Down Market Ranks	B – C	Redemption Fee (max.)	None
Annual Expenses (total)	1.15%	Annual 12b-1 Fee	0.25%

American - Tax-Exempt Bond $1.37 billion

80% A-rated and higher municipals • Portfolio Manager: Multiple Managers
333 South Hope Street, Los Angeles CA 90071 • 800-421-9900
Founded in 1979 • Ticker symbol: AFTEX • Telephone Switching: Unlimited; free
Minimum Initial Investment: $1,000 • Minimum IRA Investment: None

Portfolio	
Yield	5.0%
Average Quality	AA-
Average Maturity	11 years
Average Duration	7.2 years
Average Coupon	6.5%
Correlation with U.S. T-Bond (R^2)	49%

Quality

AAA	33%
AA	24%
A	18%
BBB	19%
BB & Below	7%
No Rating	0%

Sectors

General Oblig.	17%
Utility	31%
Health	18%
Housing	5%
Education	6%
Transportation	17%
Other	6%

★★★ All Star Rating

Safety Rating (0-10)	9.2	Sales Load (max.)	5.0%
Up & Down Market Ranks	C – C	Redemption Fee (max.)	None
Annual Expenses (total)	0.71%	Annual 12b-1 Fee	0.25%

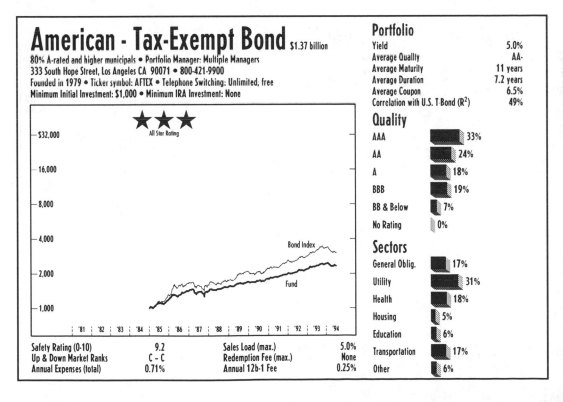

American - US Government Secs $1.39 billion

U.S. Government securities and agencies • Portfolio Manager: Multiple Managers
333 South Hope Street, Los Angeles CA 90071 • 800-421-9900
Founded in 1985 • Ticker symbol: AMUSX • Telephone Switching: Unlimited; free
Minimum Initial Investment: $1,000 • Minimum IRA Investment: $250

Portfolio

Yield	6.1%
Average Quality	AAA
Average Maturity	9.2 years
Average Duration	5.7 years
Average Coupon	8.5%
Correlation with U.S. T-Bond (R^2)	63%
Dividends Paid	Monthly (Accrue Daily)

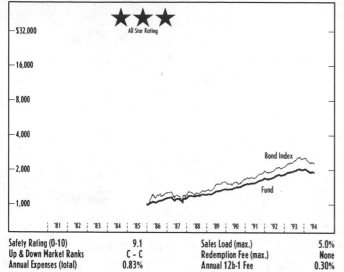

Quality

AAA	100%
AA	0%
A	0%
BBB	0%
BB	0%
B	0%
C	0%
D	0%
No Rating	0%

Safety Rating (0-10)	9.1	Sales Load (max.)	5.0%
Up & Down Market Ranks	C – C	Redemption Fee (max.)	None
Annual Expenses (total)	0.83%	Annual 12b-1 Fee	0.30%

American - Washington Mutual $12.7 billion

Prudent man rule • Portfolio Manager: Multiple Managers
333 South Hope Street, Los Angeles CA 90071 • 800-421-9900
Founded in 1952 • Ticker symbol: AWSHX • Telephone Switching: Unlimited; free
Minimum Initial Investment: $250 • Minimum IRA Investment: $250

Portfolio

	Fund	S&P
Avg. P/E Ratio	20	20
Avg. Price/Book	2.6	3.1
Avg. 5-Year Earning Growth	0.6%	5.2%
Median Mkt. Capitalization	$7.00 bil.	$3.60 bil.
Correlation v. S&P 500 (R^2)	88%	100%
Market Volatility (Beta)	0.87	1.00
Superiority Rating (Alpha)	+0%	0%

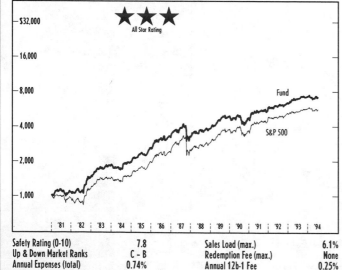

Industry Diversification

Durables	4%
Energy	9%
Finance	24%
Industrial	24%
Non-Durables	2%
Retail	0%
Health	0%
Services	4%
Technology	21%
Utilities	12%
Precious Metals	0%
Other	0%

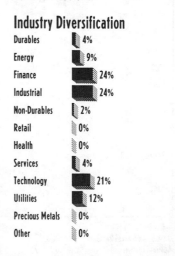

Safety Rating (0-10)	7.8	Sales Load (max.)	6.1%
Up & Down Market Ranks	C – B	Redemption Fee (max.)	None
Annual Expenses (total)	0.74%	Annual 12b-1 Fee	0.25%

American Capital Govt Secs "A" $2.91 billion

Govt securities plus option writing • Portfolio Manager: John R. Reynoldson
2800 Post Oak Blvd, Houston TX 77056 • 800-421-5666
Founded in 1984 • Ticker symbol: ACGVX • Telephone Switching: Unlimited; $5
Minimum Initial Investment: $500 • Minimum IRA Investment: $500

Portfolio

Yield	4.8%
Average Quality	AAA
Average Maturity	5.5 years
Average Duration	4.4 years
Average Coupon	9.4%
Correlation with U.S. T-Bond (R^2)	75%
Dividends Paid	Monthly

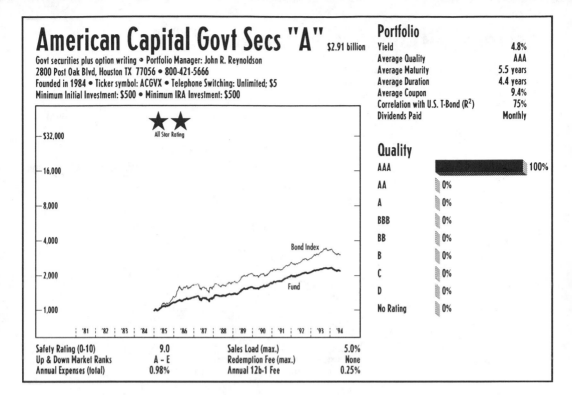

Quality

AAA	100%
AA	0%
A	0%
BBB	0%
BB	0%
B	0%
C	0%
D	0%
No Rating	0%

Safety Rating (0-10)	9.0	Sales Load (max.)	5.0%
Up & Down Market Ranks	A – E	Redemption Fee (max.)	None
Annual Expenses (total)	0.98%	Annual 12b-1 Fee	0.25%

American Capital Pace "A" $2.25 billion

Growth company stocks • Portfolio Manager: Alan T. Sachtleben
2800 Post Oak Blvd, Houston TX 77056 • 800-421-5666
Founded in 1969 • Ticker symbol: ACPAX • Telephone Switching: Unlimited; $5
Minimum Initial Investment: $500 • Minimum IRA Investment: $500

Portfolio

	Fund	S&P
Avg. P/E Ratio	20	20
Avg. Price/Book	3.4	3.1
Avg. 5-Year Earning Growth	13.9%	5.2%
Median Mkt. Capitalization	$1.39 bil.	$3.60 bil.
Correlation v. S&P 500 (R^2)	88%	100%
Market Volatility (Beta)	1.05	1.00
Superiority Rating (Alpha)	-4%	0%

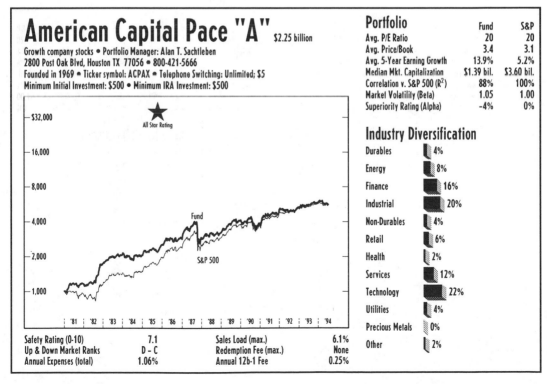

Industry Diversification

Durables	4%
Energy	8%
Finance	16%
Industrial	20%
Non-Durables	4%
Retail	6%
Health	2%
Services	12%
Technology	22%
Utilities	4%
Precious Metals	0%
Other	2%

Safety Rating (0-10)	7.1	Sales Load (max.)	6.1%
Up & Down Market Ranks	D – C	Redemption Fee (max.)	None
Annual Expenses (total)	1.06%	Annual 12b-1 Fee	0.25%

Benham GNMA $1.06 billion

Ginnie Mae securities • Portfolio Managers: Tyler/Colton
1665 Charleston Road, Mountainview CA 94043 • 800-331-8331
Founded in 1985 • Ticker symbol: BGNMX • Telephone Switching: 6 per yr; free
Minimum Initial Investment: $1,000 • Minimum IRA Investment: $100

Portfolio

Yield	7.0%
Average Quality	AAA
Average Maturity	6.7 years
Average Duration	4.9 years
Average Coupon	8.3%
Correlation with U.S. T-Bond (R^2)	43%
Dividends Paid	Monthly (Accrue Daily)

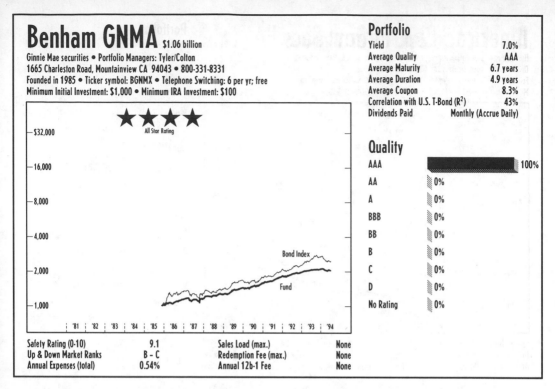

★★★★ All Star Rating

Quality

AAA	100%
AA	0%
A	0%
BBB	0%
BB	0%
B	0%
C	0%
D	0%
No Rating	0%

Safety Rating (0-10)	9.1	Sales Load (max.)	None
Up & Down Market Ranks	B – C	Redemption Fee (max.)	None
Annual Expenses (total)	0.54%	Annual 12b-1 Fee	None

Berger - One Hundred $1.87 billion

Established growth stocks • Portfolio Managers: W. Berger/R. Linafelter
210 University Blvd, Suite 900, Denver CO 80206 • 800-333-1001
Founded in 1966 • Ticker symbol: BEONX • Telephone Switching: 4 per yr; free
Minimum Initial Investment: $250 • Minimum IRA Investment: $250

Portfolio

	Fund	S&P
Avg. P/E Ratio	25	20
Avg. Price/Book	4.9	3.1
Avg. 5-Year Earning Growth	48.3%	5.2%
Median Mkt. Capitalization	$870 mil.	$3.60 bil.
Correlation v. S&P 500 (R^2)	56%	100%
Market Volatility (Beta)	1.31	1.00
Superiority Rating (Alpha)	+4%	0%

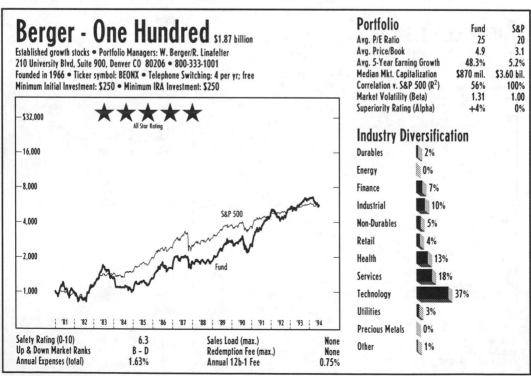

★★★★★ All Star Rating

Industry Diversification

Durables	2%
Energy	0%
Finance	7%
Industrial	10%
Non-Durables	5%
Retail	4%
Health	13%
Services	18%
Technology	37%
Utilities	3%
Precious Metals	0%
Other	1%

Safety Rating (0-10)	6.3	Sales Load (max.)	None
Up & Down Market Ranks	B – D	Redemption Fee (max.)	None
Annual Expenses (total)	1.63%	Annual 12b-1 Fee	0.75%

BlackRock 2001 Term $1.19 billion

High-qlty corps, govts & agen; retn $10 2001 • Portfolio Managers: K. Anderson/R. Kapito
One Seaport Plaza, New York NY 10292 • 800-227-7236
Founded in 1992 • Ticker symbol: BLK • Telephone Switching: Via broker
Minimum Initial Investment: $0 • Minimum IRA Investment: None

Portfolio

Yield	6.8%
Average Quality	AAA
Average Maturity	7.0 years
Average Duration	5.0 years
Average Coupon	3.8%
Correlation with U.S. T-Bond (R^2)	-2%
Dividends Paid	Monthly

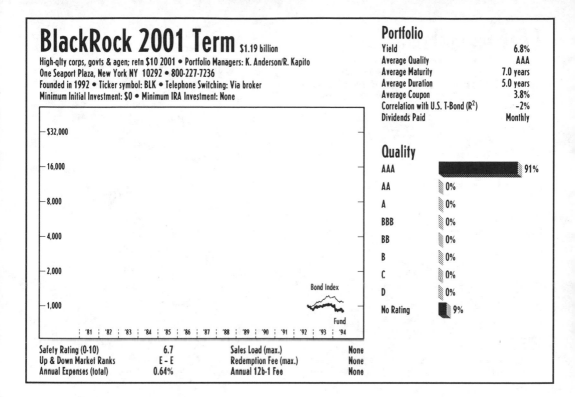

Quality

AAA	91%
AA	0%
A	0%
BBB	0%
BB	0%
B	0%
C	0%
D	0%
No Rating	9%

Safety Rating (0-10)	6.7	Sales Load (max.)	None
Up & Down Market Ranks	E – E	Redemption Fee (max.)	None
Annual Expenses (total)	0.64%	Annual 12b-1 Fee	None

Brandywine $1.96 billion

Financial strength; EPS growth • Portfolio Manager: Friess Associates
3908 Kennett Pike, Greenville DE 19807 • 800-338-1579
Founded in 1985 • Ticker symbol: BRWIX • Telephone Switching: Not available
Minimum Initial Investment: $25,000 • Minimum IRA Investment: $25,000

Portfolio

	Fund	S&P
Avg. P/E Ratio	21	20
Avg. Price/Book	4.2	3.1
Avg. 5-Year Earning Growth	32.1%	5.2%
Median Mkt. Capitalization	$240 mil.	$3.60 bil.
Correlation v. S&P 500 (R^2)	49%	100%
Market Volatility (Beta)	1.17	1.00
Superiority Rating (Alpha)	+4%	0%

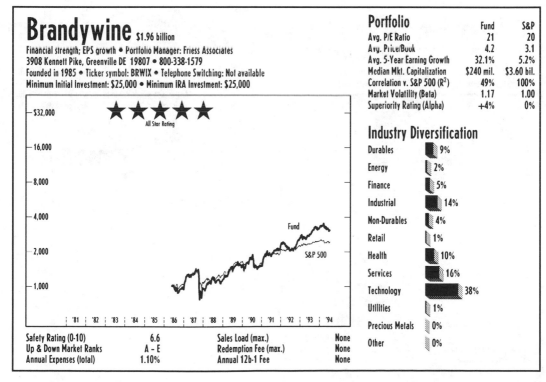

Industry Diversification

Durables	9%
Energy	2%
Finance	5%
Industrial	14%
Non-Durables	4%
Retail	1%
Health	10%
Services	16%
Technology	38%
Utilities	1%
Precious Metals	0%
Other	0%

Safety Rating (0-10)	6.6	Sales Load (max.)	None
Up & Down Market Ranks	A – E	Redemption Fee (max.)	None
Annual Expenses (total)	1.10%	Annual 12b-1 Fee	None

CGM Mutual $1.15 billion

Diversified securities • Portfolio Manager: G. Kenneth Heebner
P.O. Box #49, Back Bay Annex, Boston MA 02117 • 800-345-4048
Founded in 1929 • Ticker symbol: LOMMX • Telephone Switching: 4 per yr; free
Minimum Initial Investment: $2,500 • Minimum IRA Investment: $1,000

Portfolio	Fund	S&P
Avg. P/E Ratio	24	20
Avg. Price/Book	3.0	3.1
Avg. 5-Year Earning Growth	10.1%	5.2%
Median Mkt. Capitalization	$423 mil.	$3.60 bil.
Correlation v. S&P 500 (R^2)	64%	100%
Market Volatility (Beta)	0.84	1.00
Superiority Rating (Alpha)	+4%	0%

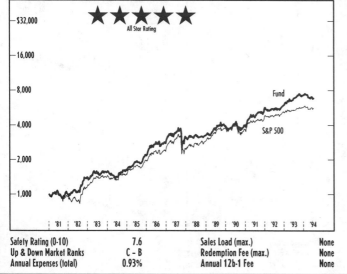

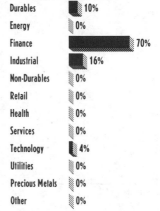

Industry Diversification

Durables	10%
Energy	0%
Finance	70%
Industrial	16%
Non-Durables	0%
Retail	0%
Health	0%
Services	0%
Technology	4%
Utilities	0%
Precious Metals	0%
Other	0%

Safety Rating (0-10)	7.6	Sales Load (max.)	None
Up & Down Market Ranks	C – B	Redemption Fee (max.)	None
Annual Expenses (total)	0.93%	Annual 12b-1 Fee	None

Colonial Federal Secs "A" $1.41 billion

Primarily U.S. Govt & agen; mtg secs; options • Portfolio Manager: Helen Peters
One Financial Center, Boston MA 02111 • 800-322-2847
Founded in 1988 • Ticker symbol: CFSAX • Telephone Switching: Unlimited; free
Minimum Initial Investment: $1,000 • Minimum IRA Investment: $25

Portfolio	
Yield	7.7%
Average Quality	AAA
Average Maturity	16 years
Average Duration	5.5 years
Average Coupon	11.3%
Correlation with U.S. T-Bond (R^2)	66%
Dividends Paid	Monthly (Accrue Daily)

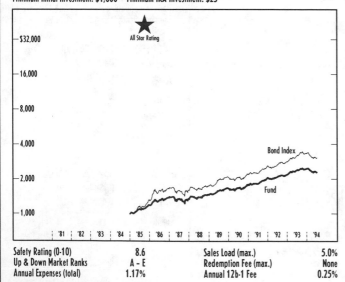

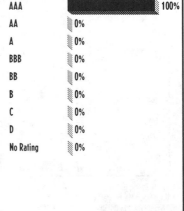

Quality

AAA	100%
AA	0%
A	0%
BBB	0%
BB	0%
B	0%
C	0%
D	0%
No Rating	0%

Safety Rating (0-10)	8.6	Sales Load (max.)	5.0%
Up & Down Market Ranks	A – E	Redemption Fee (max.)	None
Annual Expenses (total)	1.17%	Annual 12b-1 Fee	0.25%

Colonial Tax-Exempt "A" $3.17 billion

Investment-grade municipals • Portfolio Managers: Hardie/Boatman
One Financial Center, Boston MA 02111 • 800-322-2847
Founded in 1978 • Ticker symbol: COLTX • Telephone Switching: Unlimited; free
Minimum Initial Investment: $1,000 • Minimum IRA Investment: None

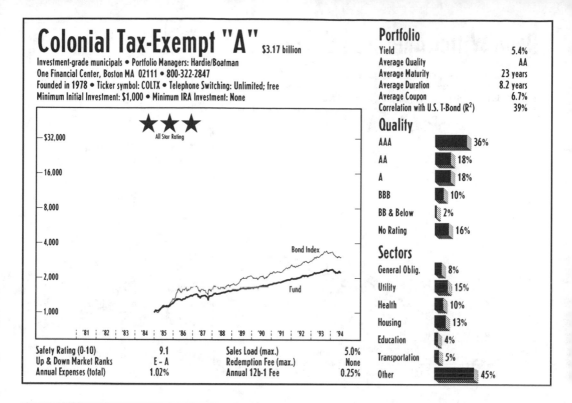

★★★
All Star Rating

$32,000
16,000
8,000
4,000
2,000
1,000

Bond Index
Fund

'81 '82 '83 '84 '85 '86 '87 '88 '89 '90 '91 '92 '93 '94

Safety Rating (0-10)	9.1	Sales Load (max.)	5.0%
Up & Down Market Ranks	E – A	Redemption Fee (max.)	None
Annual Expenses (total)	1.02%	Annual 12b-1 Fee	0.25%

Portfolio

Yield	5.4%
Average Quality	AA
Average Maturity	23 years
Average Duration	8.2 years
Average Coupon	6.7%
Correlation with U.S. T-Bond (R^2)	39%

Quality

AAA	36%
AA	18%
A	18%
BBB	10%
BB & Below	2%
No Rating	16%

Sectors

General Oblig.	8%
Utility	15%
Health	10%
Housing	13%
Education	4%
Transportation	5%
Other	45%

Common Sense Growth $2.13 billion

Diversified stocks; no alcohol, tobacco • Portfolio Manager: Stephen L. Boyd
3120 Breckinridge Blvd, Duluth GA 30199 • 800-544-5445
Founded in 1987 • Ticker symbol: CSGWX • Telephone Switching: Mail only
Minimum Initial Investment: $250 • Minimum IRA Investment: $250

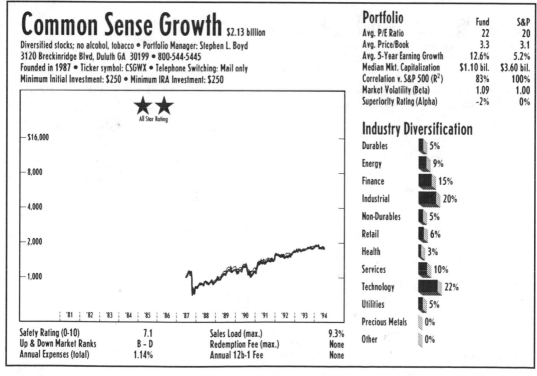

★★
All Star Rating

$16,000
8,000
4,000
2,000
1,000

'81 '82 '83 '84 '85 '86 '87 '88 '89 '90 '91 '92 '93 '94

Safety Rating (0-10)	7.1	Sales Load (max.)	9.3%
Up & Down Market Ranks	B – D	Redemption Fee (max.)	None
Annual Expenses (total)	1.14%	Annual 12b-1 Fee	None

Portfolio

	Fund	S&P
Avg. P/E Ratio	22	20
Avg. Price/Book	3.3	3.1
Avg. 5-Year Earning Growth	12.6%	5.2%
Median Mkt. Capitalization	$1.10 bil.	$3.60 bil.
Correlation v. S&P 500 (R^2)	83%	100%
Market Volatility (Beta)	1.09	1.00
Superiority Rating (Alpha)	–2%	0%

Industry Diversification

Durables	5%
Energy	9%
Finance	15%
Industrial	20%
Non-Durables	5%
Retail	6%
Health	3%
Services	10%
Technology	22%
Utilities	5%
Precious Metals	0%
Other	0%

Dean Witter American Value $1.42 billion

Undervalued industries ● Portfolio Manager: Anita Kolleeny
Two World Trade Center, New York NY 10048 ● 800-869-3863
Founded in 1980 ● Ticker symbol: DWIVX ● Telephone Switching: See prospectus
Minimum Initial Investment: $1,000 ● Minimum IRA Investment: $1,000

Portfolio

	Fund	S&P
Avg. P/E Ratio	24	20
Avg. Price/Book	4.7	3.1
Avg. 5-Year Earning Growth	27.0%	5.2%
Median Mkt. Capitalization	$1.65 bil.	$3.60 bil.
Correlation v. S&P 500 (R²)	61%	100%
Market Volatility (Beta)	1.20	1.00
Superiority Rating (Alpha)	+2%	0%

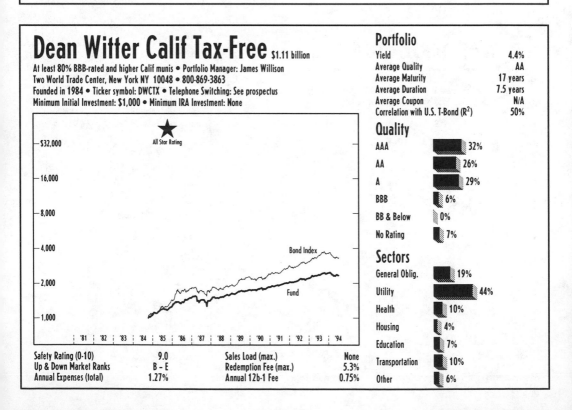

★ ★ ★ ★
All Star Rating

$32,000
16,000
8,000
4,000
2,000
1,000

S&P 500

Fund

'81 '82 '83 '84 '85 '86 '87 '88 '89 '90 '91 '92 '93 '94

Industry Diversification

Durables	1%
Energy	1%
Finance	5%
Industrial	19%
Non-Durables	5%
Retail	4%
Health	4%
Services	15%
Technology	46%
Utilities	0%
Precious Metals	0%
Other	0%

Safety Rating (0-10)	7.0	Sales Load (max.)	None
Up & Down Market Ranks	A – D	Redemption Fee (max.)	5.3%
Annual Expenses (total)	1.61%	Annual 12b-1 Fee	1.00%

Dean Witter Calif Tax-Free $1.11 billion

At least 80% BBB-rated and higher Calif munis ● Portfolio Manager: James Willison
Two World Trade Center, New York NY 10048 ● 800-869-3863
Founded in 1984 ● Ticker symbol: DWCTX ● Telephone Switching: See prospectus
Minimum Initial Investment: $1,000 ● Minimum IRA Investment: None

Portfolio

Yield	4.4%
Average Quality	AA
Average Maturity	17 years
Average Duration	7.5 years
Average Coupon	N/A
Correlation with U.S. T-Bond (R²)	50%

★
All Star Rating

$32,000
16,000
8,000
4,000
2,000
1,000

Bond Index

Fund

'81 '82 '83 '84 '85 '86 '87 '88 '89 '90 '91 '92 '93 '94

Quality

AAA	32%
AA	26%
A	29%
BBB	6%
BB & Below	0%
No Rating	7%

Sectors

General Oblig.	19%
Utility	44%
Health	10%
Housing	4%
Education	7%
Transportation	10%
Other	6%

Safety Rating (0-10)	9.0	Sales Load (max.)	None
Up & Down Market Ranks	B – E	Redemption Fee (max.)	5.3%
Annual Expenses (total)	1.27%	Annual 12b-1 Fee	0.75%

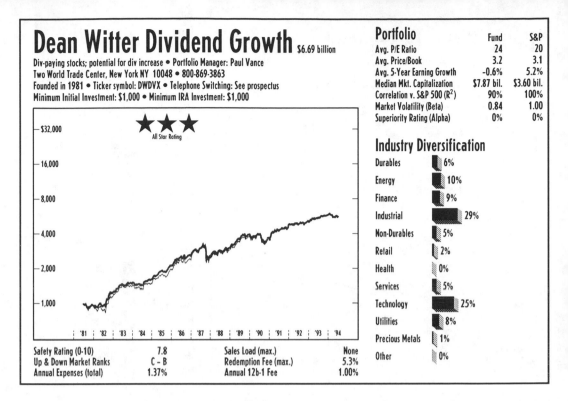

Dean Witter Dividend Growth $6.69 billion

Div-paying stocks; potential for div increase • Portfolio Manager: Paul Vance
Two World Trade Center, New York NY 10048 • 800-869-3863
Founded in 1981 • Ticker symbol: DWDVX • Telephone Switching: See prospectus
Minimum Initial Investment: $1,000 • Minimum IRA Investment: $1,000

★★★
All Star Rating

$32,000
16,000
8,000
4,000
2,000
1,000

'81 '82 '83 '84 '85 '86 '87 '88 '89 '90 '91 '92 '93 '94

Safety Rating (0-10)	7.8	Sales Load (max.)	None
Up & Down Market Ranks	C - B	Redemption Fee (max.)	5.3%
Annual Expenses (total)	1.37%	Annual 12b-1 Fee	1.00%

Portfolio

	Fund	S&P
Avg. P/E Ratio	24	20
Avg. Price/Book	3.2	3.1
Avg. 5-Year Earning Growth	-0.6%	5.2%
Median Mkt. Capitalization	$7.87 bil.	$3.60 bil.
Correlation v. S&P 500 (R^2)	90%	100%
Market Volatility (Beta)	0.84	1.00
Superiority Rating (Alpha)	0%	0%

Industry Diversification

Durables	6%
Energy	10%
Finance	9%
Industrial	29%
Non-Durables	5%
Retail	2%
Health	0%
Services	5%
Technology	25%
Utilities	8%
Precious Metals	1%
Other	0%

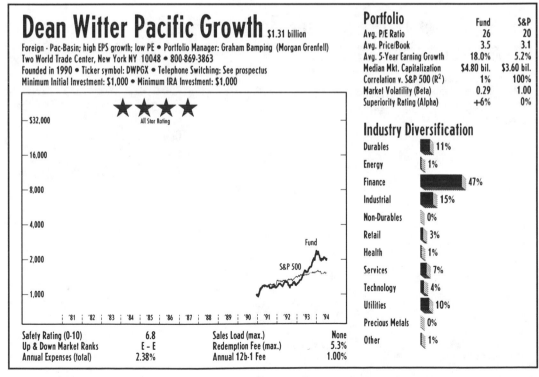

Dean Witter Pacific Growth $1.31 billion

Foreign - Pac-Basin; high EPS growth; low PE • Portfolio Manager: Graham Bamping (Morgan Grenfell)
Two World Trade Center, New York NY 10048 • 800-869-3863
Founded in 1990 • Ticker symbol: DWPGX • Telephone Switching: See prospectus
Minimum Initial Investment: $1,000 • Minimum IRA Investment: $1,000

★★★★
All Star Rating

$32,000
16,000
8,000
4,000
2,000
1,000

Fund
S&P 500

'81 '82 '83 '84 '85 '86 '87 '88 '89 '90 '91 '92 '93 '94

Safety Rating (0-10)	6.8	Sales Load (max.)	None
Up & Down Market Ranks	E - E	Redemption Fee (max.)	5.3%
Annual Expenses (total)	2.38%	Annual 12b-1 Fee	1.00%

Portfolio

	Fund	S&P
Avg. P/E Ratio	26	20
Avg. Price/Book	3.5	3.1
Avg. 5-Year Earning Growth	18.0%	5.2%
Median Mkt. Capitalization	$4.80 bil.	$3.60 bil.
Correlation v. S&P 500 (R^2)	1%	100%
Market Volatility (Beta)	0.29	1.00
Superiority Rating (Alpha)	+6%	0%

Industry Diversification

Durables	11%
Energy	1%
Finance	47%
Industrial	15%
Non-Durables	0%
Retail	3%
Health	1%
Services	7%
Technology	4%
Utilities	10%
Precious Metals	0%
Other	1%

Dean Witter Tax-Exempt Secs $1.46 billion

BBB-rated and higher municipal bonds • Portfolio Manager: James Willison
Two World Trade Center, New York NY 10048 • 800-869-3863
Founded in 1980 • Ticker symbol: DWTEX • Telephone Switching: See prospectus
Minimum Initial Investment: $1,000 • Minimum IRA Investment: None

Portfolio

Yield	5.1%
Average Quality	AA-
Average Maturity	18 years
Average Duration	8.4 years
Average Coupon	6.4%
Correlation with U.S. T-Bond (R^2)	50%

Quality

AAA	28%
AA	29%
A	31%
BBB	7%
BB & Below	0%
No Rating	5%

Sectors

General Oblig.	14%
Utility	39%
Health	11%
Housing	7%
Education	9%
Transportation	17%
Other	3%

★★★
All Star Rating

Bond Index

Fund

Safety Rating (0-10)	9.0	Sales Load (max.)	4.2%
Up & Down Market Ranks	B – D	Redemption Fee (max.)	None
Annual Expenses (total)	0.47%	Annual 12b-1 Fee	None

Dean Witter TCW No Amer Govt $2.09 billion

U.S., Canadian and Mexican govt & mortg secs • Portfolio Manager: Phil Barach (TCW)
Two World Trade Center, New York NY 10048 • 800-869-3863
Founded in 1992 • Ticker symbol: TCGIX • Telephone Switching: See prospectus
Minimum Initial Investment: $1,000 • Minimum IRA Investment: $1,000

Portfolio

Yield	8.0%
Average Quality	AA
Average Maturity	2.8 years
Average Duration	N/A
Average Coupon	N/A
Correlation with U.S. T-Bond (R^2)	22%
Dividends Paid	Monthly

Quality

AAA	0%
AA	100%
A	0%
BBB	0%
BB	0%
B	0%
C	0%
D	0%
No Rating	0%

Bond Index

Fund

Safety Rating (0-10)	9.2	Sales Load (max.)	None
Up & Down Market Ranks	E – C	Redemption Fee (max.)	None
Annual Expenses (total)	1.54%	Annual 12b-1 Fee	0.75%

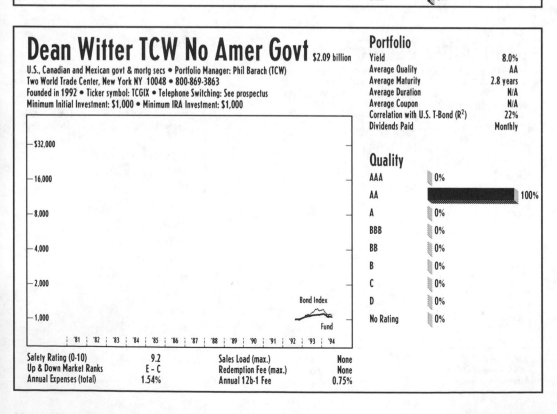

Dean Witter US Government $10.4 billion

US Government securities; Ginnie Maes • Portfolio Manager: Rajesh K. Gupta
Two World Trade Center, New York NY 10048 • 800-869-3863
Founded in 1984 • Ticker symbol: DWUSX • Telephone Switching: See prospectus
Minimum Initial Investment: $1,000 • Minimum IRA Investment: $1,000

Portfolio

Yield	6.1%
Average Quality	AAA
Average Maturity	6.8 years
Average Duration	4.9 years
Average Coupon	6.9%
Correlation with U.S. T-Bond (R^2)	56%
Dividends Paid	Monthly (Accrue Daily)

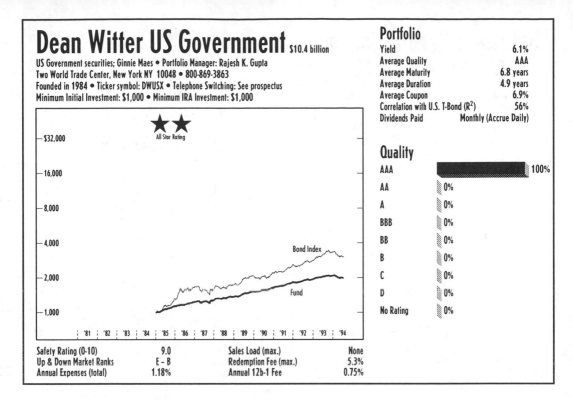

Quality

AAA	100%
AA	0%
A	0%
BBB	0%
BB	0%
B	0%
C	0%
D	0%
No Rating	0%

Safety Rating (0-10)	9.0	Sales Load (max.)	None
Up & Down Market Ranks	E – B	Redemption Fee (max.)	5.3%
Annual Expenses (total)	1.18%	Annual 12b-1 Fee	0.75%

Dean Witter Utilities $3.31 billion

Utility stocks • Portfolio Manager: Ed Gaylor
Two World Trade Center, New York NY 10048 • 800-869-3863
Founded in 1988 • Ticker symbol: DWUTX • Telephone Switching: See prospectus
Minimum Initial Investment: $1,000 • Minimum IRA Investment: $1,000

Portfolio

	Fund	S&P
Avg. P/E Ratio	16	20
Avg. Price/Book	2.0	3.1
Avg. 5-Year Earning Growth	0.6%	5.2%
Median Mkt. Capitalization	$3.05 bil.	$3.60 bil.
Correlation v. S&P 500 (R^2)	43%	100%
Market Volatility (Beta)	0.55	1.00
Superiority Rating (Alpha)	+3%	0%

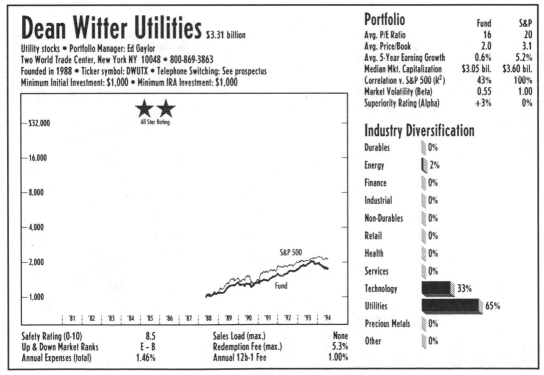

Industry Diversification

Durables	0%
Energy	2%
Finance	0%
Industrial	0%
Non-Durables	0%
Retail	0%
Health	0%
Services	0%
Technology	33%
Utilities	65%
Precious Metals	0%
Other	0%

Safety Rating (0-10)	8.5	Sales Load (max.)	None
Up & Down Market Ranks	E – B	Redemption Fee (max.)	5.3%
Annual Expenses (total)	1.46%	Annual 12b-1 Fee	1.00%

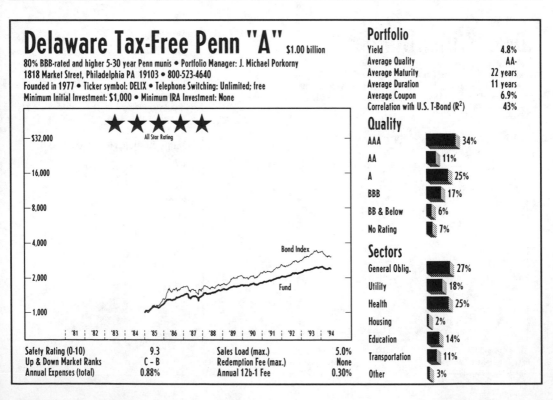

Delaware Decatur Income $1.46 billion

Quality stocks, high yield • Portfolio Manager: John B. Fields
1818 Market Street, Philadelphia PA 19103 • 800-523-4640
Founded in 1957 • Ticker symbol: DELDX • Telephone Switching: Unlimited; free
Minimum Initial Investment: $250 • Minimum IRA Investment: $250

Portfolio

	Fund	S&P
Avg. P/E Ratio	31	20
Avg. Price/Book	3.0	3.1
Avg. 5-Year Earning Growth	−5.6%	5.2%
Median Mkt. Capitalization	$6.57 bil.	$3.60 bil.
Correlation v. S&P 500 (R^2)	77%	100%
Market Volatility (Beta)	0.84	1.00
Superiority Rating (Alpha)	−2%	0%

Industry Diversification

Durables	4%
Energy	15%
Finance	28%
Industrial	28%
Non-Durables	0%
Retail	3%
Health	0%
Services	1%
Technology	16%
Utilities	5%
Precious Metals	0%
Other	0%

★★ All Star Rating

Fund

S&P 500

'81 '82 '83 '84 '85 '86 '87 '88 '89 '90 '91 '92 '93 '94

Safety Rating (0-10)	7.6	Sales Load (max.)	6.1%
Up & Down Market Ranks	D – B	Redemption Fee (max.)	None
Annual Expenses (total)	0.81%	Annual 12b-1 Fee	0.30%

Delaware Tax-Free Penn "A" $1.00 billion

80% BBB-rated and higher 5-30 year Penn munis • Portfolio Manager: J. Michael Porkorny
1818 Market Street, Philadelphia PA 19103 • 800-523-4640
Founded in 1977 • Ticker symbol: DELIX • Telephone Switching: Unlimited; free
Minimum Initial Investment: $1,000 • Minimum IRA Investment: None

Portfolio

Yield	4.8%
Average Quality	AA-
Average Maturity	22 years
Average Duration	11 years
Average Coupon	6.9%
Correlation with U.S. T-Bond (R^2)	43%

Quality

AAA	34%
AA	11%
A	25%
BBB	17%
BB & Below	6%
No Rating	7%

Sectors

General Oblig.	27%
Utility	18%
Health	25%
Housing	2%
Education	14%
Transportation	11%
Other	3%

★★★★★ All Star Rating

Bond Index

Fund

'81 '82 '83 '84 '85 '86 '87 '88 '89 '90 '91 '92 '93 '94

Safety Rating (0-10)	9.3	Sales Load (max.)	5.0%
Up & Down Market Ranks	C – B	Redemption Fee (max.)	None
Annual Expenses (total)	0.88%	Annual 12b-1 Fee	0.30%

Dreyfus California Tax-Exempt $1.65 billion

At least 60% BBB-rated & higher Calif munis • Portfolio Manager: L. Lawrence Troutman
144 Glenn Curtis Blvd, Uniondale NY 11556 • 800-645-6561
Founded in 1983 • Ticker symbol: DRCAX • Telephone Switching: Unlimited; free
Minimum Initial Investment: $2,500 • Minimum IRA Investment: None

Portfolio

Yield	5.5%
Average Quality	AA
Average Maturity	20 years
Average Duration	N/A
Average Coupon	6.4%
Correlation with U.S. T-Bond (R^2)	50%

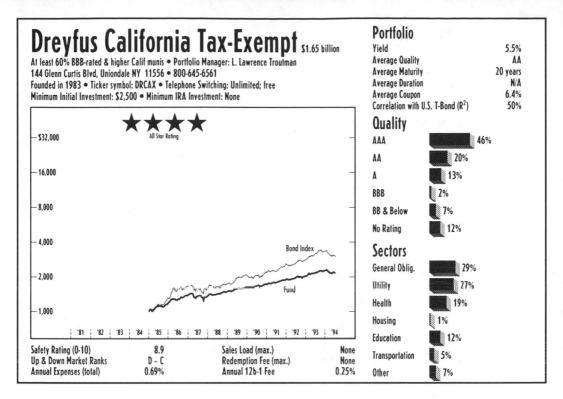

★★★★
All Star Rating

Quality

AAA	46%
AA	20%
A	13%
BBB	2%
BB & Below	7%
No Rating	12%

Sectors

General Oblig.	29%
Utility	27%
Health	19%
Housing	1%
Education	12%
Transportation	5%
Other	7%

Safety Rating (0-10)	8.9	Sales Load (max.)	None
Up & Down Market Ranks	D – C	Redemption Fee (max.)	None
Annual Expenses (total)	0.69%	Annual 12b-1 Fee	0.25%

Dreyfus Fund $2.67 billion

Diversified stocks • Portfolio Manager: Wolodymyr Wronskyj
144 Glenn Curtis Blvd, Uniondale NY 11556 • 800-645-6561
Founded in 1951 • Ticker symbol: DREVX • Telephone Switching: Unlimited; free
Minimum Initial Investment: $2,500 • Minimum IRA Investment: $750

Portfolio

	Fund	S&P
Avg. P/E Ratio	18	20
Avg. Price/Book	3.1	3.1
Avg. 5-Year Earning Growth	11.8%	5.2%
Median Mkt. Capitalization	$6.58 bil.	$3.60 bil.
Correlation v. S&P 500 (R^2)	84%	100%
Market Volatility (Beta)	0.88	1.00
Superiority Rating (Alpha)	–3%	0%

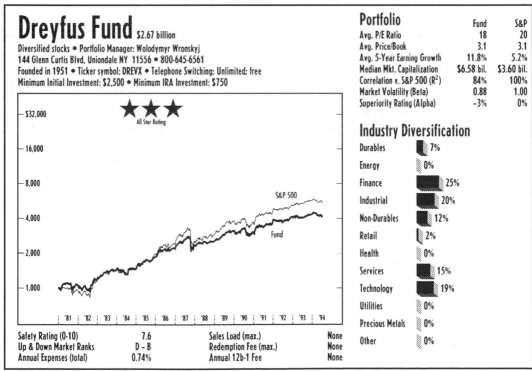

★★★
All Star Rating

Industry Diversification

Durables	7%
Energy	0%
Finance	25%
Industrial	20%
Non-Durables	12%
Retail	2%
Health	0%
Services	15%
Technology	19%
Utilities	0%
Precious Metals	0%
Other	0%

Safety Rating (0-10)	7.6	Sales Load (max.)	None
Up & Down Market Ranks	D – B	Redemption Fee (max.)	None
Annual Expenses (total)	0.74%	Annual 12b-1 Fee	None

Dreyfus GNMA $1.58 billion

65% Ginnie Maes; government securities • Portfolio Manager: Garitt Kono
144 Glenn Curtis Blvd, Uniondale NY 11556 • 800-645-6561
Founded in 1985 • Ticker symbol: DRGMX • Telephone Switching: Unlimited; free
Minimum Initial Investment: $2,500 • Minimum IRA Investment: $250

Portfolio

Yield	6.3%
Average Quality	AAA
Average Maturity	8.0 years
Average Duration	N/A
Average Coupon	6.7%
Correlation with U.S. T-Bond (R^2)	56%
Dividends Paid	Monthly

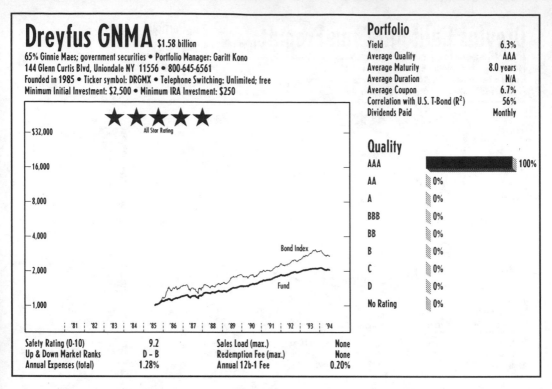

★ ★ ★ ★ ★
All Star Rating

Quality

AAA	100%
AA	0%
A	0%
BBB	0%
BB	0%
B	0%
C	0%
D	0%
No Rating	0%

Safety Rating (0-10)	9.2	Sales Load (max.)	None
Up & Down Market Ranks	D – B	Redemption Fee (max.)	None
Annual Expenses (total)	1.28%	Annual 12b-1 Fee	0.20%

Dreyfus Growth & Income (Conv) $1.66 billion

Foreign & US - stocks; inv-gr bonds; mny mkts • Portfolio Manager: Richard B. Hoey
144 Glenn Curtis Blvd, Uniondale NY 11556 • 800-645-6561
Founded in 1971 • Ticker symbol: DGRIX • Telephone Switching: Unlimited; free
Minimum Initial Investment: $2,500 • Minimum IRA Investment: $750

Portfolio

	Fund	S&P
Avg. P/E Ratio	23	20
Avg. Price/Book	3.1	3.1
Avg. 5-Year Earning Growth	7.8%	5.2%
Median Mkt. Capitalization	$1.34 bil.	$3.60 bil.
Correlation v. S&P 500 (R^2)	57%	100%
Market Volatility (Beta)	0.67	1.00
Superiority Rating (Alpha)	–2%	0%

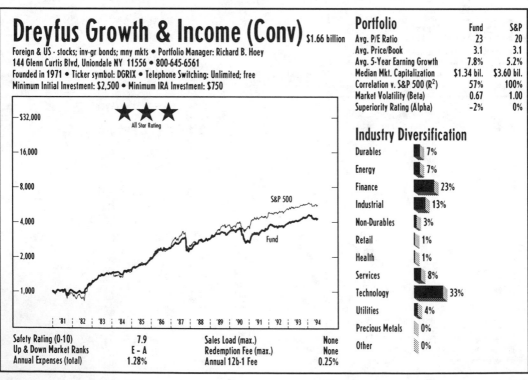

★ ★ ★
All Star Rating

Industry Diversification

Durables	7%
Energy	7%
Finance	23%
Industrial	13%
Non-Durables	3%
Retail	1%
Health	1%
Services	8%
Technology	33%
Utilities	4%
Precious Metals	0%
Other	0%

Safety Rating (0-10)	7.9	Sales Load (max.)	None
Up & Down Market Ranks	E – A	Redemption Fee (max.)	None
Annual Expenses (total)	1.28%	Annual 12b-1 Fee	0.25%

Dreyfus Inter Municipal Bond $1.74 billion

80% A-rated and higher municipals • Portfolio Manager: Monica S. Wieboldt
144 Glenn Curtis Blvd, Uniondale NY 11556 • 800-645-6561
Founded in 1983 • Ticker symbol: DITEX • Telephone Switching: Unlimited; free
Minimum Initial Investment: $2,500 • Minimum IRA Investment: None

Portfolio

Yield	5.1%
Average Quality	AA
Average Maturity	10.0 years
Average Duration	N/A
Average Coupon	6.4%
Correlation with U.S. T-Bond (R^2)	47%

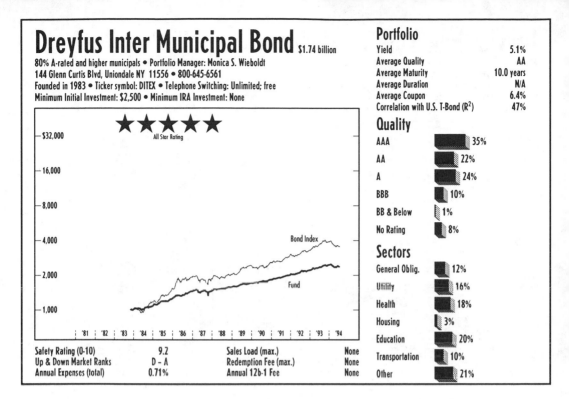

★★★★★
All Star Rating

Quality

AAA	35%
AA	22%
A	24%
BBB	10%
BB & Below	1%
No Rating	8%

Sectors

General Oblig.	12%
Utility	16%
Health	18%
Housing	3%
Education	20%
Transportation	10%
Other	21%

Safety Rating (0-10)	9.2	Sales Load (max.)	None
Up & Down Market Ranks	D – A	Redemption Fee (max.)	None
Annual Expenses (total)	0.71%	Annual 12b-1 Fee	None

Dreyfus Municipal Bond $4.07 billion

80% long-term municipals • Portfolio Manager: Richard J. Moynihan
144 Glenn Curtis Blvd, Uniondale NY 11556 • 800-645-6561
Founded in 1976 • Ticker symbol: DRTAX • Telephone Switching: Unlimited; free
Minimum Initial Investment: $2,500 • Minimum IRA Investment: None

Portfolio

Yield	5.8%
Average Quality	AA-
Average Maturity	23 years
Average Duration	N/A
Average Coupon	6.9%
Correlation with U.S. T-Bond (R^2)	50%

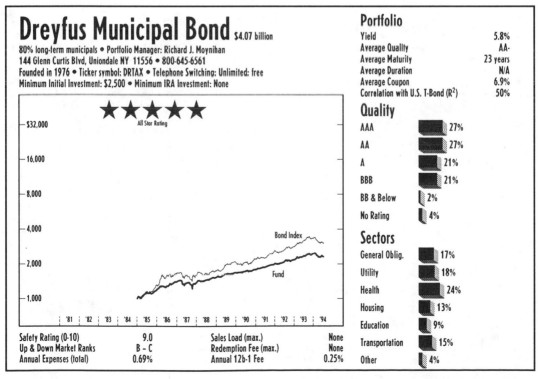

★★★★★
All Star Rating

Quality

AAA	27%
AA	27%
A	21%
BBB	21%
BB & Below	2%
No Rating	4%

Sectors

General Oblig.	17%
Utility	18%
Health	24%
Housing	13%
Education	9%
Transportation	15%
Other	4%

Safety Rating (0-10)	9.0	Sales Load (max.)	None
Up & Down Market Ranks	B – C	Redemption Fee (max.)	None
Annual Expenses (total)	0.69%	Annual 12b-1 Fee	0.25%

Dreyfus New York Tax-Exempt $1.95 billion

At least 65% BBB-rated and higher N.Y. munis • Portfolio Manager: Monica S. Wieboldt
144 Glenn Curtis Blvd, Uniondale NY 11556 • 800-645-6561
Founded in 1983 • Ticker symbol: DRNYX • Telephone Switching: Unlimited; free
Minimum Initial Investment: $2,500 • Minimum IRA Investment: None

Portfolio

Yield	5.3%
Average Quality	A+
Average Maturity	20 years
Average Duration	N/A
Average Coupon	6.7%
Correlation with U.S. T-Bond (R^2)	51%

Quality

AAA	16%
AA	23%
A	27%
BBB	22%
BB & Below	5%
No Rating	1%

Sectors

General Oblig.	31%
Utility	21%
Health	4%
Housing	6%
Education	12%
Transportation	22%
Other	4%

★★★★ All Star Rating

(Chart: $32,000 / 16,000 / 8,000 / 4,000 / 2,000 / 1,000 — years '81 to '94, Bond Index, Fund)

Safety Rating (0-10)	9.0	Sales Load (max.)	None
Up & Down Market Ranks	B – D	Redemption Fee (max.)	None
Annual Expenses (total)	0.70%	Annual 12b-1 Fee	None

Duff & Phelps Utilities Icm $1.56 billion

Utility securities • Portfolio Manager: Richard J. Spletzer
55 E. Monroe, Room 3800, Chicago IL 60603 • 800-426-5523
Founded in 1987 • Ticker symbol: DNP • Telephone Switching: Via broker
Minimum Initial Investment: $0 • Minimum IRA Investment: None

Portfolio

	Fund	S&P
Avg. P/E Ratio	13	20
Avg. Price/Book	1.6	3.1
Avg. 5-Year Earning Growth	0.9%	5.2%
Median Mkt. Capitalization	$3.34 bil.	$3.60 bil.
Correlation v. S&P 500 (R^2)	7%	100%
Market Volatility (Beta)	0.47	1.00
Superiority Rating (Alpha)	+1%	0%

Industry Diversification

Durables	0%
Energy	0%
Finance	0%
Industrial	0%
Non-Durables	0%
Retail	0%
Health	0%
Services	0%
Technology	16%
Utilities	84%
Precious Metals	0%
Other	0%

★ All Star Rating

(Chart: $32,000 / 16,000 / 8,000 / 4,000 / 2,000 / 1,000 — years '81 to '94, S&P 500, Fund)

Safety Rating (0-10)	7.5	Sales Load (max.)	None
Up & Down Market Ranks	E – A	Redemption Fee (max.)	None
Annual Expenses (total)	1.04%	Annual 12b-1 Fee	None

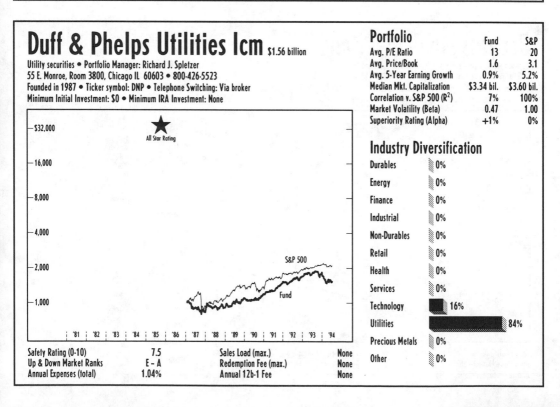

Evergreen Total Return $1.06 billion

Diversified securities • Portfolio Manager: Nola M. Falcone
2500 Westchester Avenue, Purchase NY 10577 • 800-235-0064
Founded in 1978 • Ticker symbol: EVTRX • Telephone Switching: 4 per yr.fr; $5
Minimum Initial Investment: $2,000 • Minimum IRA Investment: None

Portfolio

	Fund	S&P
Avg. P/E Ratio	23	20
Avg. Price/Book	2.1	3.1
Avg. 5-Year Earning Growth	–5.7%	5.2%
Median Mkt. Capitalization	$1.11 bil.	$3.60 bil.
Correlation v. S&P 500 (R^2)	79%	100%
Market Volatility (Beta)	0.68	1.00
Superiority Rating (Alpha)	+1%	0%

Industry Diversification

Durables	3%
Energy	8%
Finance	17%
Industrial	13%
Non-Durables	0%
Retail	0%
Health	0%
Services	4%
Technology	18%
Utilities	36%
Precious Metals	1%
Other	0%

★★★ All Star Rating

Safety Rating (0-10)	8.4	Sales Load (max.)	None
Up & Down Market Ranks	E – B	Redemption Fee (max.)	None
Annual Expenses (total)	1.18%	Annual 12b-1 Fee	None

Federated GNMA Trust $1.70 billion

Ginnie Mae securities • Portfolio Manager: Gary Madish
Federated Investors Tower, Pittsburgh PA 15222 • 800-245-2423
Founded in 1982 • Ticker symbol: FGMAX • Telephone Switching: Unlimited; free
Minimum Initial Investment: $25,000 • Minimum IRA Investment: $2,000

Portfolio

Yield	6.6%
Average Quality	AAA
Average Maturity	5.9 years
Average Duration	3.8 years
Average Coupon	7.9%
Correlation with U.S. T-Bond (R^2)	51%
Dividends Paid	Monthly (Accrue Daily)

Quality

AAA	100%
AA	0%
A	0%
BBB	0%
BB	0%
B	0%
C	0%
D	0%
No Rating	0%

★★★ All Star Rating

Safety Rating (0-10)	8.9	Sales Load (max.)	None
Up & Down Market Ranks	C – D	Redemption Fee (max.)	None
Annual Expenses (total)	0.57%	Annual 12b-1 Fee	0.25%

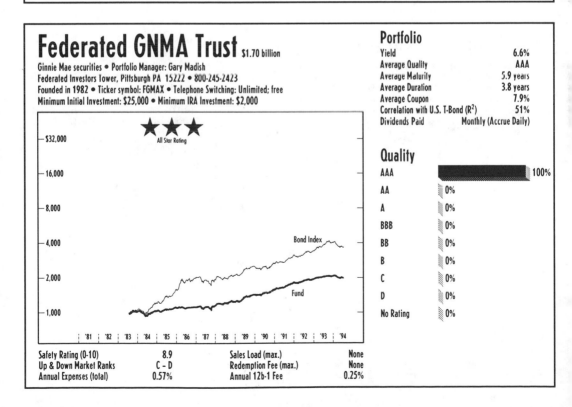

Federated Income Trust Inst $1.52 billion

U.S. Govt securities and agencies • Portfolio Manager: Gary Madich
Federated Investors Tower, Pittsburgh PA 15222 • 800-245-2423
Founded in 1982 • Ticker symbol: FICMX • Telephone Switching: Unlimited; free
Minimum Initial Investment: $25,000 • Minimum IRA Investment: $2,000

Portfolio

Yield	5.6%
Average Quality	AAA
Average Maturity	3.7 years
Average Duration	2.9 years
Average Coupon	6.2%
Correlation with U.S. T-Bond (R^2)	45%
Dividends Paid	Monthly (Accrue Daily)

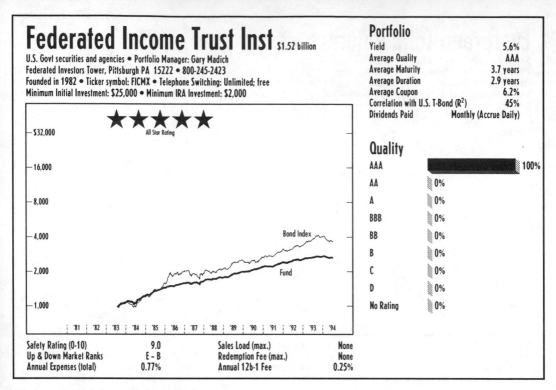

★★★★★ All Star Rating

Quality

AAA	100%
AA	0%
A	0%
BBB	0%
BB	0%
B	0%
C	0%
D	0%
No Rating	0%

Safety Rating (0-10)	9.0	Sales Load (max.)	None
Up & Down Market Ranks	E - B	Redemption Fee (max.)	None
Annual Expenses (total)	0.77%	Annual 12b-1 Fee	0.25%

Fidel Adv Growth Oppor "A" $3.37 billion

Diversified stocks • Portfolio Manager: George A. Vanderheiden
164 Northern Avenue, Boston MA 02210 • 800-522-7297
Founded in 1987 • Ticker symbol: FAGOX • Telephone Switching: Unlimited; free
Minimum Initial Investment: $2,500 • Minimum IRA Investment: $500

Portfolio

	Fund	S&P
Avg. P/E Ratio	20	20
Avg. Price/Book	3.0	3.1
Avg. 5-Year Earning Growth	13.0%	5.2%
Median Mkt. Capitalization	$1.51 bil.	$3.60 bil.
Correlation v. S&P 500 (R^2)	78%	100%
Market Volatility (Beta)	1.03	1.00
Superiority Rating (Alpha)	+5%	0%

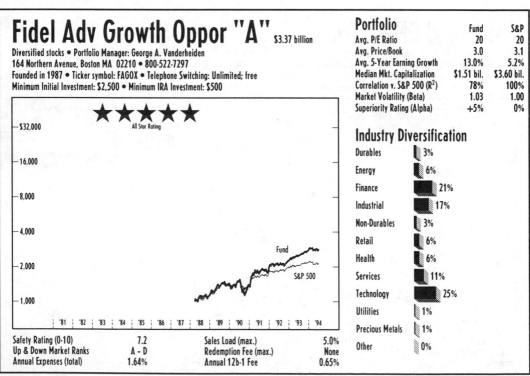

★★★★★ All Star Rating

Industry Diversification

Durables	3%
Energy	6%
Finance	21%
Industrial	17%
Non-Durables	3%
Retail	6%
Health	6%
Services	11%
Technology	25%
Utilities	1%
Precious Metals	1%
Other	0%

Safety Rating (0-10)	7.2	Sales Load (max.)	5.0%
Up & Down Market Ranks	A - D	Redemption Fee (max.)	None
Annual Expenses (total)	1.64%	Annual 12b-1 Fee	0.65%

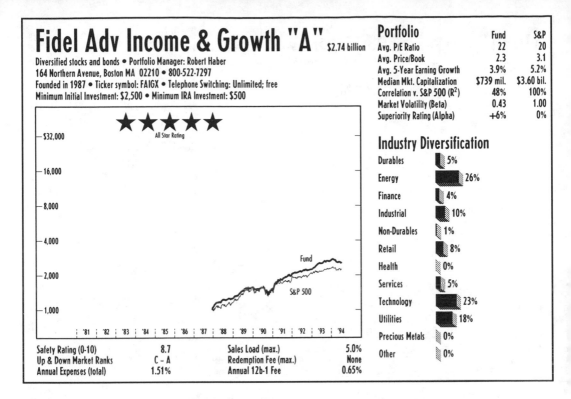

Fidel Adv Income & Growth "A" $2.74 billion

Diversified stocks and bonds • Portfolio Manager: Robert Haber
164 Northern Avenue, Boston MA 02210 • 800-522-7297
Founded in 1987 • Ticker symbol: FAIGX • Telephone Switching: Unlimited; free
Minimum Initial Investment: $2,500 • Minimum IRA Investment: $500

Portfolio

	Fund	S&P
Avg. P/E Ratio	22	20
Avg. Price/Book	2.3	3.1
Avg. 5-Year Earning Growth	3.9%	5.2%
Median Mkt. Capitalization	$739 mil.	$3.60 bil.
Correlation v. S&P 500 (R^2)	48%	100%
Market Volatility (Beta)	0.43	1.00
Superiority Rating (Alpha)	+6%	0%

★★★★★
All Star Rating

Industry Diversification

Durables	5%
Energy	26%
Finance	4%
Industrial	10%
Non-Durables	1%
Retail	8%
Health	0%
Services	5%
Technology	23%
Utilities	18%
Precious Metals	0%
Other	0%

Safety Rating (0-10)	8.7	Sales Load (max.)	5.0%
Up & Down Market Ranks	C – A	Redemption Fee (max.)	None
Annual Expenses (total)	1.51%	Annual 12b-1 Fee	0.65%

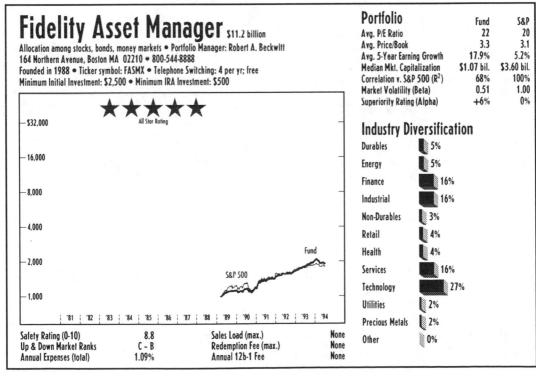

Fidelity Asset Manager $11.2 billion

Allocation among stocks, bonds, money markets • Portfolio Manager: Robert A. Beckwitt
164 Northern Avenue, Boston MA 02210 • 800-544-8888
Founded in 1988 • Ticker symbol: FASMX • Telephone Switching: 4 per yr; free
Minimum Initial Investment: $2,500 • Minimum IRA Investment: $500

Portfolio

	Fund	S&P
Avg. P/E Ratio	22	20
Avg. Price/Book	3.3	3.1
Avg. 5-Year Earning Growth	17.9%	5.2%
Median Mkt. Capitalization	$1.07 bil.	$3.60 bil.
Correlation v. S&P 500 (R^2)	68%	100%
Market Volatility (Beta)	0.51	1.00
Superiority Rating (Alpha)	+6%	0%

★★★★★
All Star Rating

Industry Diversification

Durables	5%
Energy	5%
Finance	16%
Industrial	16%
Non-Durables	3%
Retail	4%
Health	4%
Services	16%
Technology	27%
Utilities	2%
Precious Metals	2%
Other	0%

Safety Rating (0-10)	8.8	Sales Load (max.)	None
Up & Down Market Ranks	C – B	Redemption Fee (max.)	None
Annual Expenses (total)	1.09%	Annual 12b-1 Fee	None

Fidelity Asset Manager Growth $2.86 billion

Asset allocation: stocks, bonds, short term • Portfolio Manager: Robert A. Beckwitt
164 Northern Avenue, Boston MA 02210 • 800-544-8888
Founded in 1991 • Ticker symbol: FASGX • Telephone Switching: 4 per yr; free
Minimum Initial Investment: $2,500 • Minimum IRA Investment: $500

Portfolio

	Fund	S&P
Avg. P/E Ratio	20	20
Avg. Price/Book	2.9	3.1
Avg. 5-Year Earning Growth	9.2%	5.2%
Median Mkt. Capitalization	$4.10 bil.	$3.60 bil.
Correlation v. S&P 500 (R^2)	61%	100%
Market Volatility (Beta)	0.67	1.00
Superiority Rating (Alpha)	+6%	0%

Industry Diversification

Durables	8%
Energy	5%
Finance	20%
Industrial	4%
Non-Durables	4%
Retail	7%
Health	8%
Services	4%
Technology	31%
Utilities	9%
Precious Metals	0%
Other	0%

Safety Rating (0-10)	8.0	Sales Load (max.)	None
Up & Down Market Ranks	E – D	Redemption Fee (max.)	None
Annual Expenses (total)	1.20%	Annual 12b-1 Fee	None

Fidelity Balanced $5.29 billion

Div-paying stocks; 25% investment-grade bonds • Portfolio Manager: Robert J. Haber
164 Northern Avenue, Boston MA 02210 • 800-544-8888
Founded in 1986 • Ticker symbol: FBALX • Telephone Switching: 4 per yr; free
Minimum Initial Investment: $2,500 • Minimum IRA Investment: $500

Portfolio

	Fund	S&P
Avg. P/E Ratio	29	20
Avg. Price/Book	2.2	3.1
Avg. 5-Year Earning Growth	-4.9%	5.2%
Median Mkt. Capitalization	$1.01 bil.	$3.60 bil.
Correlation v. S&P 500 (R^2)	45%	100%
Market Volatility (Beta)	0.37	1.00
Superiority Rating (Alpha)	+6%	0%

Industry Diversification

Durables	16%
Energy	24%
Finance	9%
Industrial	13%
Non-Durables	2%
Retail	3%
Health	0%
Services	0%
Technology	22%
Utilities	10%
Precious Metals	1%
Other	0%

Safety Rating (0-10)	8.9	Sales Load (max.)	None
Up & Down Market Ranks	E – A	Redemption Fee (max.)	None
Annual Expenses (total)	0.93%	Annual 12b-1 Fee	None

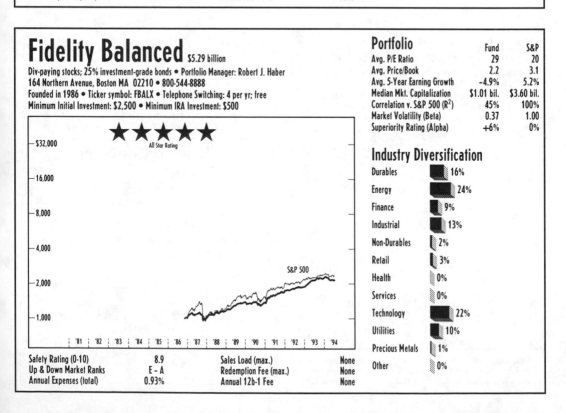

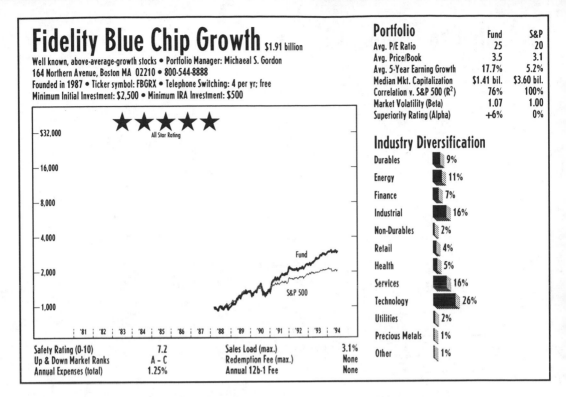

Fidelity Blue Chip Growth $1.91 billion

Well known, above-average-growth stocks • Portfolio Manager: Michaeal S. Gordon
164 Northern Avenue, Boston MA 02210 • 800-544-8888
Founded in 1987 • Ticker symbol: FBGRX • Telephone Switching: 4 per yr; free
Minimum Initial Investment: $2,500 • Minimum IRA Investment: $500

★★★★★
All Star Rating

Fund

S&P 500

Portfolio	Fund	S&P
Avg. P/E Ratio	25	20
Avg. Price/Book	3.5	3.1
Avg. 5-Year Earning Growth	17.7%	5.2%
Median Mkt. Capitalization	$1.41 bil.	$3.60 bil.
Correlation v. S&P 500 (R^2)	76%	100%
Market Volatility (Beta)	1.07	1.00
Superiority Rating (Alpha)	+6%	0%

Industry Diversification

Durables	9%
Energy	11%
Finance	7%
Industrial	16%
Non-Durables	2%
Retail	4%
Health	5%
Services	16%
Technology	26%
Utilities	2%
Precious Metals	1%
Other	1%

Safety Rating (0-10)	7.2	Sales Load (max.)	3.1%
Up & Down Market Ranks	A – C	Redemption Fee (max.)	None
Annual Expenses (total)	1.25%	Annual 12b-1 Fee	None

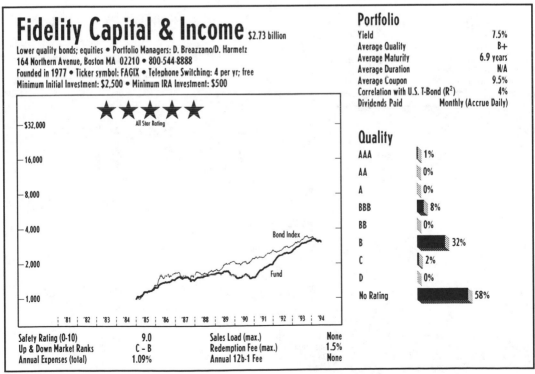

Fidelity Capital & Income $2.73 billion

Lower quality bonds; equities • Portfolio Managers: D. Breazzano/D. Harmetz
164 Northern Avenue, Boston MA 02210 • 800-544-8888
Founded in 1977 • Ticker symbol: FAGIX • Telephone Switching: 4 per yr; free
Minimum Initial Investment: $2,500 • Minimum IRA Investment: $500

★★★★★
All Star Rating

Bond Index

Fund

Portfolio	
Yield	7.5%
Average Quality	B+
Average Maturity	6.9 years
Average Duration	N/A
Average Coupon	9.5%
Correlation with U.S. T-Bond (R^2)	4%
Dividends Paid	Monthly (Accrue Daily)

Quality

AAA	1%
AA	0%
A	0%
BBB	8%
BB	0%
B	32%
C	2%
D	0%
No Rating	58%

Safety Rating (0-10)	9.0	Sales Load (max.)	None
Up & Down Market Ranks	C – B	Redemption Fee (max.)	1.5%
Annual Expenses (total)	1.09%	Annual 12b-1 Fee	None

Fidelity Capital Appreciation $1.91 billion

Diversified securities • Portfolio Manager: Thomas Sweeney
164 Northern Avenue, Boston MA 02210 • 800-544-8888
Founded in 1986 • Ticker symbol: FDCAX • Telephone Switching: 4 per yr; free
Minimum Initial Investment: $2,500 • Minimum IRA Investment: $500

Portfolio

	Fund	S&P
Avg. P/E Ratio	29	20
Avg. Price/Book	2.7	3.1
Avg. 5-Year Earning Growth	-4.6%	5.2%
Median Mkt. Capitalization	$310 mil.	$3.60 bil.
Correlation v. S&P 500 (R^2)	39%	100%
Market Volatility (Beta)	0.64	1.00
Superiority Rating (Alpha)	+2%	0%

★★★★★
All Star Rating

Fund

S&P 500

$32,000
16,000
8,000
4,000
2,000
1,000

'81 '82 '83 '84 '85 '86 '87 '88 '89 '90 '91 '92 '93 '94

Industry Diversification

Durables	19%
Energy	7%
Finance	2%
Industrial	4%
Non-Durables	15%
Retail	7%
Health	0%
Services	22%
Technology	3%
Utilities	16%
Precious Metals	5%
Other	0%

Safety Rating (0-10)	7.8	Sales Load (max.)	3.1%
Up & Down Market Ranks	C - C	Redemption Fee (max.)	None
Annual Expenses (total)	0.86%	Annual 12b-1 Fee	None

Fidelity Contrafund $7.71 billion

Out-of-favor stocks • Portfolio Manager: William Danoff
164 Northern Avenue, Boston MA 02210 • 800-544-8888
Founded in 1967 • Ticker symbol: FCNTX • Telephone Switching: 4 per yr; free
Minimum Initial Investment: $2,500 • Minimum IRA Investment: $500

Portfolio

	Fund	S&P
Avg. P/E Ratio	25	20
Avg. Price/Book	3.5	3.1
Avg. 5-Year Earning Growth	11.1%	5.2%
Median Mkt. Capitalization	$648 mil.	$3.60 bil.
Correlation v. S&P 500 (R^2)	65%	100%
Market Volatility (Beta)	0.97	1.00
Superiority Rating (Alpha)	+6%	0%

★★★★★
All Star Rating

Fund

S&P 500

$32,000
16,000
8,000
4,000
2,000
1,000

'81 '82 '83 '84 '85 '86 '87 '88 '89 '90 '91 '92 '93 '94

Industry Diversification

Durables	6%
Energy	10%
Finance	5%
Industrial	21%
Non-Durables	6%
Retail	3%
Health	4%
Services	12%
Technology	26%
Utilities	3%
Precious Metals	3%
Other	1%

Safety Rating (0-10)	7.5	Sales Load (max.)	3.1%
Up & Down Market Ranks	B - C	Redemption Fee (max.)	None
Annual Expenses (total)	1.06%	Annual 12b-1 Fee	None

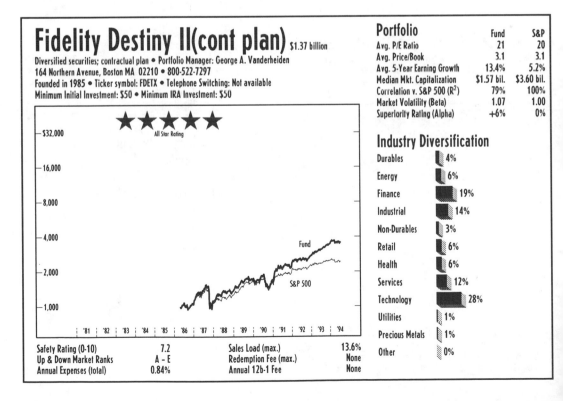

Fidelity Destiny I (cont plan) $3.24 billion

Diversified securities; contractual plan ● Portfolio Manager: George A. Vanderheiden
164 Northern Avenue, Boston MA 02210 ● 800-522-7297
Founded in 1970 ● Ticker symbol: FDESX ● Telephone Switching: Not available
Minimum Initial Investment: $50 ● Minimum IRA Investment: $50

★★★★★
All Star Rating

Safety Rating (0-10)	7.3	Sales Load (max.)	13.6%
Up & Down Market Ranks	A – D	Redemption Fee (max.)	None
Annual Expenses (total)	0.65%	Annual 12b-1 Fee	None

Portfolio

	Fund	S&P
Avg. P/E Ratio	19	20
Avg. Price/Book	2.9	3.1
Avg. 5-Year Earning Growth	8.1%	5.2%
Median Mkt. Capitalization	$5.23 bil.	$3.60 bil.
Correlation v. S&P 500 (R^2)	81%	100%
Market Volatility (Beta)	1.03	1.00
Superiority Rating (Alpha)	+5%	0%

Industry Diversification

Durables	4%
Energy	9%
Finance	22%
Industrial	4%
Non-Durables	5%
Retail	5%
Health	4%
Services	4%
Technology	15%
Utilities	9%
Precious Metals	0%
Other	19%

Fidelity Destiny II(cont plan) $1.37 billion

Diversified securities; contractual plan ● Portfolio Manager: George A. Vanderheiden
164 Northern Avenue, Boston MA 02210 ● 800-522-7297
Founded in 1985 ● Ticker symbol: FDETX ● Telephone Switching: Not available
Minimum Initial Investment: $50 ● Minimum IRA Investment: $50

★★★★★
All Star Rating

Safety Rating (0-10)	7.2	Sales Load (max.)	13.6%
Up & Down Market Ranks	A – E	Redemption Fee (max.)	None
Annual Expenses (total)	0.84%	Annual 12b-1 Fee	None

Portfolio

	Fund	S&P
Avg. P/E Ratio	21	20
Avg. Price/Book	3.1	3.1
Avg. 5-Year Earning Growth	13.4%	5.2%
Median Mkt. Capitalization	$1.57 bil.	$3.60 bil.
Correlation v. S&P 500 (R^2)	79%	100%
Market Volatility (Beta)	1.07	1.00
Superiority Rating (Alpha)	+6%	0%

Industry Diversification

Durables	4%
Energy	6%
Finance	19%
Industrial	14%
Non-Durables	3%
Retail	6%
Health	6%
Services	12%
Technology	28%
Utilities	1%
Precious Metals	1%
Other	0%

Fidelity Emerging Markets $1.55 billion

Foreign - 65% emerging market securities • Portfolio Manager: Richard Hazelwood
164 Northern Avenue, Boston MA 02210 • 800-544-8888
Founded in 1990 • Ticker symbol: FEMKX • Telephone Switching: 4 per yr; free
Minimum Initial Investment: $2,500 • Minimum IRA Investment: $500

Portfolio	Fund	S&P
Avg. P/E Ratio	27	20
Avg. Price/Book	4.7	3.1
Avg. 5-Year Earning Growth	N/A	5.2%
Median Mkt. Capitalization	$2.60 bil.	$3.60 bil.
Correlation v. S&P 500 (R^2)	7%	100%
Market Volatility (Beta)	0.67	1.00
Superiority Rating (Alpha)	+6%	0%

Industry Diversification

Durables	0%
Energy	3%
Finance	0%
Industrial	0%
Non-Durables	4%
Retail	10%
Health	6%
Services	2%
Technology	40%
Utilities	19%
Precious Metals	0%
Other	16%

Fund

S&P 500

Safety Rating (0-10)	5.2	Sales Load (max.)	3.1%
Up & Down Market Ranks	E – E	Redemption Fee (max.)	1.5%
Annual Expenses (total)	1.91%	Annual 12b-1 Fee	None

Fidelity Equity-Income $6.94 billion

High-yield conservative stocks • Portfolio Manager: Stephen R. Petersen
164 Northern Avenue, Boston MA 02210 • 800-544-8888
Founded in 1966 • Ticker symbol: FEQIX • Telephone Switching: 4 per yr; free
Minimum Initial Investment: $2,500 • Minimum IRA Investment: $500

Portfolio	Fund	S&P
Avg. P/E Ratio	21	20
Avg. Price/Book	2.5	3.1
Avg. 5-Year Earning Growth	2.1%	5.2%
Median Mkt. Capitalization	$3.22 bil.	$3.60 bil.
Correlation v. S&P 500 (R^2)	80%	100%
Market Volatility (Beta)	0.77	1.00
Superiority Rating (Alpha)	+4%	0%

★ ★ ★ ★ ★
All Star Rating

Fund

S&P 500

Industry Diversification

Durables	2%
Energy	9%
Finance	27%
Industrial	18%
Non-Durables	5%
Retail	2%
Health	1%
Services	3%
Technology	25%
Utilities	8%
Precious Metals	0%
Other	0%

Safety Rating (0-10)	8.0	Sales Load (max.)	None
Up & Down Market Ranks	D – A	Redemption Fee (max.)	None
Annual Expenses (total)	0.72%	Annual 12b-1 Fee	None

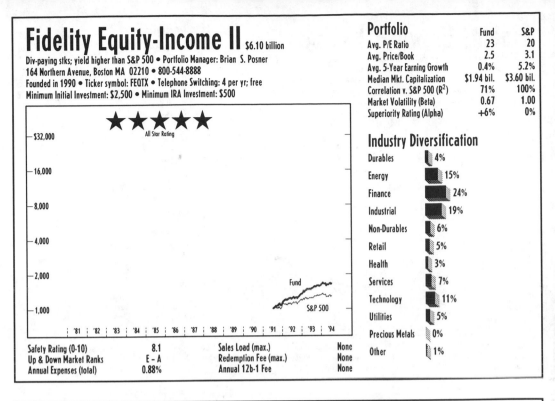

Fidelity Equity-Income II $6.10 billion

Div-paying stks; yield higher than S&P 500 • Portfolio Manager: Brian S. Posner
164 Northern Avenue, Boston MA 02210 • 800-544-8888
Founded in 1990 • Ticker symbol: FEQTX • Telephone Switching: 4 per yr; free
Minimum Initial Investment: $2,500 • Minimum IRA Investment: $500

Portfolio

	Fund	S&P
Avg. P/E Ratio	23	20
Avg. Price/Book	2.5	3.1
Avg. 5-Year Earning Growth	0.4%	5.2%
Median Mkt. Capitalization	$1.94 bil.	$3.60 bil.
Correlation v. S&P 500 (R^2)	71%	100%
Market Volatility (Beta)	0.67	1.00
Superiority Rating (Alpha)	+6%	0%

Industry Diversification

Durables	4%
Energy	15%
Finance	24%
Industrial	19%
Non-Durables	6%
Retail	5%
Health	3%
Services	7%
Technology	11%
Utilities	5%
Precious Metals	0%
Other	1%

Safety Rating (0-10)	8.1	Sales Load (max.)	None
Up & Down Market Ranks	E – A	Redemption Fee (max.)	None
Annual Expenses (total)	0.88%	Annual 12b-1 Fee	None

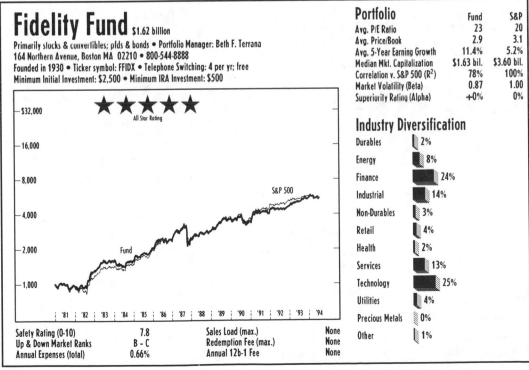

Fidelity Fund $1.62 billion

Primarily stocks & convertibles; pfds & bonds • Portfolio Manager: Beth F. Terrana
164 Northern Avenue, Boston MA 02210 • 800-544-8888
Founded in 1930 • Ticker symbol: FFIDX • Telephone Switching: 4 per yr; free
Minimum Initial Investment: $2,500 • Minimum IRA Investment: $500

Portfolio

	Fund	S&P
Avg. P/E Ratio	23	20
Avg. Price/Book	2.9	3.1
Avg. 5-Year Earning Growth	11.4%	5.2%
Median Mkt. Capitalization	$1.63 bil.	$3.60 bil.
Correlation v. S&P 500 (R^2)	78%	100%
Market Volatility (Beta)	0.87	1.00
Superiority Rating (Alpha)	+0%	0%

Industry Diversification

Durables	2%
Energy	8%
Finance	24%
Industrial	14%
Non-Durables	3%
Retail	4%
Health	2%
Services	13%
Technology	25%
Utilities	4%
Precious Metals	0%
Other	1%

Safety Rating (0-10)	7.8	Sales Load (max.)	None
Up & Down Market Ranks	B – C	Redemption Fee (max.)	None
Annual Expenses (total)	0.66%	Annual 12b-1 Fee	None

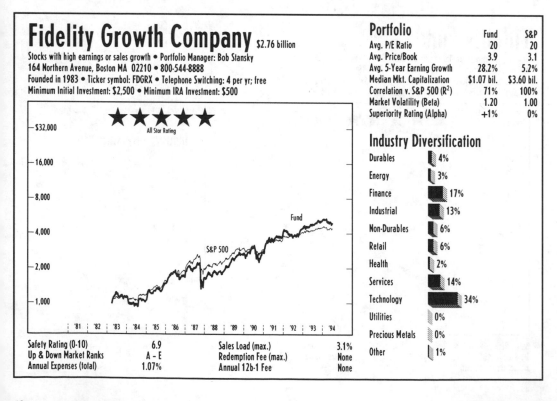

Fidelity Growth & Income $8.44 billion

Dividend-paying growth stocks • Portfolio Manager: Steven Kaye
164 Northern Avenue, Boston MA 02210 • 800-544-8888
Founded in 1985 • Ticker symbol: FGRIX • Telephone Switching: 4 per yr; free
Minimum Initial Investment: $2,500 • Minimum IRA Investment: $2,500

★★★★★
All Star Rating

Fund

S&P 500

Portfolio	Fund	S&P
Avg. P/E Ratio	22	20
Avg. Price/Book	3.0	3.1
Avg. 5-Year Earning Growth	10.6%	5.2%
Median Mkt. Capitalization	$1.73 bil.	$3.60 bil.
Correlation v. S&P 500 (R^2)	80%	100%
Market Volatility (Beta)	0.86	1.00
Superiority Rating (Alpha)	+4%	0%

Industry Diversification

Durables	4%
Energy	8%
Finance	21%
Industrial	15%
Non-Durables	2%
Retail	5%
Health	4%
Services	8%
Technology	27%
Utilities	6%
Precious Metals	0%
Other	0%

Safety Rating (0-10)	7.8	Sales Load (max.)	3.1%
Up & Down Market Ranks	B – C	Redemption Fee (max.)	None
Annual Expenses (total)	0.83%	Annual 12b-1 Fee	None

Fidelity Growth Company $2.76 billion

Stocks with high earnings or sales growth • Portfolio Manager: Bob Stansky
164 Northern Avenue, Boston MA 02210 • 800-544-8888
Founded in 1983 • Ticker symbol: FDGRX • Telephone Switching: 4 per yr; free
Minimum Initial Investment: $2,500 • Minimum IRA Investment: $500

★★★★★
All Star Rating

Fund

S&P 500

Portfolio	Fund	S&P
Avg. P/E Ratio	20	20
Avg. Price/Book	3.9	3.1
Avg. 5-Year Earning Growth	28.2%	5.2%
Median Mkt. Capitalization	$1.07 bil.	$3.60 bil.
Correlation v. S&P 500 (R^2)	71%	100%
Market Volatility (Beta)	1.20	1.00
Superiority Rating (Alpha)	+1%	0%

Industry Diversification

Durables	4%
Energy	3%
Finance	17%
Industrial	13%
Non-Durables	6%
Retail	6%
Health	2%
Services	14%
Technology	34%
Utilities	0%
Precious Metals	0%
Other	1%

Safety Rating (0-10)	6.9	Sales Load (max.)	3.1%
Up & Down Market Ranks	A – E	Redemption Fee (max.)	None
Annual Expenses (total)	1.07%	Annual 12b-1 Fee	None

Fidelity High Yield Tax-Free $1.91 billion

Long-term, medium-low quality municipals • Portfolio Manager: Anne Punzak
164 Northern Avenue, Boston MA 02210 • 800-544-8888
Founded in 1977 • Ticker symbol: FHIGX • Telephone Switching: 4 per yr; free
Minimum Initial Investment: $2,500 • Minimum IRA Investment: None

Portfolio
Yield	6.2%
Average Quality	A+
Average Maturity	19 years
Average Duration	8.9 years
Average Coupon	6.2%
Correlation with U.S. T-Bond (R^2)	42%

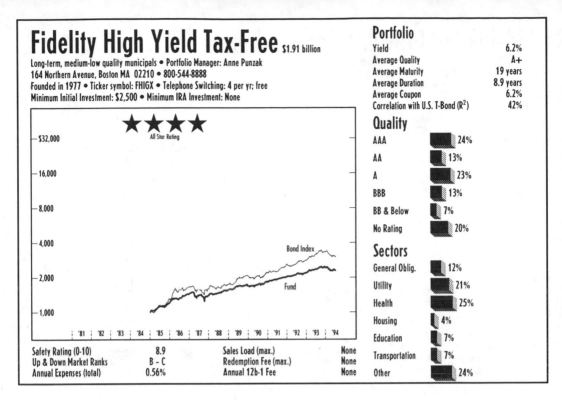

★★★★
All Star Rating

Quality
AAA	24%
AA	13%
A	23%
BBB	13%
BB & Below	7%
No Rating	20%

Sectors
General Oblig.	12%
Utility	21%
Health	25%
Housing	4%
Education	7%
Transportation	7%
Other	24%

Safety Rating (0-10)	8.9	Sales Load (max.)	None
Up & Down Market Ranks	B – C	Redemption Fee (max.)	None
Annual Expenses (total)	0.56%	Annual 12b-1 Fee	None

Fidelity Intermediate Bond $1.82 billion

BBB-rated and higher 3-10 year corporates • Portfolio Manager: Michael Gray
164 Northern Avenue, Boston MA 02210 • 800-544-8888
Founded in 1975 • Ticker symbol: FTHRX • Telephone Switching: 4 per yr; free
Minimum Initial Investment: $2,500 • Minimum IRA Investment: $500

Portfolio
Yield	6.2%
Average Quality	AA+
Average Maturity	7.7 years
Average Duration	2.9 years
Average Coupon	7.7%
Correlation with U.S. T-Bond (R^2)	64%
Dividends Paid	Monthly (Accrue Daily)

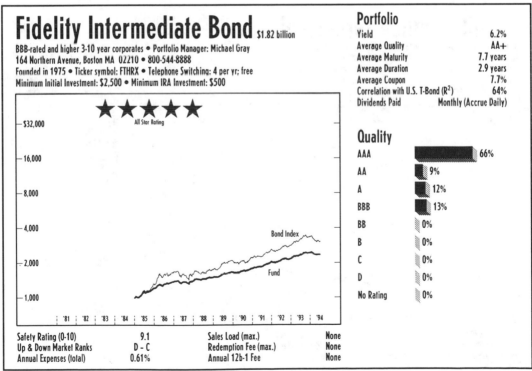

★★★★★
All Star Rating

Quality
AAA	66%
AA	9%
A	12%
BBB	13%
BB	0%
B	0%
C	0%
D	0%
No Rating	0%

Safety Rating (0-10)	9.1	Sales Load (max.)	None
Up & Down Market Ranks	D – C	Redemption Fee (max.)	None
Annual Expenses (total)	0.61%	Annual 12b-1 Fee	None

Fidelity Intl Growth & Income $1.48 billion

Foreign - EPS, dividend growth stocks • Portfolio Manager: Rick Mace
164 Northern Avenue, Boston MA 02210 • 800-544-8888
Founded in 1986 • Ticker symbol: FIGRX • Telephone Switching: 2 per yr; free
Minimum Initial Investment: $2,500 • Minimum IRA Investment: $500

Portfolio

	Fund	S&P
Avg. P/E Ratio	29	20
Avg. Price/Book	2.4	3.1
Avg. 5-Year Earning Growth	N/A	5.2%
Median Mkt. Capitalization	$5.40 bil.	$3.60 bil.
Correlation v. S&P 500 (R²)	15%	100%
Market Volatility (Beta)	0.41	1.00
Superiority Rating (Alpha)	+1%	0%

Industry Diversification

Durables	15%
Energy	4%
Finance	10%
Industrial	3%
Non-Durables	2%
Retail	3%
Health	1%
Services	8%
Technology	8%
Utilities	4%
Precious Metals	0%
Other	42%

★★★ All Star Rating

[Chart: $32,000 / 16,000 / 8,000 / 4,000 / 2,000 / 1,000 — '81 '82 '83 '84 '85 '86 '87 '88 '89 '90 '91 '92 '93 '94 — S&P 500, Fund]

Safety Rating (0-10)	7.8	Sales Load (max.)	None
Up & Down Market Ranks	E – A	Redemption Fee (max.)	None
Annual Expenses (total)	1.52%	Annual 12b-1 Fee	None

Fidelity Limited Term Muni $1.02 billion

High-medium quality municipals • Portfolio Manager: David L. Murphy
164 Northern Avenue, Boston MA 02210 • 800-544-8888
Founded in 1977 • Ticker symbol: FLTMX • Telephone Switching: 4 per yr; free
Minimum Initial Investment: $2,500 • Minimum IRA Investment: None

Portfolio

Yield	5.4%
Average Quality	AA-
Average Maturity	9.6 years
Average Duration	8.1 years
Average Coupon	4.1%
Correlation with U.S. T-Bond (R²)	45%

Quality

AAA	39%
AA	11%
A	21%
BBB	17%
BB & Below	0%
No Rating	12%

Sectors

General Oblig.	19%
Utility	26%
Health	10%
Housing	26%
Education	6%
Transportation	9%
Other	4%

★★★★★ All Star Rating

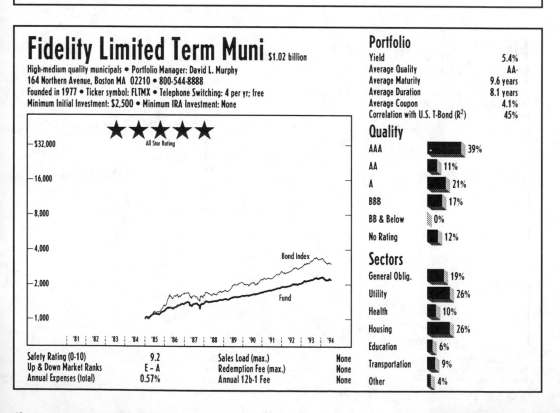

[Chart: $32,000 / 16,000 / 8,000 / 4,000 / 2,000 / 1,000 — '81 '82 '83 '84 '85 '86 '87 '88 '89 '90 '91 '92 '93 '94 — Bond Index, Fund]

Safety Rating (0-10)	9.2	Sales Load (max.)	None
Up & Down Market Ranks	E – A	Redemption Fee (max.)	None
Annual Expenses (total)	0.57%	Annual 12b-1 Fee	None

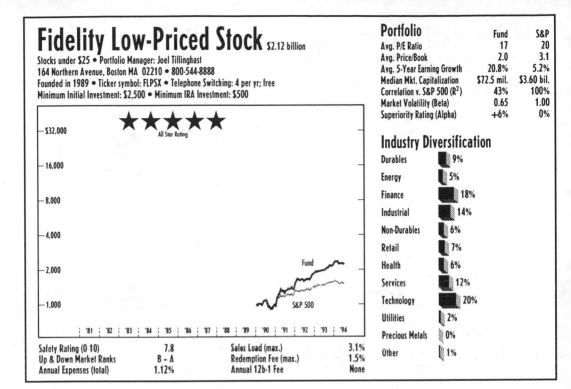

Fidelity Low-Priced Stock $2.12 billion

Stocks under $25 • Portfolio Manager: Joel Tillinghast
164 Northern Avenue, Boston MA 02210 • 800-544-8888
Founded in 1989 • Ticker symbol: FLPSX • Telephone Switching: 4 per yr; free
Minimum Initial Investment: $2,500 • Minimum IRA Investment: $500

★★★★★
All Star Rating

Portfolio	Fund	S&P
Avg. P/E Ratio	17	20
Avg. Price/Book	2.0	3.1
Avg. 5-Year Earning Growth	20.8%	5.2%
Median Mkt. Capitalization	$72.5 mil.	$3.60 bil.
Correlation v. S&P 500 (R^2)	43%	100%
Market Volatility (Beta)	0.65	1.00
Superiority Rating (Alpha)	+6%	0%

Industry Diversification

Durables	9%
Energy	5%
Finance	18%
Industrial	14%
Non-Durables	6%
Retail	7%
Health	6%
Services	12%
Technology	20%
Utilities	2%
Precious Metals	0%
Other	1%

Safety Rating (0-10)	7.8	Sales Load (max.)	3.1%
Up & Down Market Ranks	B – A	Redemption Fee (max.)	1.5%
Annual Expenses (total)	1.12%	Annual 12b-1 Fee	None

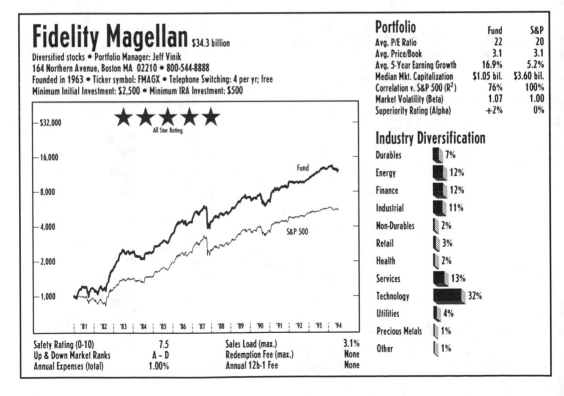

Fidelity Magellan $34.3 billion

Diversified stocks • Portfolio Manager: Jeff Vinik
164 Northern Avenue, Boston MA 02210 • 800-544-8888
Founded in 1963 • Ticker symbol: FMAGX • Telephone Switching: 4 per yr; free
Minimum Initial Investment: $2,500 • Minimum IRA Investment: $500

★★★★★
All Star Rating

Portfolio	Fund	S&P
Avg. P/E Ratio	22	20
Avg. Price/Book	3.1	3.1
Avg. 5-Year Earning Growth	16.9%	5.2%
Median Mkt. Capitalization	$1.05 bil.	$3.60 bil.
Correlation v. S&P 500 (R^2)	76%	100%
Market Volatility (Beta)	1.07	1.00
Superiority Rating (Alpha)	+2%	0%

Industry Diversification

Durables	7%
Energy	12%
Finance	12%
Industrial	11%
Non-Durables	2%
Retail	3%
Health	2%
Services	13%
Technology	32%
Utilities	4%
Precious Metals	1%
Other	1%

Safety Rating (0-10)	7.5	Sales Load (max.)	3.1%
Up & Down Market Ranks	A – D	Redemption Fee (max.)	None
Annual Expenses (total)	1.00%	Annual 12b-1 Fee	None

Fidelity Mass Tax-Free $1.16 billion

Investment-grade Massachusetts municipals • Portfolio Manager: Guy E. Wickwire
164 Northern Avenue, Boston MA 02210 • 800-544-8888
Founded in 1983 • Ticker symbol: FDMMX • Telephone Switching: 4 per yr; free
Minimum Initial Investment: $2,500 • Minimum IRA Investment: None

Portfolio
Yield	6.1%
Average Quality	AA-
Average Maturity	20 years
Average Duration	8.3 years
Average Coupon	N/A
Correlation with U.S. T-Bond (R^2)	40%

Quality
AAA	21%
AA	9%
A	29%
BBB	9%
BB & Below	2%
No Rating	31%

Sectors
General Oblig.	16%
Utility	17%
Health	22%
Housing	8%
Education	14%
Transportation	7%
Other	16%

★ ★ ★ ★ ★
All Star Rating

Safety Rating (0-10)	9.1	Sales Load (max.)	None
Up & Down Market Ranks	D - A	Redemption Fee (max.)	None
Annual Expenses (total)	0.55%	Annual 12b-1 Fee	None

Fidelity Municipal Bond $1.14 billion

Investment-grade municipals • Portfolio Manager: Gary Swayze
164 Northern Avenue, Boston MA 02210 • 800-544-8888
Founded in 1976 • Ticker symbol: FMBDX • Telephone Switching: 4 per yr; free
Minimum Initial Investment: $2,500 • Minimum IRA Investment: None

Portfolio
Yield	5.6%
Average Quality	AA-
Average Maturity	20 years
Average Duration	9.9 years
Average Coupon	6.2%
Correlation with U.S. T-Bond (R^2)	47%

Quality
AAA	34%
AA	20%
A	31%
BBB	11%
BB & Below	0%
No Rating	4%

Sectors
General Oblig.	6%
Utility	37%
Health	26%
Housing	3%
Education	15%
Transportation	9%
Other	4%

★ ★ ★ ★
All Star Rating

Safety Rating (0-10)	8.9	Sales Load (max.)	None
Up & Down Market Ranks	A - E	Redemption Fee (max.)	None
Annual Expenses (total)	0.50%	Annual 12b-1 Fee	None

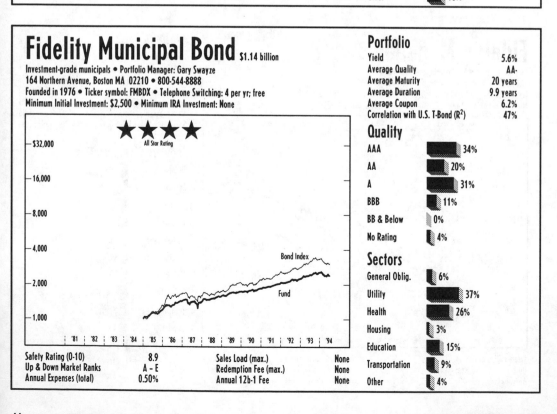

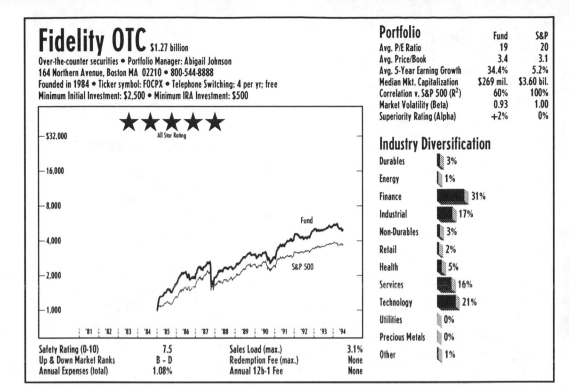

Fidelity OTC $1.27 billion

Over-the-counter securities • Portfolio Manager: Abigail Johnson
164 Northern Avenue, Boston MA 02210 • 800-544-8888
Founded in 1984 • Ticker symbol: FOCPX • Telephone Switching: 4 per yr; free
Minimum Initial Investment: $2,500 • Minimum IRA Investment: $500

★★★★★
All Star Rating

Portfolio	Fund	S&P
Avg. P/E Ratio	19	20
Avg. Price/Book	3.4	3.1
Avg. 5-Year Earning Growth	34.4%	5.2%
Median Mkt. Capitalization	$269 mil.	$3.60 bil.
Correlation v. S&P 500 (R^2)	60%	100%
Market Volatility (Beta)	0.93	1.00
Superiority Rating (Alpha)	+2%	0%

Industry Diversification

Durables	3%
Energy	1%
Finance	31%
Industrial	17%
Non-Durables	3%
Retail	2%
Health	5%
Services	16%
Technology	21%
Utilities	0%
Precious Metals	0%
Other	1%

Safety Rating (0-10)	7.5	Sales Load (max.)	3.1%
Up & Down Market Ranks	B – D	Redemption Fee (max.)	None
Annual Expenses (total)	1.08%	Annual 12b-1 Fee	None

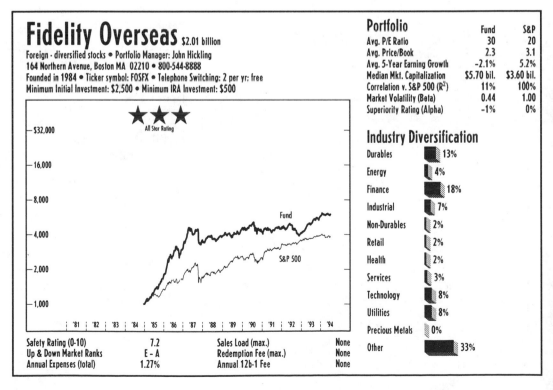

Fidelity Overseas $2.01 billion

Foreign - diversified stocks • Portfolio Manager: John Hickling
164 Northern Avenue, Boston MA 02210 • 800-544-8888
Founded in 1984 • Ticker symbol: FOSFX • Telephone Switching: 2 per yr; free
Minimum Initial Investment: $2,500 • Minimum IRA Investment: $500

★★★
All Star Rating

Portfolio	Fund	S&P
Avg. P/E Ratio	30	20
Avg. Price/Book	2.3	3.1
Avg. 5-Year Earning Growth	-2.1%	5.2%
Median Mkt. Capitalization	$5.70 bil.	$3.60 bil.
Correlation v. S&P 500 (R^2)	11%	100%
Market Volatility (Beta)	0.44	1.00
Superiority Rating (Alpha)	-1%	0%

Industry Diversification

Durables	13%
Energy	4%
Finance	18%
Industrial	7%
Non-Durables	2%
Retail	2%
Health	2%
Services	3%
Technology	8%
Utilities	8%
Precious Metals	0%
Other	33%

Safety Rating (0-10)	7.2	Sales Load (max.)	None
Up & Down Market Ranks	E – A	Redemption Fee (max.)	None
Annual Expenses (total)	1.27%	Annual 12b-1 Fee	None

Fidelity Puritan $10.4 billion

High-yield stocks and bonds • Portfolio Manager: Richard Fentin
164 Northern Avenue, Boston MA 02210 • 800-544-8888
Founded in 1947 • Ticker symbol: FPURX • Telephone Switching: 4 per yr; free
Minimum Initial Investment: $2,500 • Minimum IRA Investment: $500

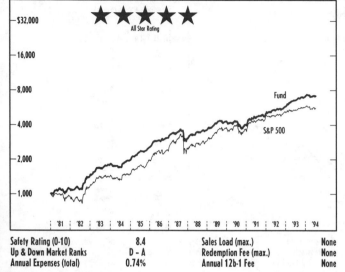

Safety Rating (0-10)	8.4	Sales Load (max.)	None
Up & Down Market Ranks	D - A	Redemption Fee (max.)	None
Annual Expenses (total)	0.74%	Annual 12b-1 Fee	None

Portfolio

	Fund	S&P
Avg. P/E Ratio	31	20
Avg. Price/Book	2.4	3.1
Avg. 5-Year Earning Growth	-6.7%	5.2%
Median Mkt. Capitalization	$1.72 bil.	$3.60 bil.
Correlation v. S&P 500 (R^2)	66%	100%
Market Volatility (Beta)	0.57	1.00
Superiority Rating (Alpha)	+6%	0%

Industry Diversification

Durables	4%
Energy	15%
Finance	14%
Industrial	24%
Non-Durables	6%
Retail	4%
Health	2%
Services	4%
Technology	23%
Utilities	0%
Precious Metals	2%
Other	2%

Fidelity Retirement Growth $2.95 billion

For retirement plans only • Portfolio Manager: Harris Leviton
164 Northern Avenue, Boston MA 02210 • 800-544-8888
Founded in 1983 • Ticker symbol: FDFFX • Telephone Switching: 4 per yr; free
Minimum Initial Investment: $500 • Minimum IRA Investment: $500

Safety Rating (0-10)	7.5	Sales Load (max.)	None
Up & Down Market Ranks	A - D	Redemption Fee (max.)	None
Annual Expenses (total)	1.05%	Annual 12b-1 Fee	None

Portfolio

	Fund	S&P
Avg. P/E Ratio	19	20
Avg. Price/Book	2.8	3.1
Avg. 5-Year Earning Growth	13.2%	5.2%
Median Mkt. Capitalization	$503 mil.	$3.60 bil.
Correlation v. S&P 500 (R^2)	71%	100%
Market Volatility (Beta)	0.91	1.00
Superiority Rating (Alpha)	+2%	0%

Industry Diversification

Durables	9%
Energy	6%
Finance	12%
Industrial	15%
Non-Durables	3%
Retail	6%
Health	1%
Services	13%
Technology	32%
Utilities	1%
Precious Metals	1%
Other	1%

Fidelity Short Term Bond $1.96 billion

Investment-grade corporates; under 3yr maty • Portfolio Manager: Donald G. Taylor
164 Northern Avenue, Boston MA 02210 • 800-544-8888
Founded in 1986 • Ticker symbol: FSHBX • Telephone Switching: 4 per yr; free
Minimum Initial Investment: $2,500 • Minimum IRA Investment: $500

Portfolio

Yield	6.2%
Average Quality	A+
Average Maturity	2.6 years
Average Duration	2.0 years
Average Coupon	7.9%
Correlation with U.S. T-Bond (R^2)	21%
Dividends Paid	Monthly (Accrue Daily)

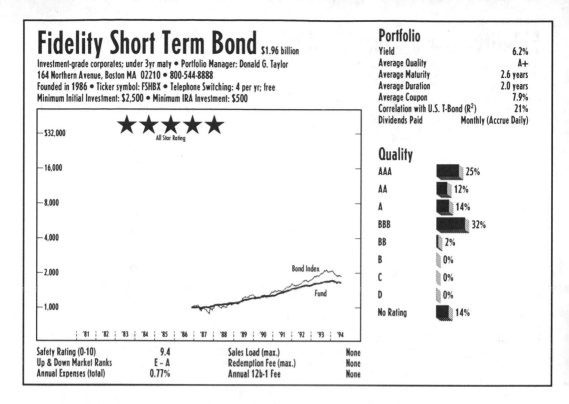

★★★★★
All Star Rating

Quality

AAA	25%
AA	12%
A	14%
BBB	32%
BB	2%
B	0%
C	0%
D	0%
No Rating	14%

Safety Rating (0-10)	9.4	Sales Load (max.)	None
Up & Down Market Ranks	E – A	Redemption Fee (max.)	None
Annual Expenses (total)	0.77%	Annual 12b-1 Fee	None

Fidelity Spartan Ltd Maturity $1.07 billion

U.S. Government secs; less than 10yrs maty • Portfolio Manager: Curtis Hollingsworth
164 Northern Avenue, Boston MA 02210 • 800-544-8888
Founded in 1988 • Ticker symbol: FSTGX • Telephone Switching: 4 per yr; $5
Minimum Initial Investment: $10,000 • Minimum IRA Investment: $10,000

Portfolio

Yield	5.7%
Average Quality	AAA
Average Maturity	4.0 years
Average Duration	2.5 years
Average Coupon	8.7%
Correlation with U.S. T-Bond (R^2)	45%
Dividends Paid	Monthly (Accrue Daily)

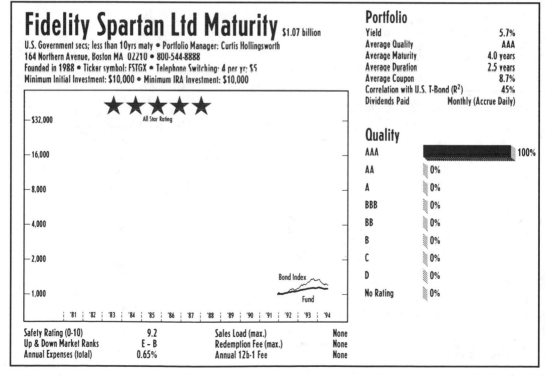

★★★★★
All Star Rating

Quality

AAA	100%
AA	0%
A	0%
BBB	0%
BB	0%
B	0%
C	0%
D	0%
No Rating	0%

Safety Rating (0-10)	9.2	Sales Load (max.)	None
Up & Down Market Ranks	E – B	Redemption Fee (max.)	None
Annual Expenses (total)	0.65%	Annual 12b-1 Fee	None

Fidelity Spartan Shrt-Int Muni $1.08 billion

Investment-grade municipals • Portfolio Manager: David L. Murphy
164 Northern Avenue, Boston MA 02210 • 800-544-8888
Founded in 1986 • Ticker symbol: FSTFX • Telephone Switching: 4 per yr; $5
Minimum Initial Investment: $10,000 • Minimum IRA Investment: None

Portfolio

Yield	4.4%
Average Quality	AA
Average Maturity	3.5 years
Average Duration	3.4 years
Average Coupon	5.6%
Correlation with U.S. T-Bond (R^2)	36%

Quality

AAA	35%
AA	8%
A	31%
BBB	1%
BB & Below	0%
No Rating	24%

Sectors

General Oblig.	41%
Utility	19%
Health	6%
Housing	3%
Education	25%
Transportation	1%
Other	5%

★★★★ All Star Rating

(chart: Bond Index, Fund — years '81 through '94, $32,000 to $1,000)

Safety Rating (0-10)	9.5	Sales Load (max.)	None
Up & Down Market Ranks	E – A	Redemption Fee (max.)	None
Annual Expenses (total)	0.55%	Annual 12b-1 Fee	None

Fidelity Trend $1.27 billion

Diversified stocks • Portfolio Manager: Alan Leifer
164 Northern Avenue, Boston MA 02210 • 800-544-8888
Founded in 1958 • Ticker symbol: FTRNX • Telephone Switching: 4 per yr; free
Minimum Initial Investment: $2,500 • Minimum IRA Investment: $500

Portfolio

	Fund	S&P
Avg. P/E Ratio	25	20
Avg. Price/Book	3.2	3.1
Avg. 5-Year Earning Growth	15.5%	5.2%
Median Mkt. Capitalization	$1.11 bil.	$3.60 bil.
Correlation v. S&P 500 (R^2)	75%	100%
Market Volatility (Beta)	1.15	1.00
Superiority Rating (Alpha)	0%	0%

Industry Diversification

Durables	6%
Energy	9%
Finance	23%
Industrial	11%
Non-Durables	4%
Retail	6%
Health	6%
Services	11%
Technology	16%
Utilities	4%
Precious Metals	0%
Other	4%

★★★★★ All Star Rating

(chart: S&P 500, Fund — years '81 through '94, $32,000 to $1,000)

Safety Rating (0-10)	7.1	Sales Load (max.)	None
Up & Down Market Ranks	A – E	Redemption Fee (max.)	None
Annual Expenses (total)	0.92%	Annual 12b-1 Fee	None

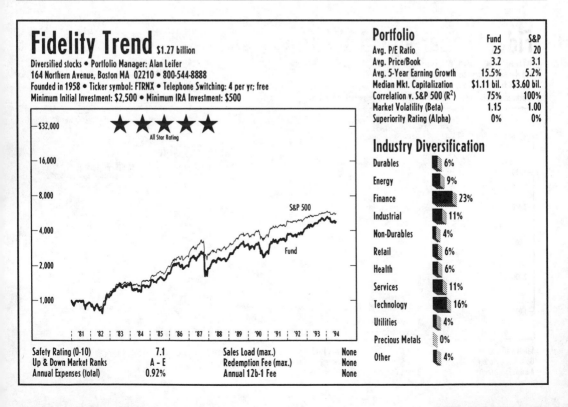

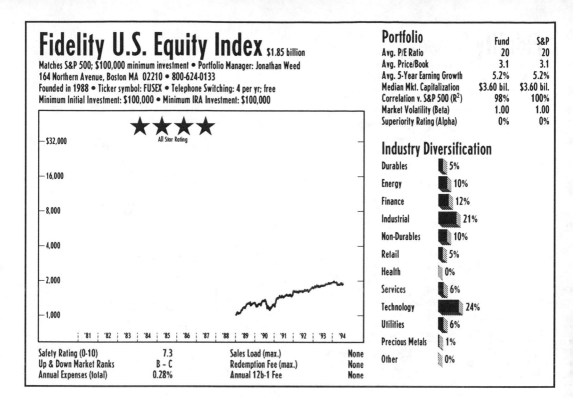

Fidelity U.S. Equity Index $1.85 billion

Matches S&P 500; $100,000 minimum investment • Portfolio Manager: Jonathan Weed
164 Northern Avenue, Boston MA 02210 • 800-624-0133
Founded in 1988 • Ticker symbol: FUSEX • Telephone Switching: 4 per yr; free
Minimum Initial Investment: $100,000 • Minimum IRA Investment: $100,000

★★★★
All Star Rating

Portfolio	Fund	S&P
Avg. P/E Ratio	20	20
Avg. Price/Book	3.1	3.1
Avg. 5-Year Earning Growth	5.2%	5.2%
Median Mkt. Capitalization	$3.60 bil.	$3.60 bil.
Correlation v. S&P 500 (R^2)	98%	100%
Market Volatility (Beta)	1.00	1.00
Superiority Rating (Alpha)	0%	0%

Industry Diversification

Durables	5%
Energy	10%
Finance	12%
Industrial	21%
Non-Durables	10%
Retail	5%
Health	0%
Services	6%
Technology	24%
Utilities	6%
Precious Metals	1%
Other	0%

Safety Rating (0-10)	7.3	Sales Load (max.)	None
Up & Down Market Ranks	B – C	Redemption Fee (max.)	None
Annual Expenses (total)	0.28%	Annual 12b-1 Fee	None

Fidelity Utilities Income $1.24 billion

Utility securities • Portfolio Manager: John Muresianu
164 Northern Avenue, Boston MA 02210 • 800-544-8888
Founded in 1987 • Ticker symbol: FIUIX • Telephone Switching: 4 per yr; free
Minimum Initial Investment: $2,500 • Minimum IRA Investment: $500

★★★★
All Star Rating

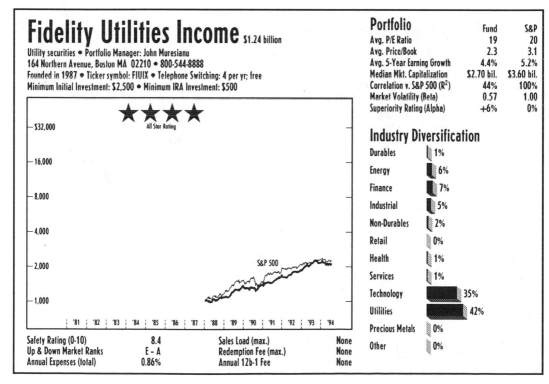

S&P 500

Portfolio	Fund	S&P
Avg. P/E Ratio	19	20
Avg. Price/Book	2.3	3.1
Avg. 5-Year Earning Growth	4.4%	5.2%
Median Mkt. Capitalization	$2.70 bil.	$3.60 bil.
Correlation v. S&P 500 (R^2)	44%	100%
Market Volatility (Beta)	0.57	1.00
Superiority Rating (Alpha)	+6%	0%

Industry Diversification

Durables	1%
Energy	6%
Finance	7%
Industrial	5%
Non-Durables	2%
Retail	0%
Health	1%
Services	1%
Technology	35%
Utilities	42%
Precious Metals	0%
Other	0%

Safety Rating (0-10)	8.4	Sales Load (max.)	None
Up & Down Market Ranks	E – A	Redemption Fee (max.)	None
Annual Expenses (total)	0.86%	Annual 12b-1 Fee	None

Fidelity Value $2.33 billion

Undervalued stocks • Portfolio Manager: Jeffery Ubben
164 Northern Avenue, Boston MA 02210 • 800-544-8888
Founded in 1978 • Ticker symbol: FDVLX • Telephone Switching: 4 per yr; free
Minimum Initial Investment: $2,500 • Minimum IRA Investment: $500

Portfolio

	Fund	S&P
Avg. P/E Ratio	26	20
Avg. Price/Book	2.6	3.1
Avg. 5-Year Earning Growth	0.3%	5.2%
Median Mkt. Capitalization	$1.22 bil.	$3.60 bil.
Correlation v. S&P 500 (R^2)	68%	100%
Market Volatility (Beta)	0.79	1.00
Superiority Rating (Alpha)	+6%	0%

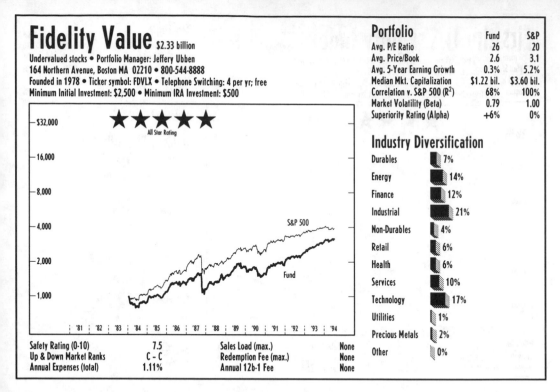

Industry Diversification

Durables	7%
Energy	14%
Finance	12%
Industrial	21%
Non-Durables	4%
Retail	6%
Health	6%
Services	10%
Technology	17%
Utilities	1%
Precious Metals	2%
Other	0%

Safety Rating (0-10)	7.5	Sales Load (max.)	None
Up & Down Market Ranks	C – C	Redemption Fee (max.)	None
Annual Expenses (total)	1.11%	Annual 12b-1 Fee	None

First Australia Prime Income $1.17 billion

AA-rated & higher Australian bonds; leveraged • Portfolio Manager: Brian M. Sherman
199 Water Street, 25th Floor, New York NY 10292 • 800-451-6788
Founded in 1986 • Ticker symbol: FAX • Telephone Switching: Via broker
Minimum Initial Investment: $0 • Minimum IRA Investment: None

Portfolio

Yield	10.7%
Average Quality	AAA-
Average Maturity	N/A
Average Duration	1.0 years
Average Coupon	11.4%
Correlation with U.S. T-Bond (R^2)	0%
Dividends Paid	Monthly

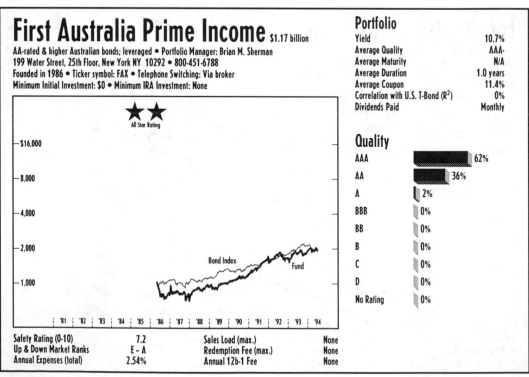

Quality

AAA	62%
AA	36%
A	2%
BBB	0%
BB	0%
B	0%
C	0%
D	0%
No Rating	0%

Safety Rating (0-10)	7.2	Sales Load (max.)	None
Up & Down Market Ranks	E – A	Redemption Fee (max.)	None
Annual Expenses (total)	2.54%	Annual 12b-1 Fee	None

First Investors Insured Tax-Ex $1.40 billion

80% municipals; all quality ratings • Portfolio Manager: Clark D. Wagner
95 Wall Street, New York NY 10005 • 800-423-4026
Founded in 1977 • Ticker symbol: FITAX • Telephone Switching: 1 per month; free
Minimum Initial Investment: $1,000 • Minimum IRA Investment: None

Portfolio

Yield	5.3%
Average Quality	AAA-
Average Maturity	20 years
Average Duration	7.7 years
Average Coupon	7.5%
Correlation with U.S. T-Bond (R^2)	40%

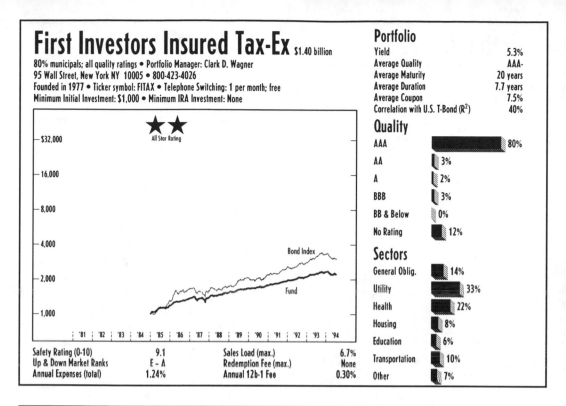

Quality

AAA	80%
AA	3%
A	2%
BBB	3%
BB & Below	0%
No Rating	12%

Sectors

General Oblig.	14%
Utility	33%
Health	22%
Housing	8%
Education	6%
Transportation	10%
Other	7%

Safety Rating (0-10)	9.1	Sales Load (max.)	6.7%
Up & Down Market Ranks	E – A	Redemption Fee (max.)	None
Annual Expenses (total)	1.24%	Annual 12b-1 Fee	0.30%

Fortress Govt Income Secs $3.35 billion

U.S. Government securities • Portfolio Manager: Gary Madich
Federated Investors Tower, Pittsburgh PA 15222 • 800-245-5051
Founded in 1986 • Ticker symbol: FGOIX • Telephone Switching: Unlimited; free
Minimum Initial Investment: $1,500 • Minimum IRA Investment: $50

Portfolio

Yield	5.9%
Average Quality	AAA
Average Maturity	6.6 years
Average Duration	4.4 years
Average Coupon	10.0%
Correlation with U.S. T-Bond (R^2)	57%
Dividends Paid	Monthly

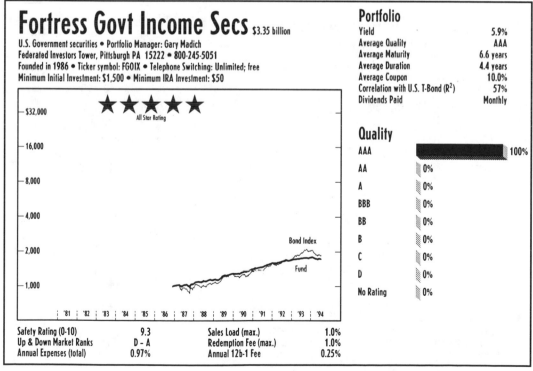

Quality

AAA	100%
AA	0%
A	0%
BBB	0%
BB	0%
B	0%
C	0%
D	0%
No Rating	0%

Safety Rating (0-10)	9.3	Sales Load (max.)	1.0%
Up & Down Market Ranks	D – A	Redemption Fee (max.)	1.0%
Annual Expenses (total)	0.97%	Annual 12b-1 Fee	0.25%

Franklin Age $1.82 billion

BBB-rated and lower corporate bonds • Portfolio Managers: R. Wiskemann/Molumphy
777 Mariners Island Blvd, San Mateo CA 94404 • 800-342-5236
Founded in 1969 • Ticker symbol: AGEFX • Telephone Switching: Unlimited; free
Minimum Initial Investment: $100 • Minimum IRA Investment: $100

Portfolio

Yield	8.9%
Average Quality	B+
Average Maturity	8.6 years
Average Duration	4.5 years
Average Coupon	9.9%
Correlation with U.S. T-Bond (R^2)	3%
Dividends Paid	Monthly

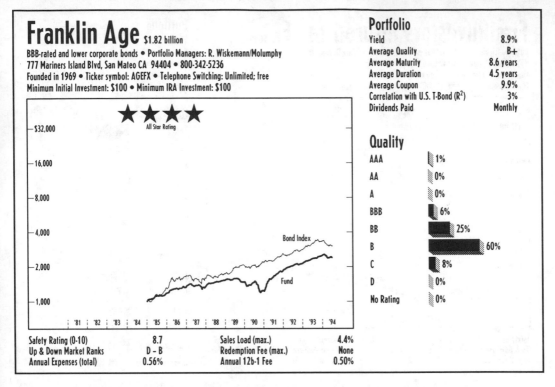

Quality

AAA	1%
AA	0%
A	0%
BBB	6%
BB	25%
B	60%
C	8%
D	0%
No Rating	0%

Safety Rating (0-10)	8.7	Sales Load (max.)	4.4%
Up & Down Market Ranks	D – B	Redemption Fee (max.)	None
Annual Expenses (total)	0.56%	Annual 12b-1 Fee	0.50%

Franklin California Tax-Free $13.4 billion

California 20-25 year municipals • Portfolio Manager: Bernie Schroer
777 Mariners Island Blvd, San Mateo CA 94404 • 800-342-5236
Founded in 1977 • Ticker symbol: FKTFX • Telephone Switching: Unlimited; free
Minimum Initial Investment: $100 • Minimum IRA Investment: None

Portfolio

Yield	5.5%
Average Quality	AA-
Average Maturity	19 years
Average Duration	10 years
Average Coupon	7.1%
Correlation with U.S. T-Bond (R^2)	46%

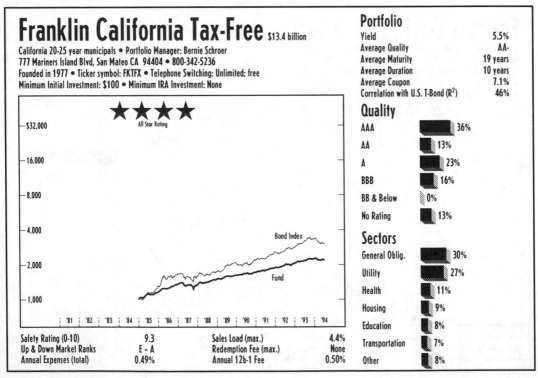

Quality

AAA	36%
AA	13%
A	23%
BBB	16%
BB & Below	0%
No Rating	13%

Sectors

General Oblig.	30%
Utility	27%
Health	11%
Housing	9%
Education	8%
Transportation	7%
Other	8%

Safety Rating (0-10)	9.3	Sales Load (max.)	4.4%
Up & Down Market Ranks	E – A	Redemption Fee (max.)	None
Annual Expenses (total)	0.49%	Annual 12b-1 Fee	0.50%

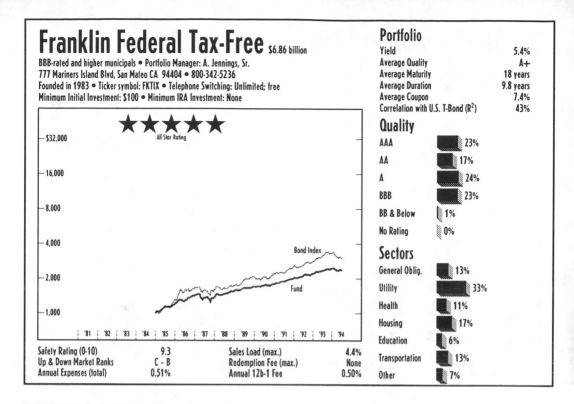

Franklin Federal Tax-Free $6.86 billion

BBB-rated and higher municipals • Portfolio Manager: A. Jennings, Sr.
777 Mariners Island Blvd, San Mateo CA 94404 • 800-342-5236
Founded in 1983 • Ticker symbol: FKTIX • Telephone Switching: Unlimited; free
Minimum Initial Investment: $100 • Minimum IRA Investment: None

★★★★★
All Star Rating

Bond Index

Fund

Safety Rating (0-10)	9.3	Sales Load (max.)	4.4%
Up & Down Market Ranks	C – B	Redemption Fee (max.)	None
Annual Expenses (total)	0.51%	Annual 12b-1 Fee	0.50%

Portfolio

Yield	5.4%
Average Quality	A+
Average Maturity	18 years
Average Duration	9.8 years
Average Coupon	7.4%
Correlation with U.S. T-Bond (R^2)	43%

Quality

AAA	23%
AA	17%
A	24%
BBB	23%
BB & Below	1%
No Rating	0%

Sectors

General Oblig.	13%
Utility	33%
Health	11%
Housing	17%
Education	6%
Transportation	13%
Other	7%

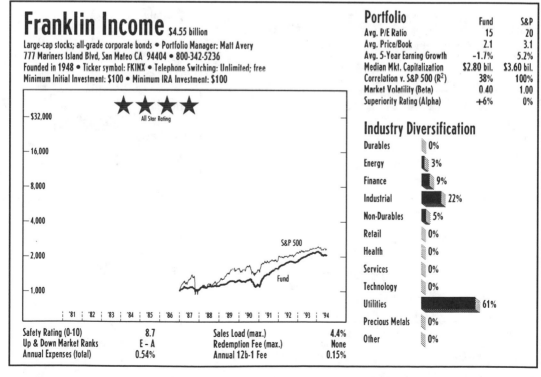

Franklin Income $4.55 billion

Large-cap stocks; all-grade corporate bonds • Portfolio Manager: Matt Avery
777 Mariners Island Blvd, San Mateo CA 94404 • 800-342-5236
Founded in 1948 • Ticker symbol: FKINX • Telephone Switching: Unlimited; free
Minimum Initial Investment: $100 • Minimum IRA Investment: $100

★★★★
All Star Rating

S&P 500

Fund

Safety Rating (0-10)	8.7	Sales Load (max.)	4.4%
Up & Down Market Ranks	E – A	Redemption Fee (max.)	None
Annual Expenses (total)	0.54%	Annual 12b-1 Fee	0.15%

Portfolio

	Fund	S&P
Avg. P/E Ratio	15	20
Avg. Price/Book	2.1	3.1
Avg. 5-Year Earning Growth	-1.7%	5.2%
Median Mkt. Capitalization	$2.80 bil.	$3.60 bil.
Correlation v. S&P 500 (R^2)	38%	100%
Market Volatility (Beta)	0.40	1.00
Superiority Rating (Alpha)	+6%	0%

Industry Diversification

Durables	0%
Energy	3%
Finance	9%
Industrial	22%
Non-Durables	5%
Retail	0%
Health	0%
Services	0%
Technology	0%
Utilities	61%
Precious Metals	0%
Other	0%

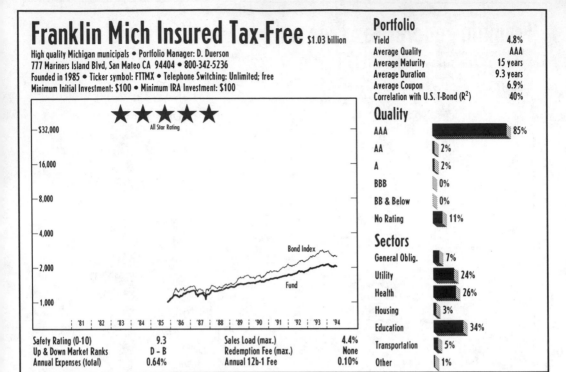

Franklin Mich Insured Tax-Free $1.03 billion

High quality Michigan municipals • Portfolio Manager: D. Duerson
777 Mariners Island Blvd, San Mateo CA 94404 • 800-342-5236
Founded in 1985 • Ticker symbol: FTTMX • Telephone Switching: Unlimited; free
Minimum Initial Investment: $100 • Minimum IRA Investment: $100

★★★★★
All Star Rating

Bond Index
Fund

Safety Rating (0-10)	9.3	Sales Load (max.)	4.4%
Up & Down Market Ranks	D – B	Redemption Fee (max.)	None
Annual Expenses (total)	0.64%	Annual 12b-1 Fee	0.10%

Portfolio

Yield	4.8%
Average Quality	AAA
Average Maturity	15 years
Average Duration	9.3 years
Average Coupon	6.9%
Correlation with U.S. T-Bond (R^2)	40%

Quality

AAA	85%
AA	2%
A	2%
BBB	0%
BB & Below	0%
No Rating	11%

Sectors

General Oblig.	7%
Utility	24%
Health	26%
Housing	3%
Education	34%
Transportation	5%
Other	1%

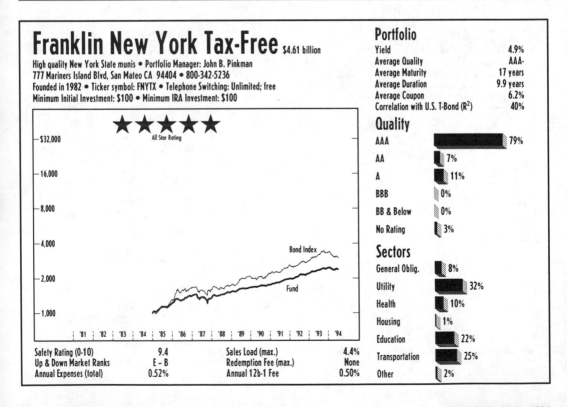

Franklin New York Tax-Free $4.61 billion

High quality New York State munis • Portfolio Manager: John B. Pinkman
777 Mariners Island Blvd, San Mateo CA 94404 • 800-342-5236
Founded in 1982 • Ticker symbol: FNYTX • Telephone Switching: Unlimited; free
Minimum Initial Investment: $100 • Minimum IRA Investment: $100

★★★★★
All Star Rating

Bond Index
Fund

Safety Rating (0-10)	9.4	Sales Load (max.)	4.4%
Up & Down Market Ranks	E – B	Redemption Fee (max.)	None
Annual Expenses (total)	0.52%	Annual 12b-1 Fee	0.50%

Portfolio

Yield	4.9%
Average Quality	AAA-
Average Maturity	17 years
Average Duration	9.9 years
Average Coupon	6.2%
Correlation with U.S. T-Bond (R^2)	40%

Quality

AAA	79%
AA	7%
A	11%
BBB	0%
BB & Below	0%
No Rating	3%

Sectors

General Oblig.	8%
Utility	32%
Health	10%
Housing	1%
Education	22%
Transportation	25%
Other	2%

Franklin U.S. Government $12.6 billion

U.S. Government securities; Ginnie Maes • Portfolio Manager: J. Lemein
777 Mariners Island Blvd, San Mateo CA 94404 • 800-342-5236
Founded in 1987 • Ticker symbol: FKUSX • Telephone Switching: Unlimited; free
Minimum Initial Investment: $100 • Minimum IRA Investment: $100

Portfolio

Yield	6.4%
Average Quality	AAA
Average Maturity	26 years
Average Duration	4.1 years
Average Coupon	8.0%
Correlation with U.S. T-Bond (R^2)	53%
Dividends Paid	Monthly

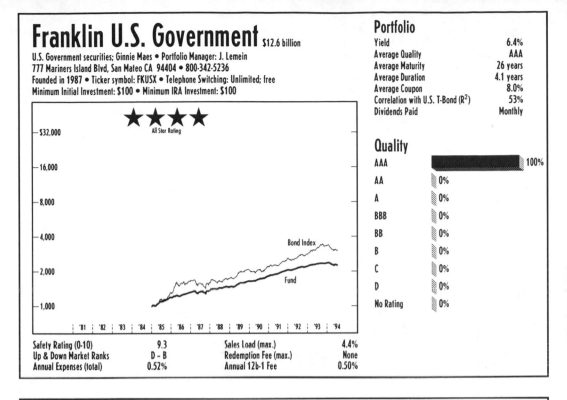

Quality

AAA	100%
AA	0%
A	0%
BBB	0%
BB	0%
B	0%
C	0%
D	0%
No Rating	0%

Safety Rating (0-10)	9.3	Sales Load (max.)	4.4%
Up & Down Market Ranks	D – B	Redemption Fee (max.)	None
Annual Expenses (total)	0.52%	Annual 12b-1 Fee	0.50%

Franklin Utilities $2.79 billion

Utility growth securities • Portfolio Managers: Johnson/Edwards
777 Mariners Island Blvd, San Mateo CA 94404 • 800-342-5236
Founded in 1948 • Ticker symbol: FKUTX • Telephone Switching: Unlimited; free
Minimum Initial Investment: $100 • Minimum IRA Investment: $100

Portfolio

	Fund	S&P
Avg. P/E Ratio	14	20
Avg. Price/Book	1.4	3.1
Avg. 5-Year Earning Growth	-2.8%	5.2%
Median Mkt. Capitalization	$2.48 bil.	$3.60 bil.
Correlation v. S&P 500 (R^2)	30%	100%
Market Volatility (Beta)	0.57	1.00
Superiority Rating (Alpha)	+2%	0%

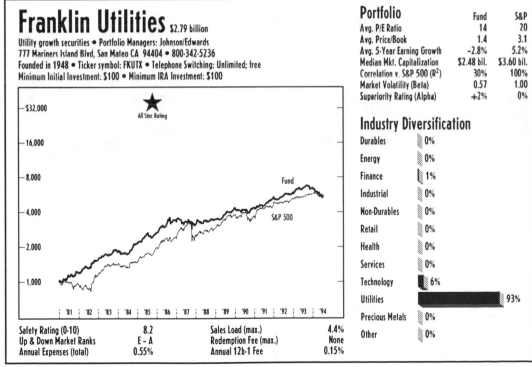

Industry Diversification

Durables	0%
Energy	0%
Finance	1%
Industrial	0%
Non-Durables	0%
Retail	0%
Health	0%
Services	0%
Technology	6%
Utilities	93%
Precious Metals	0%
Other	0%

Safety Rating (0-10)	8.2	Sales Load (max.)	4.4%
Up & Down Market Ranks	E – A	Redemption Fee (max.)	None
Annual Expenses (total)	0.55%	Annual 12b-1 Fee	0.15%

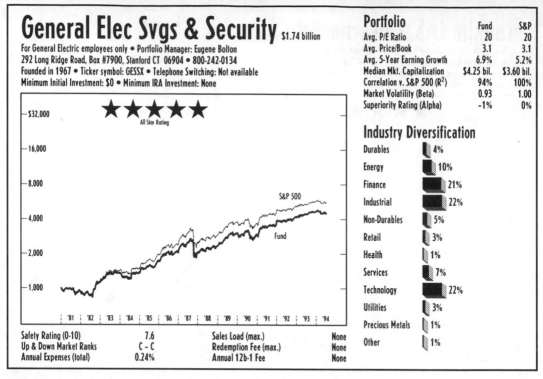

General Elec Svgs & Security $1.74 billion

For General Electric employees only • Portfolio Manager: Eugene Bolton
292 Long Ridge Road, Box #7900, Stanford CT 06904 • 800-242-0134
Founded in 1967 • Ticker symbol: GESSX • Telephone Switching: Not available
Minimum Initial Investment: $0 • Minimum IRA Investment: None

Portfolio	Fund	S&P
Avg. P/E Ratio	20	20
Avg. Price/Book	3.1	3.1
Avg. 5-Year Earning Growth	6.9%	5.2%
Median Mkt. Capitalization	$4.25 bil.	$3.60 bil.
Correlation v. S&P 500 (R^2)	94%	100%
Market Volatility (Beta)	0.93	1.00
Superiority Rating (Alpha)	-1%	0%

★ ★ ★ ★ ★
All Star Rating

Industry Diversification

Durables	4%
Energy	10%
Finance	21%
Industrial	22%
Non-Durables	5%
Retail	3%
Health	1%
Services	7%
Technology	22%
Utilities	3%
Precious Metals	1%
Other	1%

Safety Rating (0-10)	7.6	Sales Load (max.)	None
Up & Down Market Ranks	C – C	Redemption Fee (max.)	None
Annual Expenses (total)	0.24%	Annual 12b-1 Fee	None

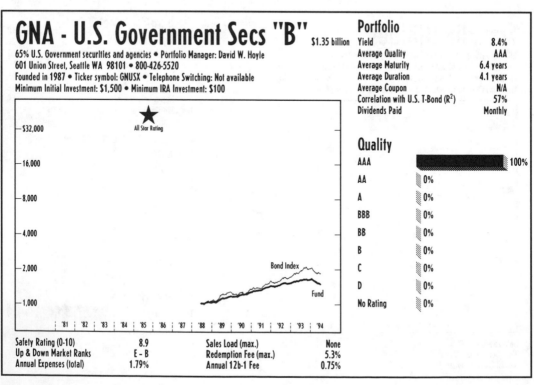

GNA - U.S. Government Secs "B" $1.35 billion

65% U.S. Government securities and agencies • Portfolio Manager: David W. Hoyle
601 Union Street, Seattle WA 98101 • 800-426-5520
Founded in 1987 • Ticker symbol: GNUSX • Telephone Switching: Not available
Minimum Initial Investment: $1,500 • Minimum IRA Investment: $100

Portfolio

Yield	8.4%
Average Quality	AAA
Average Maturity	6.4 years
Average Duration	4.1 years
Average Coupon	N/A
Correlation with U.S. T-Bond (R^2)	57%
Dividends Paid	Monthly

★
All Star Rating

Quality

AAA	100%
AA	0%
A	0%
BBB	0%
BB	0%
B	0%
C	0%
D	0%
No Rating	0%

Safety Rating (0-10)	8.9	Sales Load (max.)	None
Up & Down Market Ranks	E – B	Redemption Fee (max.)	5.3%
Annual Expenses (total)	1.79%	Annual 12b-1 Fee	0.75%

Goldman Sachs Inst Adjust Govt $1.32 billion

65% adjust rate secs; U.S. Govt & agencies • Portfolio Manager: Multiple Managers
32 Old Slip, 34th Floor, New York NY 10005 • 800-621-2550
Founded in 1991 • Ticker symbol: GSARX • Telephone Switching: Unlimited; free
Minimum Initial Investment: $50,000 • Minimum IRA Investment: None

Portfolio

Yield	4.4%
Average Quality	AAA
Average Maturity	N/A
Average Duration	1.1 years
Average Coupon	N/A
Correlation with U.S. T-Bond (R^2)	11%
Dividends Paid	Monthly (Accrue Daily)

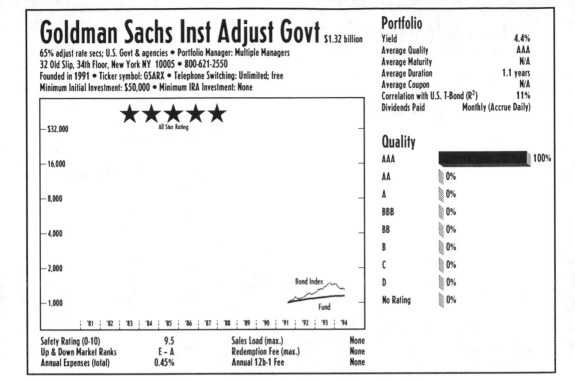

Quality

AAA	100%
AA	0%
A	0%
BBB	0%
BB	0%
B	0%
C	0%
D	0%
No Rating	0%

Safety Rating (0-10)	9.5	Sales Load (max.)	None
Up & Down Market Ranks	E – A	Redemption Fee (max.)	None
Annual Expenses (total)	0.45%	Annual 12b-1 Fee	None

G.T. Global Telecomm "A" $1.49 billion

Foreign - telecommunications stocks • Portfolio Manager: Multiple Managers
50 California Street, 27th Flr, San Francisco CA 94111 • 800-824-1580
Founded in 1992 • Ticker symbol: GTTCX • Telephone Switching: See prospectus
Minimum Initial Investment: $500 • Minimum IRA Investment: $250

Portfolio

	Fund	S&P
Avg. P/E Ratio	23	20
Avg. Price/Book	3.9	3.1
Avg. 5-Year Earning Growth	27.3%	5.2%
Median Mkt. Capitalization	$1.96 bil.	$3.60 bil.
Correlation v. S&P 500 (R^2)	38%	100%
Market Volatility (Beta)	0.81	1.00
Superiority Rating (Alpha)	+6%	0%

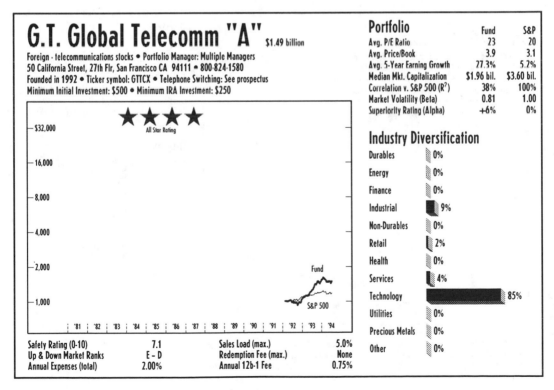

Industry Diversification

Durables	0%
Energy	0%
Finance	0%
Industrial	9%
Non-Durables	0%
Retail	2%
Health	0%
Services	4%
Technology	85%
Utilities	0%
Precious Metals	0%
Other	0%

Safety Rating (0-10)	7.1	Sales Load (max.)	5.0%
Up & Down Market Ranks	E – D	Redemption Fee (max.)	None
Annual Expenses (total)	2.00%	Annual 12b-1 Fee	0.75%

Harbor - International $2.65 billion

Foreign - Europe & Pac emrg industrl nations • Portfolio Manager: Hakan Castegren
One Seagate, 15th Floor, Toledo OH 43666 • 800-422-1050
Founded in 1987 • Ticker symbol: HAINX • Telephone Switching: See prospectus
This fund is currently not accepting new accounts.

Portfolio

	Fund	S&P
Avg. P/E Ratio	22	20
Avg. Price/Book	2.3	3.1
Avg. 5-Year Earning Growth	-7.0%	5.2%
Median Mkt. Capitalization	$3.41 bil.	$3.60 bil.
Correlation v. S&P 500 (R^2)	17%	100%
Market Volatility (Beta)	0.58	1.00
Superiority Rating (Alpha)	+3%	0%

Industry Diversification

Durables	0%
Energy	86%
Finance	0%
Industrial	0%
Non-Durables	0%
Retail	0%
Health	0%
Services	0%
Technology	14%
Utilities	0%
Precious Metals	0%
Other	0%

★★★★ All Star Rating

Safety Rating (0-10)	7.4	Sales Load (max.)	None
Up & Down Market Ranks	C – B	Redemption Fee (max.)	None
Annual Expenses (total)	1.20%	Annual 12b-1 Fee	None

IDS Bond $2.24 billion

50% BBB-rated and higher; 25% foreign • Portfolio Manager: Frederick C. Quirsfeld
IDS Tower 10, Minneapolis MN 55402 • 800-437-4332
Founded in 1974 • Ticker symbol: INBNX • Telephone Switching: 3 per month; free
Minimum Initial Investment: $2,000 • Minimum IRA Investment: $50

Portfolio

Yield	7.6%
Average Quality	BBB
Average Maturity	15 years
Average Duration	7.1 years
Average Coupon	8.4%
Correlation with U.S. T-Bond (R^2)	59%
Dividends Paid	Monthly (Accrue Daily)

Quality

AAA	3%
AA	11%
A	18%
BBB	32%
BB	14%
B	20%
C	0%
D	0%
No Rating	1%

★★★ All Star Rating

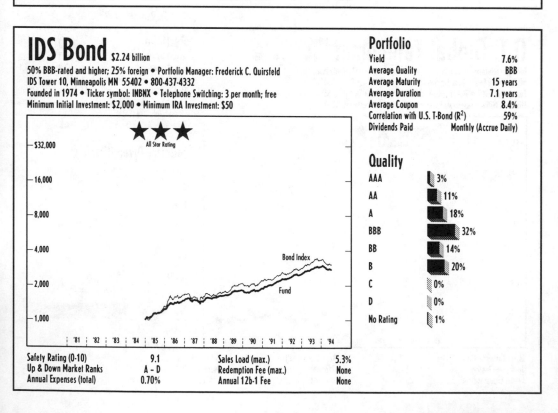

Safety Rating (0-10)	9.1	Sales Load (max.)	5.3%
Up & Down Market Ranks	A – D	Redemption Fee (max.)	None
Annual Expenses (total)	0.70%	Annual 12b-1 Fee	None

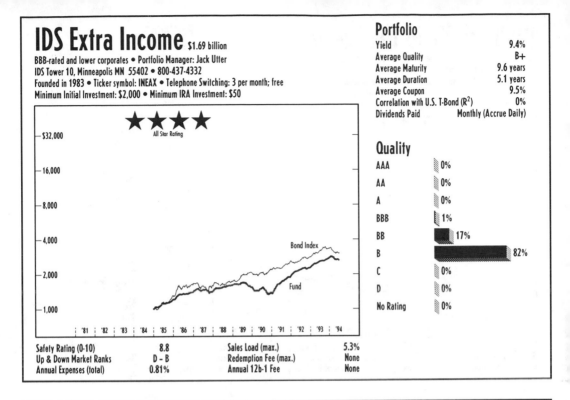

IDS Extra Income $1.69 billion

BBB-rated and lower corporates • Portfolio Manager: Jack Utter
IDS Tower 10, Minneapolis MN 55402 • 800-437-4332
Founded in 1983 • Ticker symbol: INEAX • Telephone Switching: 3 per month; free
Minimum Initial Investment: $2,000 • Minimum IRA Investment: $50

Portfolio

Yield	9.4%
Average Quality	B+
Average Maturity	9.6 years
Average Duration	5.1 years
Average Coupon	9.5%
Correlation with U.S. T-Bond (R^2)	0%
Dividends Paid	Monthly (Accrue Daily)

Quality

AAA	0%
AA	0%
A	0%
BBB	1%
BB	17%
B	82%
C	0%
D	0%
No Rating	0%

★★★★ All Star Rating

Bond Index
Fund

Safety Rating (0-10)	8.8	Sales Load (max.)	5.3%
Up & Down Market Ranks	D – B	Redemption Fee (max.)	None
Annual Expenses (total)	0.81%	Annual 12b-1 Fee	None

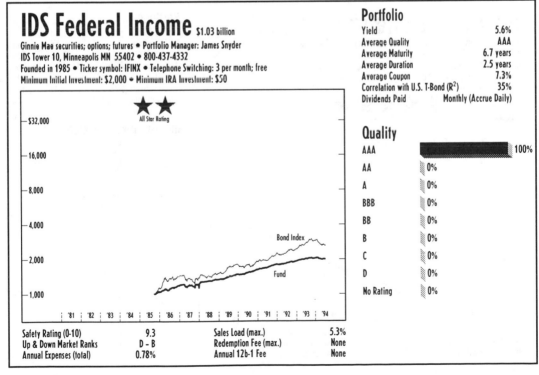

IDS Federal Income $1.03 billion

Ginnie Mae securities; options; futures • Portfolio Manager: James Snyder
IDS Tower 10, Minneapolis MN 55402 • 800-437-4332
Founded in 1985 • Ticker symbol: IFINX • Telephone Switching: 3 per month; free
Minimum Initial Investment: $2,000 • Minimum IRA Investment: $50

Portfolio

Yield	5.6%
Average Quality	AAA
Average Maturity	6.7 years
Average Duration	2.5 years
Average Coupon	7.3%
Correlation with U.S. T-Bond (R^2)	35%
Dividends Paid	Monthly (Accrue Daily)

Quality

AAA	100%
AA	0%
A	0%
BBB	0%
BB	0%
B	0%
C	0%
D	0%
No Rating	0%

★★ All Star Rating

Bond Index
Fund

Safety Rating (0-10)	9.3	Sales Load (max.)	5.3%
Up & Down Market Ranks	D – B	Redemption Fee (max.)	None
Annual Expenses (total)	0.78%	Annual 12b-1 Fee	None

IDS High Yield Tax-Exempt $6.38 billion

75% BBB-rated & higher corps; optns; futures • Portfolio Manager: Kurt Larson
IDS Tower 10, Minneapolis MN 55402 • 800-437-4332
Founded in 1979 • Ticker symbol: INHYX • Telephone Switching: 3 per month; free
Minimum Initial Investment: $2,000 • Minimum IRA Investment: None

Portfolio

Yield	5.4%
Average Quality	A+
Average Maturity	21 years
Average Duration	7.0 years
Average Coupon	7.4%
Correlation with U.S. T-Bond (R^2)	38%

Quality

AAA	22%
AA	15%
A	25%
BBB	25%
BB & Below	8%
No Rating	3%

Sectors

General Oblig.	6%
Utility	60%
Health	11%
Housing	3%
Education	3%
Transportation	12%
Other	5%

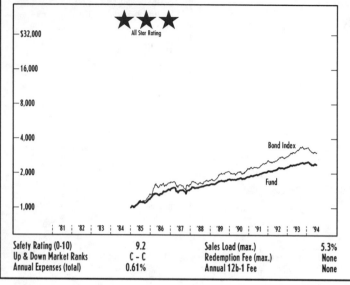

★★★ All Star Rating

Bond Index

Fund

Safety Rating (0-10)	9.2	Sales Load (max.)	5.3%
Up & Down Market Ranks	C – C	Redemption Fee (max.)	None
Annual Expenses (total)	0.61%	Annual 12b-1 Fee	None

IDS Managed Retirement $2.08 billion

Divsf; 65% U.S. stks; pfds, converts & bonds • Portfolio Manager: Richard Lazarchic
IDS Tower 10, Minneapolis MN 55402 • 800-437-4332
Founded in 1985 • Ticker symbol: IMRFX • Telephone Switching: 3 per month; free
Minimum Initial Investment: $2,000 • Minimum IRA Investment: $50

Portfolio

	Fund	S&P
Avg. P/E Ratio	23	20
Avg. Price/Book	3.4	3.1
Avg. 5-Year Earning Growth	13.7%	5.2%
Median Mkt. Capitalization	$4.07 bil.	$3.60 bil.
Correlation v. S&P 500 (R^2)	79%	100%
Market Volatility (Beta)	0.95	1.00
Superiority Rating (Alpha)	+1%	0%

Industry Diversification

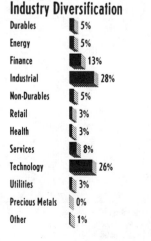

Durables	5%
Energy	5%
Finance	13%
Industrial	28%
Non-Durables	5%
Retail	3%
Health	3%
Services	8%
Technology	26%
Utilities	3%
Precious Metals	0%
Other	1%

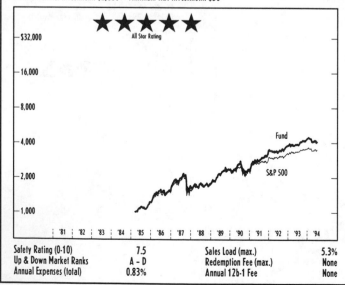

★★★★★ All Star Rating

Fund

S&P 500

Safety Rating (0-10)	7.5	Sales Load (max.)	5.3%
Up & Down Market Ranks	A – D	Redemption Fee (max.)	None
Annual Expenses (total)	0.83%	Annual 12b-1 Fee	None

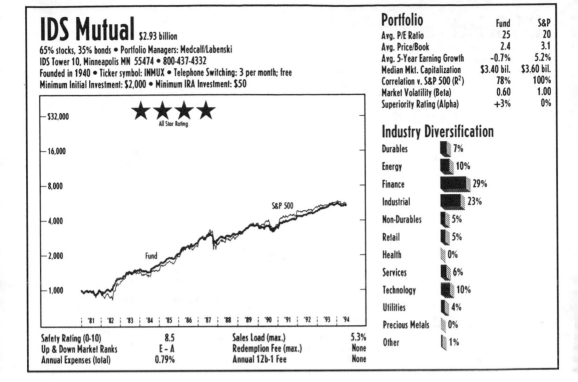

IDS Mutual $2.93 billion

65% stocks, 35% bonds • Portfolio Managers: Medcalf/Labenski
IDS Tower 10, Minneapolis MN 55474 • 800-437-4332
Founded in 1940 • Ticker symbol: INMUX • Telephone Switching: 3 per month; free
Minimum Initial Investment: $2,000 • Minimum IRA Investment: $50

★★★★
All Star Rating

	Fund	S&P
Portfolio		
Avg. P/E Ratio	25	20
Avg. Price/Book	2.4	3.1
Avg. 5-Year Earning Growth	-0.7%	5.2%
Median Mkt. Capitalization	$3.40 bil.	$3.60 bil.
Correlation v. S&P 500 (R²)	78%	100%
Market Volatility (Beta)	0.60	1.00
Superiority Rating (Alpha)	+3%	0%

Industry Diversification

Durables	7%
Energy	10%
Finance	29%
Industrial	23%
Non-Durables	5%
Retail	5%
Health	0%
Services	6%
Technology	10%
Utilities	4%
Precious Metals	0%
Other	1%

Safety Rating (0-10)	8.5	Sales Load (max.)	5.3%
Up & Down Market Ranks	E – A	Redemption Fee (max.)	None
Annual Expenses (total)	0.79%	Annual 12b-1 Fee	None

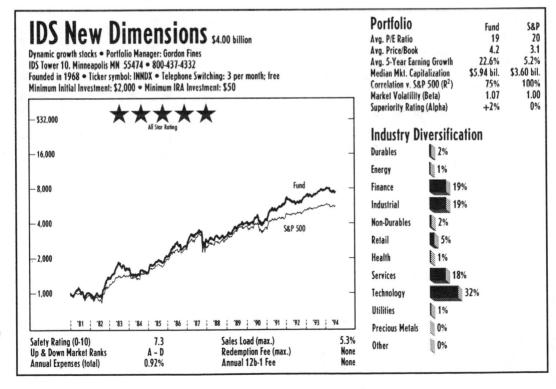

IDS New Dimensions $4.00 billion

Dynamic growth stocks • Portfolio Manager: Gordon Fines
IDS Tower 10, Minneapolis MN 55474 • 800-437-4332
Founded in 1968 • Ticker symbol: INNDX • Telephone Switching: 3 per month; free
Minimum Initial Investment: $2,000 • Minimum IRA Investment: $50

★★★★★
All Star Rating

	Fund	S&P
Portfolio		
Avg. P/E Ratio	19	20
Avg. Price/Book	4.2	3.1
Avg. 5-Year Earning Growth	22.6%	5.2%
Median Mkt. Capitalization	$5.94 bil.	$3.60 bil.
Correlation v. S&P 500 (R²)	75%	100%
Market Volatility (Beta)	1.07	1.00
Superiority Rating (Alpha)	+2%	0%

Industry Diversification

Durables	2%
Energy	1%
Finance	19%
Industrial	19%
Non-Durables	2%
Retail	5%
Health	1%
Services	18%
Technology	32%
Utilities	1%
Precious Metals	0%
Other	0%

Safety Rating (0-10)	7.3	Sales Load (max.)	5.3%
Up & Down Market Ranks	A – D	Redemption Fee (max.)	None
Annual Expenses (total)	0.92%	Annual 12b-1 Fee	None

IDS Selective $1.55 billion

A-rated and higher; 25% foreign; governments • Portfolio Manager: Ray S. Goodner
IDS Tower 10, Minneapolis MN 55402 • 800-437-4332
Founded in 1945 • Ticker symbol: INSEX • Telephone Switching: 3 per month; free
Minimum Initial Investment: $2,000 • Minimum IRA Investment: $50

Portfolio

Yield	6.3%
Average Quality	AA-
Average Maturity	15 years
Average Duration	7.4 years
Average Coupon	7.4%
Correlation with U.S. T-Bond (R^2)	76%
Dividends Paid	Monthly (Accrue Daily)

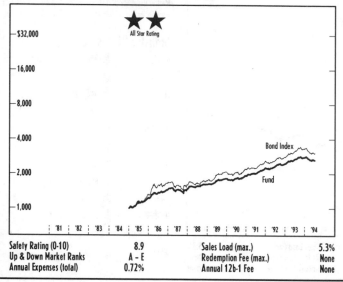

★ ★
All Star Rating

Bond Index

Fund

Quality

AAA	37%
AA	12%
A	25%
BBB	24%
BB	1%
B	0%
C	0%
D	0%
No Rating	0%

Safety Rating (0-10)	8.9	Sales Load (max.)	5.3%
Up & Down Market Ranks	A – E	Redemption Fee (max.)	None
Annual Expenses (total)	0.72%	Annual 12b-1 Fee	None

IDS Stock $2.20 billion

Diversified stocks • Portfolio Manager: Joseph M. Barsky III
IDS Tower 10, Minneapolis MN 55474 • 800-437-4332
Founded in 1945 • Ticker symbol: INSTX • Telephone Switching: 3 per month; free
Minimum Initial Investment: $2,000 • Minimum IRA Investment: $50

Portfolio

	Fund	S&P
Avg. P/E Ratio	25	20
Avg. Price/Book	2.8	3.1
Avg. 5-Year Earning Growth	0.4%	5.2%
Median Mkt. Capitalization	$6.15 bil.	$3.60 bil.
Correlation v. S&P 500 (R^2)	83%	100%
Market Volatility (Beta)	0.81	1.00
Superiority Rating (Alpha)	+2%	0%

★ ★ ★ ★ ★
All Star Rating

S&P 500

Fund

Industry Diversification

Durables	10%
Energy	10%
Finance	22%
Industrial	18%
Non-Durables	4%
Retail	0%
Health	1%
Services	6%
Technology	25%
Utilities	2%
Precious Metals	2%
Other	0%

Safety Rating (0-10)	7.9	Sales Load (max.)	5.3%
Up & Down Market Ranks	C – B	Redemption Fee (max.)	None
Annual Expenses (total)	0.73%	Annual 12b-1 Fee	None

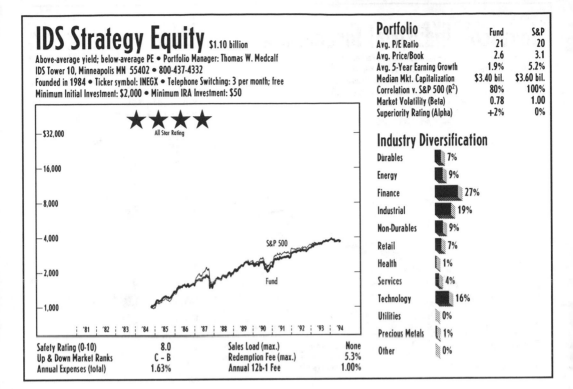

IDS Strategy Equity $1.10 billion

Above-average yield; below-average PE • Portfolio Manager: Thomas W. Medcalf
IDS Tower 10, Minneapolis MN 55402 • 800-437-4332
Founded in 1984 • Ticker symbol: INEGX • Telephone Switching: 3 per month; free
Minimum Initial Investment: $2,000 • Minimum IRA Investment: $50

★★★★
All Star Rating

S&P 500

Fund

Safety Rating (0-10)	8.0	
Up & Down Market Ranks	C – B	
Annual Expenses (total)	1.63%	
Sales Load (max.)		None
Redemption Fee (max.)		5.3%
Annual 12b-1 Fee		1.00%

Portfolio

	Fund	S&P
Avg. P/E Ratio	21	20
Avg. Price/Book	2.6	3.1
Avg. 5-Year Earning Growth	1.9%	5.2%
Median Mkt. Capitalization	$3.40 bil.	$3.60 bil.
Correlation v. S&P 500 (R^2)	80%	100%
Market Volatility (Beta)	0.78	1.00
Superiority Rating (Alpha)	+2%	0%

Industry Diversification

Durables	7%
Energy	9%
Finance	27%
Industrial	19%
Non-Durables	9%
Retail	7%
Health	1%
Services	4%
Technology	16%
Utilities	0%
Precious Metals	1%
Other	0%

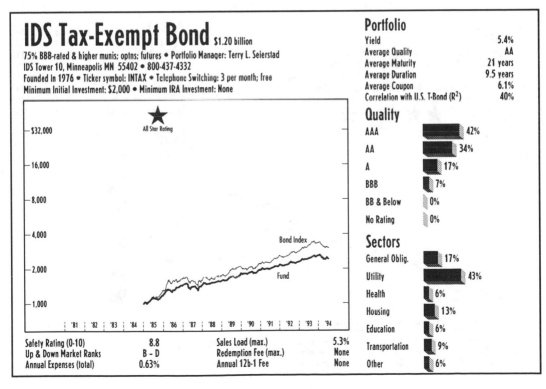

IDS Tax-Exempt Bond $1.20 billion

75% BBB-rated & higher munis; optns; futures • Portfolio Manager: Terry L. Seierstad
IDS Tower 10, Minneapolis MN 55402 • 800-437-4332
Founded in 1976 • Ticker symbol: INTAX • Telephone Switching: 3 per month; free
Minimum Initial Investment: $2,000 • Minimum IRA Investment: None

★
All Star Rating

Bond Index

Fund

Safety Rating (0-10)	8.8	
Up & Down Market Ranks	B – D	
Annual Expenses (total)	0.63%	
Sales Load (max.)		5.3%
Redemption Fee (max.)		None
Annual 12b-1 Fee		None

Portfolio

Yield	5.4%
Average Quality	AA
Average Maturity	21 years
Average Duration	9.5 years
Average Coupon	6.1%
Correlation with U.S. T-Bond (R^2)	40%

Quality

AAA	42%
AA	34%
A	17%
BBB	7%
BB & Below	0%
No Rating	0%

Sectors

General Oblig.	17%
Utility	43%
Health	6%
Housing	13%
Education	6%
Transportation	9%
Other	6%

Invesco - Industrial Income $3.97 billion

High-yield stocks; stable return • Portfolio Managers: Paul/Mayer
7800 E. Union Avenue, Ste. 300, Denver CO 80237 • 800-525-8085
Founded in 1960 • Ticker symbol: FIIIX • Telephone Switching: 4 per yr; free
Minimum Initial Investment: $1,000 • Minimum IRA Investment: $250

Portfolio

	Fund	S&P
Avg. P/E Ratio	20	20
Avg. Price/Book	2.6	3.1
Avg. 5-Year Earning Growth	7.2%	5.2%
Median Mkt. Capitalization	$4.21 bil.	$3.60 bil.
Correlation v. S&P 500 (R^2)	76%	100%
Market Volatility (Beta)	0.76	1.00
Superiority Rating (Alpha)	+3%	0%

★★★★★
All Star Rating

Fund
S&P 500

$32,000 · 16,000 · 8,000 · 4,000 · 2,000 · 1,000

'81 '82 '83 '84 '85 '86 '87 '88 '89 '90 '91 '92 '93 '94

Industry Diversification

Durables	2%
Energy	9%
Finance	14%
Industrial	20%
Non-Durables	4%
Retail	5%
Health	1%
Services	7%
Technology	28%
Utilities	8%
Precious Metals	1%
Other	1%

Safety Rating (0-10)	7.9	Sales Load (max.)	None
Up & Down Market Ranks	D – B	Redemption Fee (max.)	None
Annual Expenses (total)	0.96%	Annual 12b-1 Fee	0.25%

Janus $9.35 billion

Diversified growth stocks • Portfolio Manager: James P. Craig
100 Fillmore Street Suite 300, Denver CO 80206 • 800-525-8983
Founded in 1970 • Ticker symbol: JANSX • Telephone Switching: 4 per yr; free
Minimum Initial Investment: $1,000 • Minimum IRA Investment: $250

Portfolio

	Fund	S&P
Avg. P/E Ratio	24	20
Avg. Price/Book	3.7	3.1
Avg. 5-Year Earning Growth	12.6%	5.2%
Median Mkt. Capitalization	$6.20 bil.	$3.60 bil.
Correlation v. S&P 500 (R^2)	71%	100%
Market Volatility (Beta)	0.77	1.00
Superiority Rating (Alpha)	+2%	0%

★★★★★
All Star Rating

Fund
S&P 500

$32,000 · 16,000 · 8,000 · 4,000 · 2,000 · 1,000

'81 '82 '83 '84 '85 '86 '87 '88 '89 '90 '91 '92 '93 '94

Industry Diversification

Durables	3%
Energy	6%
Finance	24%
Industrial	14%
Non-Durables	3%
Retail	10%
Health	0%
Services	16%
Technology	22%
Utilities	2%
Precious Metals	0%
Other	0%

Safety Rating (0-10)	7.7	Sales Load (max.)	None
Up & Down Market Ranks	B – B	Redemption Fee (max.)	None
Annual Expenses (total)	0.92%	Annual 12b-1 Fee	None

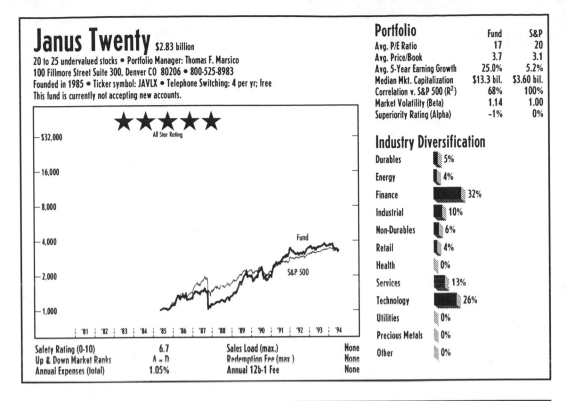

Janus Twenty $2.83 billion

20 to 25 undervalued stocks • Portfolio Manager: Thomas F. Marsico
100 Fillmore Street Suite 300, Denver CO 80206 • 800-525-8983
Founded in 1985 • Ticker symbol: JAVLX • Telephone Switching: 4 per yr; free
This fund is currently not accepting new accounts.

Portfolio	Fund	S&P
Avg. P/E Ratio	17	20
Avg. Price/Book	3.7	3.1
Avg. 5-Year Earning Growth	25.0%	5.2%
Median Mkt. Capitalization	$13.3 bil.	$3.60 bil.
Correlation v. S&P 500 (R^2)	68%	100%
Market Volatility (Beta)	1.14	1.00
Superiority Rating (Alpha)	–1%	0%

★★★★★
All Star Rating

Industry Diversification

Durables	5%
Energy	4%
Finance	32%
Industrial	10%
Non-Durables	6%
Retail	4%
Health	0%
Services	13%
Technology	26%
Utilities	0%
Precious Metals	0%
Other	0%

Safety Rating (0-10)	6.7	Sales Load (max.)	None
Up & Down Market Ranks	A – D	Redemption Fee (max)	None
Annual Expenses (total)	1.05%	Annual 12b-1 Fee	None

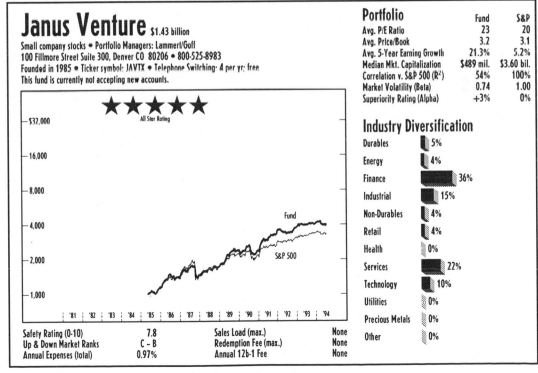

Janus Venture $1.43 billion

Small company stocks • Portfolio Managers: Lammert/Goff
100 Fillmore Street Suite 300, Denver CO 80206 • 800-525-8983
Founded in 1985 • Ticker symbol: JAVTX • Telephone Switching: 4 per yr; free
This fund is currently not accepting new accounts.

Portfolio	Fund	S&P
Avg. P/E Ratio	23	20
Avg. Price/Book	3.2	3.1
Avg. 5-Year Earning Growth	21.3%	5.2%
Median Mkt. Capitalization	$489 mil.	$3.60 bil.
Correlation v. S&P 500 (R^2)	54%	100%
Market Volatility (Beta)	0.74	1.00
Superiority Rating (Alpha)	+3%	0%

★★★★★
All Star Rating

Industry Diversification

Durables	5%
Energy	4%
Finance	36%
Industrial	15%
Non-Durables	4%
Retail	4%
Health	0%
Services	22%
Technology	10%
Utilities	0%
Precious Metals	0%
Other	0%

Safety Rating (0-10)	7.8	Sales Load (max.)	None
Up & Down Market Ranks	C – B	Redemption Fee (max.)	None
Annual Expenses (total)	0.97%	Annual 12b-1 Fee	None

Janus Worldwide $1.34 billion

Foreign & U.S. - diversified; market timing • Portfolio Manager: Helen Young Hayes
100 Fillmore Street Suite 300, Denver CO 80206 • 800-525-8983
Founded in 1991 • Ticker symbol: JAWWX • Telephone Switching: 4 per yr; free
Minimum Initial Investment: $1,000 • Minimum IRA Investment: $250

Portfolio

	Fund	S&P
Avg. P/E Ratio	23	20
Avg. Price/Book	4.1	3.1
Avg. 5-Year Earning Growth	17.5%	5.2%
Median Mkt. Capitalization	$2.12 bil.	$3.60 bil.
Correlation v. S&P 500 (R^2)	25%	100%
Market Volatility (Beta)	0.54	1.00
Superiority Rating (Alpha)	+6%	0%

Industry Diversification

Durables	9%
Energy	0%
Finance	23%
Industrial	19%
Non-Durables	23%
Retail	19%
Health	0%
Services	0%
Technology	7%
Utilities	0%
Precious Metals	0%
Other	0%

★★★★ All Star Rating

Chart: $32,000 / 16,000 / 8,000 / 4,000 / 2,000 / 1,000 — years '81 '82 '83 '84 '85 '86 '87 '88 '89 '90 '91 '92 '93 '94 — Fund, S&P 500

Safety Rating (0-10)	7.6	Sales Load (max.)	None
Up & Down Market Ranks	E – A	Redemption Fee (max.)	None
Annual Expenses (total)	1.32%	Annual 12b-1 Fee	None

John Hancock Sovrgn Bond "A" $1.39 billion

65% U.S. Government securities and agencies • Portfolio Managers: John K. Ho/Evans
101 Huntington Avenue, Boston MA 02199 • 800-225-5291
Founded in 1973 • Ticker symbol: JHNBX • Telephone Switching: Unlimited; free
Minimum Initial Investment: $1,000 • Minimum IRA Investment: $500

Portfolio

Yield	7.6%
Average Quality	A+
Average Maturity	15 years
Average Duration	5.0 years
Average Coupon	9.9%
Correlation with U.S. T-Bond (R^2)	71%
Dividends Paid	Monthly (Accrue Daily)

Quality

AAA	34%
AA	11%
A	20%
BBB	15%
BB	8%
B	10%
C	0%
D	0%
No Rating	0%

★★★★★ All Star Rating

Chart: $32,000 / 16,000 / 8,000 / 4,000 / 2,000 / 1,000 — years '81 '82 '83 '84 '85 '86 '87 '88 '89 '90 '91 '92 '93 '94 — Bond Index, Fund

Safety Rating (0-10)	9.2	Sales Load (max.)	4.7%
Up & Down Market Ranks	C – C	Redemption Fee (max.)	None
Annual Expenses (total)	1.25%	Annual 12b-1 Fee	0.50%

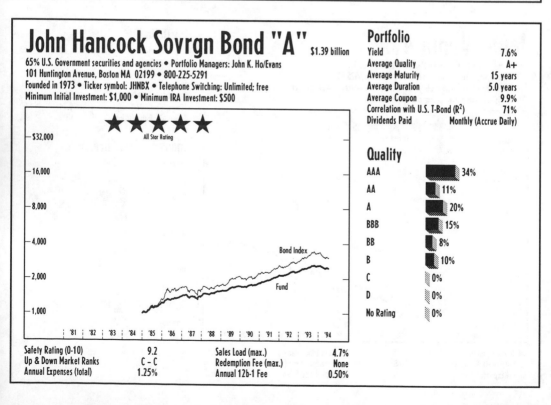

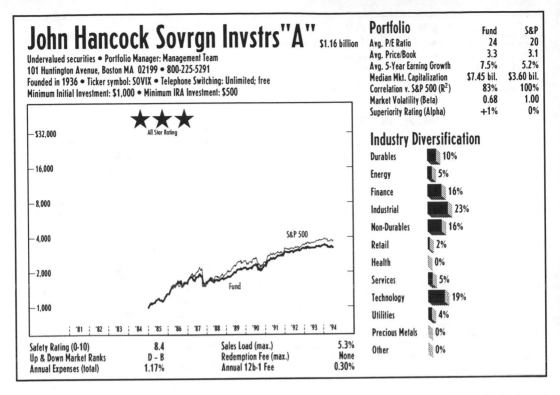

John Hancock Sovrgn Invstrs "A" $1.16 billion

Undervalued securities • Portfolio Manager: Management Team
101 Huntington Avenue, Boston MA 02199 • 800-225-5291
Founded in 1936 • Ticker symbol: SOVIX • Telephone Switching: Unlimited; free
Minimum Initial Investment: $1,000 • Minimum IRA Investment: $500

★★★
All Star Rating

Portfolio	Fund	S&P
Avg. P/E Ratio	24	20
Avg. Price/Book	3.3	3.1
Avg. 5-Year Earning Growth	7.5%	5.2%
Median Mkt. Capitalization	$7.45 bil.	$3.60 bil.
Correlation v. S&P 500 (R^2)	83%	100%
Market Volatility (Beta)	0.68	1.00
Superiority Rating (Alpha)	+1%	0%

Industry Diversification

Durables	10%
Energy	5%
Finance	16%
Industrial	23%
Non-Durables	16%
Retail	2%
Health	0%
Services	5%
Technology	19%
Utilities	4%
Precious Metals	0%
Other	0%

Safety Rating (0-10)	8.4	Sales Load (max.)	5.3%
Up & Down Market Ranks	D – B	Redemption Fee (max.)	None
Annual Expenses (total)	1.17%	Annual 12b-1 Fee	0.30%

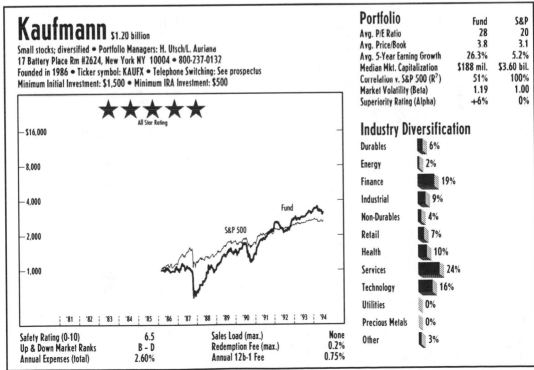

Kaufmann $1.20 billion

Small stocks; diversified • Portfolio Managers: H. Utsch/L. Auriana
17 Battery Place Rm #2624, New York NY 10004 • 800-237-0132
Founded in 1986 • Ticker symbol: KAUFX • Telephone Switching: See prospectus
Minimum Initial Investment: $1,500 • Minimum IRA Investment: $500

★★★★★
All Star Rating

Portfolio	Fund	S&P
Avg. P/E Ratio	28	20
Avg. Price/Book	3.8	3.1
Avg. 5-Year Earning Growth	26.3%	5.2%
Median Mkt. Capitalization	$188 mil.	$3.60 bil.
Correlation v. S&P 500 (R^2)	51%	100%
Market Volatility (Beta)	1.19	1.00
Superiority Rating (Alpha)	+6%	0%

Industry Diversification

Durables	6%
Energy	2%
Finance	19%
Industrial	9%
Non-Durables	4%
Retail	7%
Health	10%
Services	24%
Technology	16%
Utilities	0%
Precious Metals	0%
Other	3%

Safety Rating (0-10)	6.5	Sales Load (max.)	None
Up & Down Market Ranks	B – D	Redemption Fee (max.)	0.2%
Annual Expenses (total)	2.60%	Annual 12b-1 Fee	0.75%

Kemper "A" - Calif Tax-Free $1.19 billion

80% BBB-rated & higher California municipals ● Portfolio Managers: Beimford/Mier
120 South LaSalle Street, Chicago IL 60603 ● 800-621-1048
Founded in 1983 ● Ticker symbol: KCTAX ● Telephone Switching: 1 per 15da; fr
Minimum Initial Investment: $1,000 ● Minimum IRA Investment: None

Portfolio

Yield	5.1%
Average Quality	AA-
Average Maturity	17 years
Average Duration	9.0 years
Average Coupon	6.0%
Correlation with U.S. T-Bond (R^2)	43%

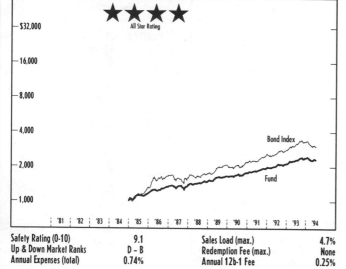

★★★★
All Star Rating

Bond Index

Fund

Quality

AAA	31%
AA	21%
A	34%
BBB	13%
BB & Below	0%
No Rating	1%

Sectors

General Oblig.	29%
Utility	24%
Health	15%
Housing	5%
Education	8%
Transportation	10%
Other	9%

Safety Rating (0-10)	9.1	Sales Load (max.)	4.7%
Up & Down Market Ranks	D – B	Redemption Fee (max.)	None
Annual Expenses (total)	0.74%	Annual 12b-1 Fee	0.25%

Kemper "A" - Growth $1.68 billion

Growth stocks; long term ● Portfolio Manager: C. Beth Conter
120 South LaSalle Street, Chicago IL 60603 ● 800-621-1048
Founded in 1966 ● Ticker symbol: KGRAX ● Telephone Switching: 1 per 15da; fr
Minimum Initial Investment: $1,000 ● Minimum IRA Investment: $250

Portfolio

	Fund	S&P
Avg. P/E Ratio	21	20
Avg. Price/Book	4.6	3.1
Avg. 5-Year Earning Growth	28.9%	5.2%
Median Mkt. Capitalization	$4.16 bil.	$3.60 bil.
Correlation v. S&P 500 (R^2)	71%	100%
Market Volatility (Beta)	1.18	1.00
Superiority Rating (Alpha)	-2%	0%

★★
All Star Rating

S&P 500

Fund

Industry Diversification

Durables	3%
Energy	2%
Finance	13%
Industrial	16%
Non-Durables	9%
Retail	3%
Health	4%
Services	23%
Technology	25%
Utilities	2%
Precious Metals	0%
Other	0%

Safety Rating (0-10)	6.7	Sales Load (max.)	6.1%
Up & Down Market Ranks	A – E	Redemption Fee (max.)	None
Annual Expenses (total)	1.00%	Annual 12b-1 Fee	0.25%

Kemper "A" - High Yield $2.32 billion

BB-rated & lower; U.S. & Canadian corporates • Portfolio Managers: McNamara/Resis
120 South LaSalle Street, Chicago IL 60603 • 800-621-1048
Founded in 1978 • Ticker symbol: KHYAX • Telephone Switching: 1 per 15da; fr
Minimum Initial Investment: $1,000 • Minimum IRA Investment: $250

Portfolio

Yield	9.4%
Average Quality	B+
Average Maturity	8.6 years
Average Duration	N/A
Average Coupon	11.2%
Correlation with U.S. T-Bond (R^2)	2%
Dividends Paid	Monthly

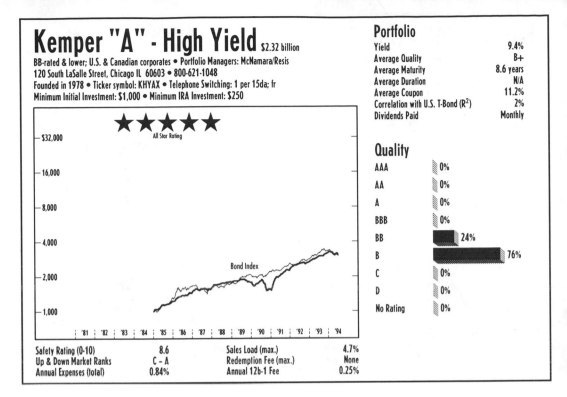

★★★★★ All Star Rating

Quality

AAA	0%
AA	0%
A	0%
BBB	0%
BB	24%
B	76%
C	0%
D	0%
No Rating	0%

Safety Rating (0-10)	8.6	Sales Load (max.)	4.7%
Up & Down Market Ranks	C – A	Redemption Fee (max.)	None
Annual Expenses (total)	0.84%	Annual 12b-1 Fee	0.25%

Kemper "A" - Municipal Bond $3.92 billion

85% BBB-rated and higher municipals • Portfolio Managers: J. Beimford, Jr./C. Mier
120 South LaSalle Street, Chicago IL 60603 • 800-621-1048
Founded in 1976 • Ticker symbol: KMBAX • Telephone Switching: 1 per 15da; fr
Minimum Initial Investment: $1,000 • Minimum IRA Investment: None

Portfolio

Yield	5.2%
Average Quality	AA
Average Maturity	17 years
Average Duration	9.1 years
Average Coupon	5.9%
Correlation with U.S. T-Bond (R^2)	50%

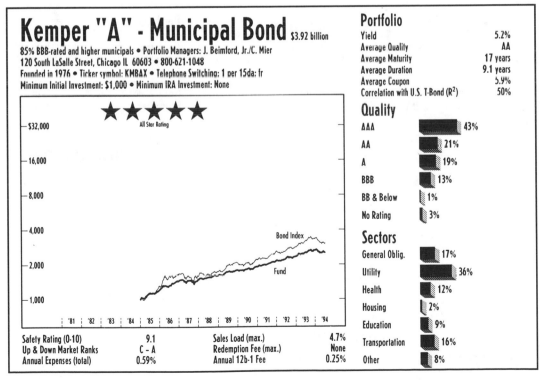

★★★★★ All Star Rating

Quality

AAA	43%
AA	21%
A	19%
BBB	13%
BB & Below	1%
No Rating	3%

Sectors

General Oblig.	17%
Utility	36%
Health	12%
Housing	2%
Education	9%
Transporation	16%
Other	8%

Safety Rating (0-10)	9.1	Sales Load (max.)	4.7%
Up & Down Market Ranks	C – A	Redemption Fee (max.)	None
Annual Expenses (total)	0.59%	Annual 12b-1 Fee	0.25%

Kemper "A" - Total Return $1.75 billion

Conservative securities; long term • Portfolio Manager: C. Beth Conter
120 South LaSalle Street, Chicago IL 60603 • 800-621-1048
Founded in 1964 • Ticker symbol: KTRAX • Telephone Switching: 1 per 15da; fr
Minimum Initial Investment: $1,000 • Minimum IRA Investment: $250

Portfolio	Fund	S&P
Avg. P/E Ratio	20	20
Avg. Price/Book	3.7	3.1
Avg. 5-Year Earning Growth	30.4%	5.2%
Median Mkt. Capitalization	$2.98 bil.	$3.60 bil.
Correlation v. S&P 500 (R^2)	71%	100%
Market Volatility (Beta)	0.81	1.00
Superiority Rating (Alpha)	0%	0%

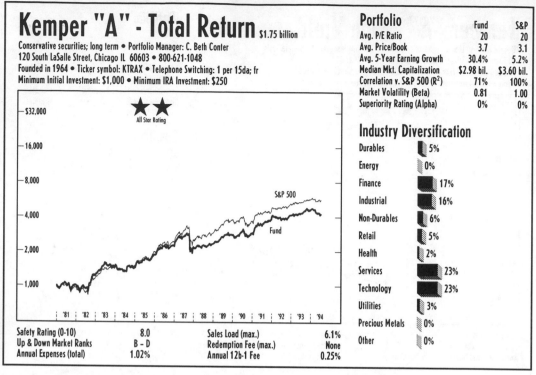

Industry Diversification

Durables	5%
Energy	0%
Finance	17%
Industrial	16%
Non-Durables	6%
Retail	5%
Health	2%
Services	23%
Technology	23%
Utilities	3%
Precious Metals	0%
Other	0%

Safety Rating (0-10)	8.0	Sales Load (max.)	6.1%
Up & Down Market Ranks	B – D	Redemption Fee (max.)	None
Annual Expenses (total)	1.02%	Annual 12b-1 Fee	0.25%

Kemper "A" - U.S. Government $5.53 billion

AAA-rated Ginnie Mae securities • Portfolio Managers: Beimford/Schumacher
120 South LaSalle Street, Chicago IL 60603 • 800-621-1048
Founded in 1979 • Ticker symbol: KUSAX • Telephone Switching: 1 per 15da; fr
Minimum Initial Investment: $1,000 • Minimum IRA Investment: $250

Portfolio	
Yield	4.4%
Average Quality	AAA
Average Maturity	7.4 years
Average Duration	4.4 years
Average Coupon	10.8%
Correlation with U.S. T-Bond (R^2)	64%
Dividends Paid	Monthly

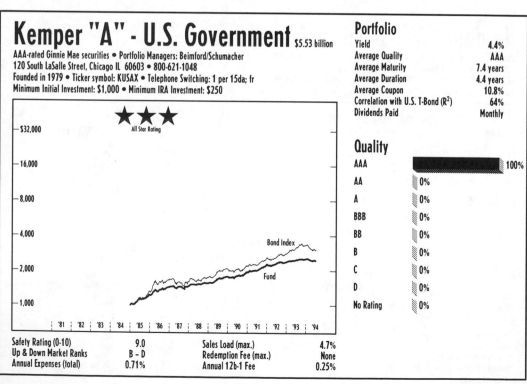

Quality

AAA	100%
AA	0%
A	0%
BBB	0%
BB	0%
B	0%
C	0%
D	0%
No Rating	0%

Safety Rating (0-10)	9.0	Sales Load (max.)	4.7%
Up & Down Market Ranks	B – D	Redemption Fee (max.)	None
Annual Expenses (total)	0.71%	Annual 12b-1 Fee	0.25%

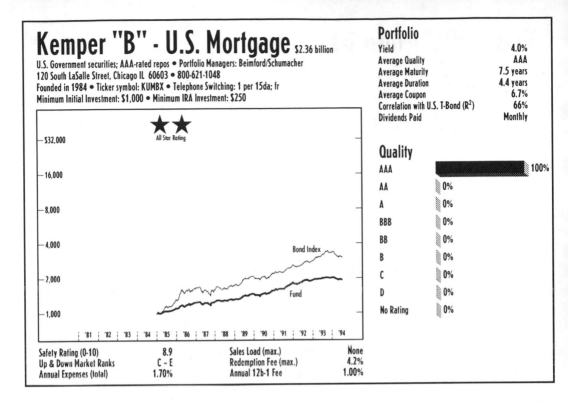

Kemper "B" - U.S. Mortgage $2.36 billion

U.S. Government securities; AAA-rated repos • Portfolio Managers: Beimford/Schumacher
120 South LaSalle Street, Chicago IL 60603 • 800-621-1048
Founded in 1984 • Ticker symbol: KUMBX • Telephone Switching: 1 per 15da; fr
Minimum Initial Investment: $1,000 • Minimum IRA Investment: $250

Portfolio

Yield	4.0%
Average Quality	AAA
Average Maturity	7.5 years
Average Duration	4.4 years
Average Coupon	6.7%
Correlation with U.S. T-Bond (R²)	66%
Dividends Paid	Monthly

Quality

AAA	100%
AA	0%
A	0%
BBB	0%
BB	0%
B	0%
C	0%
D	0%
No Rating	0%

Safety Rating (0-10)	8.9	Sales Load (max.)	None
Up & Down Market Ranks	C - E	Redemption Fee (max.)	4.2%
Annual Expenses (total)	1.70%	Annual 12b-1 Fee	1.00%

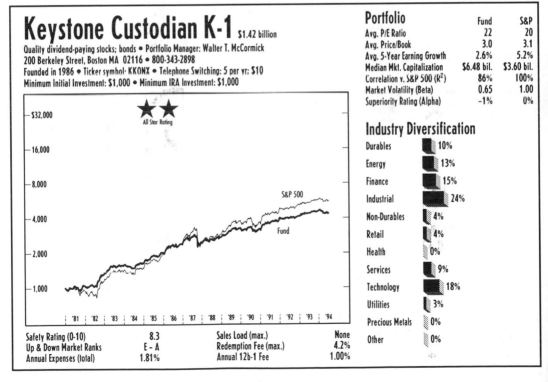

Keystone Custodian K-1 $1.42 billion

Quality dividend-paying stocks; bonds • Portfolio Manager: Walter T. McCormick
200 Berkeley Street, Boston MA 02116 • 800-343-2898
Founded in 1986 • Ticker symbol: KKONX • Telephone Switching: 5 per yr; $10
Minimum Initial Investment: $1,000 • Minimum IRA Investment: $1,000

Portfolio

	Fund	S&P
Avg. P/E Ratio	22	20
Avg. Price/Book	3.0	3.1
Avg. 5-Year Earning Growth	2.6%	5.2%
Median Mkt. Capitalization	$6.48 bil.	$3.60 bil.
Correlation v. S&P 500 (R²)	86%	100%
Market Volatility (Beta)	0.65	1.00
Superiority Rating (Alpha)	–1%	0%

Industry Diversification

Durables	10%
Energy	13%
Finance	15%
Industrial	24%
Non-Durables	4%
Retail	4%
Health	0%
Services	9%
Technology	18%
Utilities	3%
Precious Metals	0%
Other	0%

Safety Rating (0-10)	8.3	Sales Load (max.)	None
Up & Down Market Ranks	E - A	Redemption Fee (max.)	4.2%
Annual Expenses (total)	1.81%	Annual 12b-1 Fee	1.00%

Keystone Custodian S-4 $1.01 billion

Emerging and volatile stocks • Portfolio Manager: Roland Gillis
200 Berkeley Street, Boston MA 02116 • 800-343-2898
Founded in 1936 • Ticker symbol: KSFOX • Telephone Switching: 5 per yr; $10
Minimum Initial Investment: $1,000 • Minimum IRA Investment: $1,000

Portfolio

	Fund	S&P
Avg. P/E Ratio	30	20
Avg. Price/Book	4.1	3.1
Avg. 5-Year Earning Growth	40.8%	5.2%
Median Mkt. Capitalization	$482 mil.	$3.60 bil.
Correlation v. S&P 500 (R^2)	50%	100%
Market Volatility (Beta)	1.51	1.00
Superiority Rating (Alpha)	+0%	0%

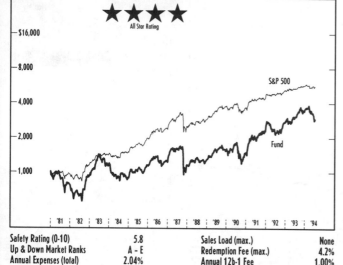

★★★★
All Star Rating

S&P 500
Fund

Industry Diversification

Durables	2%
Energy	4%
Finance	11%
Industrial	10%
Non-Durables	6%
Retail	4%
Health	2%
Services	20%
Technology	40%
Utilities	0%
Precious Metals	0%
Other	1%

Safety Rating (0-10)	5.8	Sales Load (max.)	None
Up & Down Market Ranks	A – E	Redemption Fee (max.)	4.2%
Annual Expenses (total)	2.04%	Annual 12b-1 Fee	1.00%

Keystone Tax-Free $1.38 billion

Investment-grade municipals • Portfolio Manager: Betsy A. Blacher
200 Berkeley Street, Boston MA 02116 • 800-343-2898
Founded in 1978 • Ticker symbol: KSTFX • Telephone Switching: 5 per yr; $10
This fund is currently not accepting new accounts.

Portfolio

Yield	5.1%
Average Quality	AA
Average Maturity	19 years
Average Duration	10 years
Average Coupon	6.7%
Correlation with U.S. T-Bond (R^2)	49%

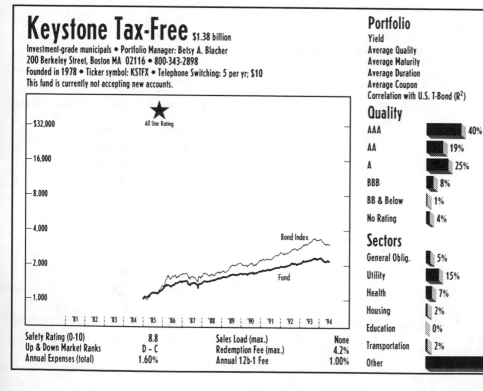

★
All Star Rating

Bond Index
Fund

Quality

AAA	40%
AA	19%
A	25%
BBB	8%
BB & Below	1%
No Rating	4%

Sectors

General Oblig.	5%
Utility	15%
Health	7%
Housing	2%
Education	0%
Transportation	2%
Other	69%

Safety Rating (0-10)	8.8	Sales Load (max.)	None
Up & Down Market Ranks	D – C	Redemption Fee (max.)	4.2%
Annual Expenses (total)	1.60%	Annual 12b-1 Fee	1.00%

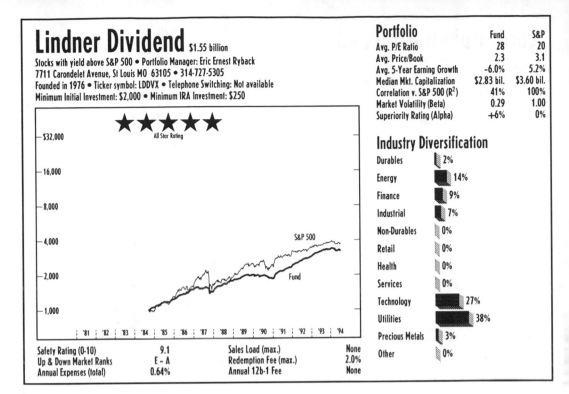

Lindner Dividend $1.55 billion

Stocks with yield above S&P 500 • Portfolio Manager: Eric Ernest Ryback
7711 Carondelet Avenue, St Louis MO 63105 • 314-727-5305
Founded in 1976 • Ticker symbol: LDDVX • Telephone Switching: Not available
Minimum Initial Investment: $2,000 • Minimum IRA Investment: $250

★★★★★
All Star Rating

Portfolio	Fund	S&P
Avg. P/E Ratio	28	20
Avg. Price/Book	2.3	3.1
Avg. 5-Year Earning Growth	–6.0%	5.2%
Median Mkt. Capitalization	$2.83 bil.	$3.60 bil.
Correlation v. S&P 500 (R^2)	41%	100%
Market Volatility (Beta)	0.29	1.00
Superiority Rating (Alpha)	+6%	0%

Industry Diversification

Durables	2%
Energy	14%
Finance	9%
Industrial	7%
Non-Durables	0%
Retail	0%
Health	0%
Services	0%
Technology	27%
Utilities	38%
Precious Metals	3%
Other	0%

Safety Rating (0-10)	9.1	Sales Load (max.)	None
Up & Down Market Ranks	E - A	Redemption Fee (max.)	2.0%
Annual Expenses (total)	0.64%	Annual 12b-1 Fee	None

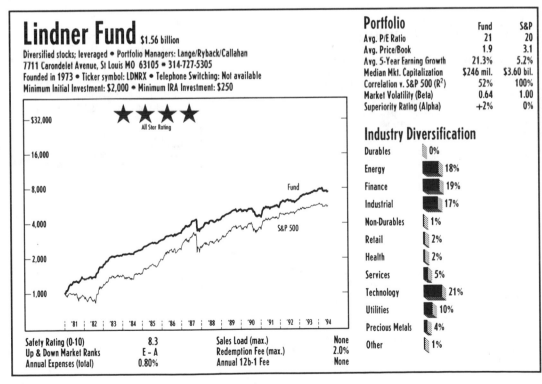

Lindner Fund $1.56 billion

Diversified stocks; leveraged • Portfolio Managers: Lange/Ryback/Callahan
7711 Carondelet Avenue, St Louis MO 63105 • 314-727-5305
Founded in 1973 • Ticker symbol: LDNRX • Telephone Switching: Not available
Minimum Initial Investment: $2,000 • Minimum IRA Investment: $250

★★★★
All Star Rating

Portfolio	Fund	S&P
Avg. P/E Ratio	21	20
Avg. Price/Book	1.9	3.1
Avg. 5-Year Earning Growth	21.3%	5.2%
Median Mkt. Capitalization	$246 mil.	$3.60 bil.
Correlation v. S&P 500 (R^2)	52%	100%
Market Volatility (Beta)	0.64	1.00
Superiority Rating (Alpha)	+2%	0%

Industry Diversification

Durables	0%
Energy	18%
Finance	19%
Industrial	17%
Non-Durables	1%
Retail	2%
Health	2%
Services	5%
Technology	21%
Utilities	10%
Precious Metals	4%
Other	1%

Safety Rating (0-10)	8.3	Sales Load (max.)	None
Up & Down Market Ranks	E - A	Redemption Fee (max.)	2.0%
Annual Expenses (total)	0.80%	Annual 12b-1 Fee	None

Lord, Abbett Affiliated $4.11 billion

Large; undervalued stocks • Portfolio Manager: Thomas Henderson
767 Fifth Avenue 11th Floor, New York NY 10153 • 800-821-5129
Founded in 1934 • Ticker symbol: LAFFX • Telephone Switching: Unlimited; free
Minimum Initial Investment: $250 • Minimum IRA Investment: $250

Portfolio

	Fund	S&P
Avg. P/E Ratio	21	20
Avg. Price/Book	2.4	3.1
Avg. 5-Year Earning Growth	2.7%	5.2%
Median Mkt. Capitalization	$6.48 bil.	$3.60 bil.
Correlation v. S&P 500 (R^2)	85%	100%
Market Volatility (Beta)	0.80	1.00
Superiority Rating (Alpha)	+0%	0%

★★★
All Star Rating

Industry Diversification

Durables	10%
Energy	7%
Finance	23%
Industrial	17%
Non-Durables	2%
Retail	4%
Health	0%
Services	5%
Technology	27%
Utilities	5%
Precious Metals	0%
Other	0%

Safety Rating (0-10)	7.9	Sales Load (max.)	6.1%
Up & Down Market Ranks	C - C	Redemption Fee (max.)	None
Annual Expenses (total)	0.63%	Annual 12b-1 Fee	0.25%

Lord, Abbett Government Secs $3.53 billion

U.S. Government securities • Portfolio Manager: Robert S. Dow
767 Fifth Avenue 11th Floor, New York NY 10153 • 800-821-5129
Founded in 1932 • Ticker symbol: LAGVX • Telephone Switching: Unlimited; free
Minimum Initial Investment: $500 • Minimum IRA Investment: $500

Portfolio

Yield	5.1%
Average Quality	AAA
Average Maturity	8.1 years
Average Duration	5.1 years
Average Coupon	7.3%
Correlation with U.S. T-Bond (R^2)	53%
Dividends Paid	Monthly (Accrue Daily)

★
All Star Rating

Quality

AAA	100%
AA	0%
A	0%
BBB	0%
BB	0%
B	0%
C	0%
D	0%
No Rating	0%

Safety Rating (0-10)	8.7	Sales Load (max.)	5.0%
Up & Down Market Ranks	A - E	Redemption Fee (max.)	None
Annual Expenses (total)	0.89%	Annual 12b-1 Fee	0.25%

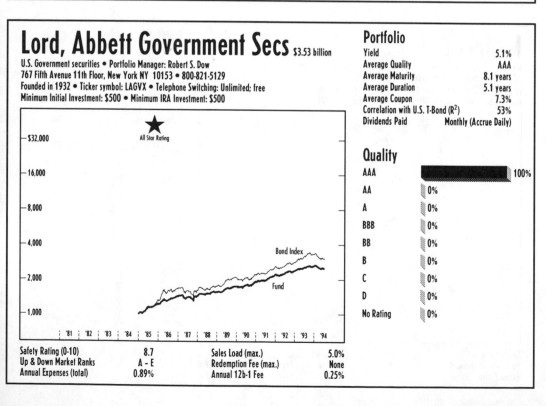

MainStay - Corporate Bond $1.01 billion

B, BB, & BBB-rated corporate bonds • Portfolio Manager: Mutiple Managers
260 Cherry Hill NY Life Inc., Parsippany NJ 07054 • 800-522-4202
Founded in 1986 • Ticker symbol: MKHCX • Telephone Switching: See prospectus
Minimum Initial Investment: $500 • Minimum IRA Investment: $500

Portfolio

Yield	8.1%
Average Quality	B+
Average Maturity	6.0 years
Average Duration	3.7 years
Average Coupon	11.0%
Correlation with U.S. T-Bond (R^2)	0%
Dividends Paid	Monthly

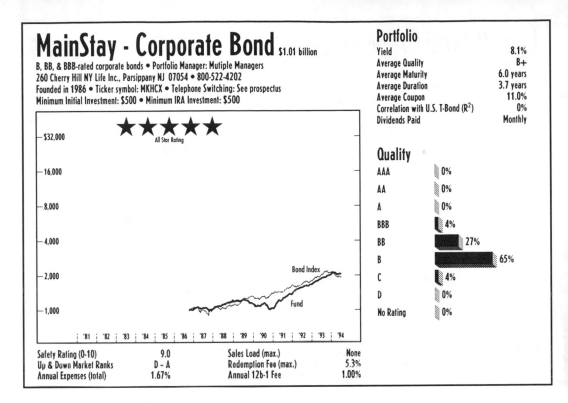

Quality

AAA	0%
AA	0%
A	0%
BBB	4%
BB	27%
B	65%
C	4%
D	0%
No Rating	0%

Safety Rating (0-10)	9.0	Sales Load (max.)	None
Up & Down Market Ranks	D – A	Redemption Fee (max.)	5.3%
Annual Expenses (total)	1.67%	Annual 12b-1 Fee	1.00%

MainStay - Government $1.14 billion

U.S. Government securities; futures; options • Portfolio Manager: Multiple Managers
260 Cherry Hill NY Life Inc., Parsippany NJ 07054 • 800-522-4202
Founded in 1986 • Ticker symbol: MCSGX • Telephone Switching: See prospectus
Minimum Initial Investment: $500 • Minimum IRA Investment: $500

Portfolio

Yield	4.5%
Average Quality	AAA
Average Maturity	4.9 years
Average Duration	4.1 years
Average Coupon	8.4%
Correlation with U.S. T-Bond (R^2)	79%
Dividends Paid	Monthly

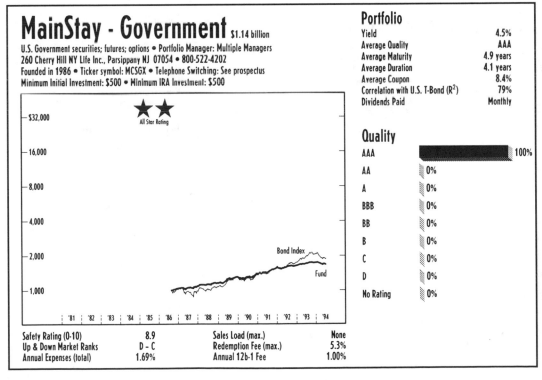

Quality

AAA	100%
AA	0%
A	0%
BBB	0%
BB	0%
B	0%
C	0%
D	0%
No Rating	0%

Safety Rating (0-10)	8.9	Sales Load (max.)	None
Up & Down Market Ranks	D – C	Redemption Fee (max.)	5.3%
Annual Expenses (total)	1.69%	Annual 12b-1 Fee	1.00%

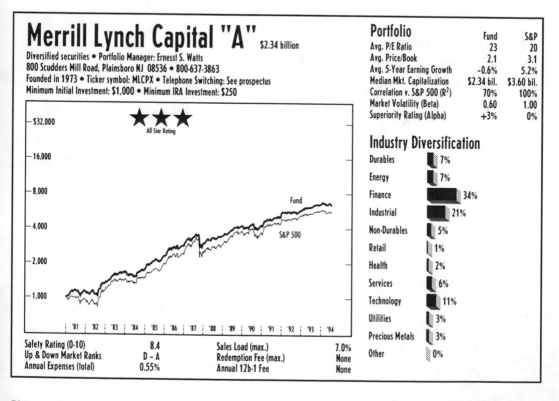

Merrill Lynch Basic Value "A" $2.31 billion

Undervalued stocks • Portfolio Manager: Paul M. Hoffmann
800 Scudders Mill Road, Plainsboro NJ 08536 • 800-637-3863
Founded in 1977 • Ticker symbol: MLBVX • Telephone Switching: See prospectus
Minimum Initial Investment: $1,000 • Minimum IRA Investment: $250

★★★★
All Star Rating

Fund

S&P 500

'81 '82 '83 '84 '85 '86 '87 '88 '89 '90 '91 '92 '93 '94

Portfolio	Fund	S&P
Avg. P/E Ratio	18	20
Avg. Price/Book	2.1	3.1
Avg. 5-Year Earning Growth	3.0%	5.2%
Median Mkt. Capitalization	$5.97 bil.	$3.60 bil.
Correlation v. S&P 500 (R²)	76%	100%
Market Volatility (Beta)	0.84	1.00
Superiority Rating (Alpha)	+1%	0%

Industry Diversification

Durables	2%
Energy	15%
Finance	34%
Industrial	15%
Non-Durables	4%
Retail	1%
Health	1%
Services	0%
Technology	20%
Utilities	7%
Precious Metals	1%
Other	0%

Safety Rating (0-10)	7.8	Sales Load (max.)	7.0%
Up & Down Market Ranks	C – B	Redemption Fee (max.)	None
Annual Expenses (total)	0.54%	Annual 12b-1 Fee	None

Merrill Lynch Capital "A" $2.34 billion

Diversified securities • Portfolio Manager: Ernesst S. Watts
800 Scudders Mill Road, Plainsboro NJ 08536 • 800-637-3863
Founded in 1973 • Ticker symbol: MLCPX • Telephone Switching: See prospectus
Minimum Initial Investment: $1,000 • Minimum IRA Investment: $250

★★★
All Star Rating

Fund

S&P 500

'81 '82 '83 '84 '85 '86 '87 '88 '89 '90 '91 '92 '93 '94

Portfolio	Fund	S&P
Avg. P/E Ratio	23	20
Avg. Price/Book	2.1	3.1
Avg. 5-Year Earning Growth	-0.6%	5.2%
Median Mkt. Capitalization	$2.34 bil.	$3.60 bil.
Correlation v. S&P 500 (R²)	70%	100%
Market Volatility (Beta)	0.60	1.00
Superiority Rating (Alpha)	+3%	0%

Industry Diversification

Durables	7%
Energy	7%
Finance	34%
Industrial	21%
Non-Durables	5%
Retail	1%
Health	2%
Services	6%
Technology	11%
Utilities	3%
Precious Metals	3%
Other	0%

Safety Rating (0-10)	8.4	Sales Load (max.)	7.0%
Up & Down Market Ranks	D – A	Redemption Fee (max.)	None
Annual Expenses (total)	0.55%	Annual 12b-1 Fee	None

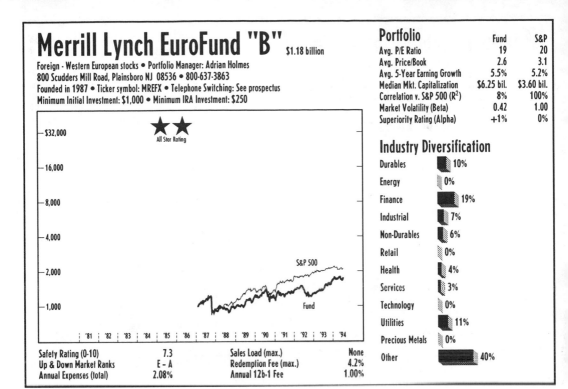

Merrill Lynch EuroFund "B" $1.18 billion

Foreign - Western European stocks ● Portfolio Manager: Adrian Holmes
800 Scudders Mill Road, Plainsboro NJ 08536 ● 800-637-3863
Founded in 1987 ● Ticker symbol: MREFX ● Telephone Switching: See prospectus
Minimum Initial Investment: $1,000 ● Minimum IRA Investment: $250

Portfolio

	Fund	S&P
Avg. P/E Ratio	19	20
Avg. Price/Book	2.6	3.1
Avg. 5-Year Earning Growth	5.5%	5.2%
Median Mkt. Capitalization	$6.25 bil.	$3.60 bil.
Correlation v. S&P 500 (R^2)	8%	100%
Market Volatility (Beta)	0.42	1.00
Superiority Rating (Alpha)	+1%	0%

★★ All Star Rating

Industry Diversification

Durables	10%
Energy	0%
Finance	19%
Industrial	7%
Non-Durables	6%
Retail	0%
Health	4%
Services	3%
Technology	0%
Utilities	11%
Precious Metals	0%
Other	40%

Safety Rating (0-10)	7.3	Sales Load (max.)	None
Up & Down Market Ranks	E – A	Redemption Fee (max.)	4.2%
Annual Expenses (total)	2.08%	Annual 12b-1 Fee	1.00%

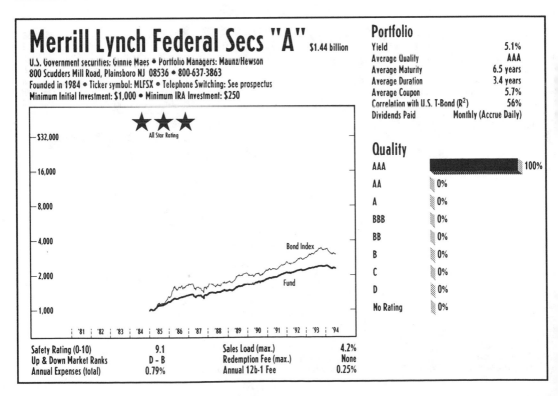

Merrill Lynch Federal Secs "A" $1.44 billion

U.S. Government securities; Ginnie Maes ● Portfolio Managers: Maunz/Hewson
800 Scudders Mill Road, Plainsboro NJ 08536 ● 800-637-3863
Founded in 1984 ● Ticker symbol: MLFSX ● Telephone Switching: See prospectus
Minimum Initial Investment: $1,000 ● Minimum IRA Investment: $250

Portfolio

Yield	5.1%
Average Quality	AAA
Average Maturity	6.5 years
Average Duration	3.4 years
Average Coupon	5.7%
Correlation with U.S. T-Bond (R^2)	56%
Dividends Paid	Monthly (Accrue Daily)

★★★ All Star Rating

Quality

AAA	100%
AA	0%
A	0%
BBB	0%
BB	0%
B	0%
C	0%
D	0%
No Rating	0%

Safety Rating (0-10)	9.1	Sales Load (max.)	4.2%
Up & Down Market Ranks	D – B	Redemption Fee (max.)	None
Annual Expenses (total)	0.79%	Annual 12b-1 Fee	0.25%

Merrill Lynch Gr Inv & Ret "B" $1.25 billion

Undervalued stocks • Portfolio Manager: Stephen C. Johnes
800 Scudders Mill Road, Plainsboro NJ 08536 • 800-637-3863
Founded in 1987 • Ticker symbol: MRQRX • Telephone Switching: See prospectus
Minimum Initial Investment: $1,000 • Minimum IRA Investment: $250

Portfolio

	Fund	S&P
Avg. P/E Ratio	33	20
Avg. Price/Book	3.0	3.1
Avg. 5-Year Earning Growth	24.6%	5.2%
Median Mkt. Capitalization	$793 mil.	$3.60 bil.
Correlation v. S&P 500 (R^2)	48%	100%
Market Volatility (Beta)	1.16	1.00
Superiority Rating (Alpha)	+2%	0%

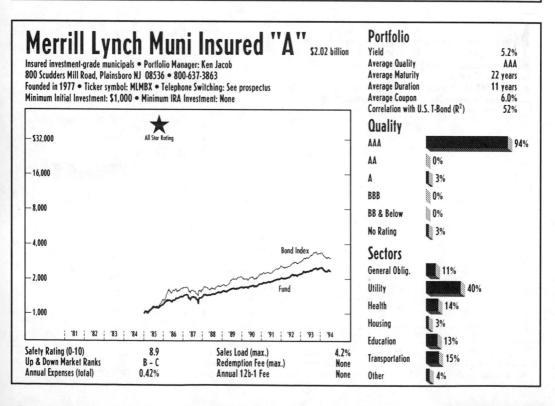

★★★★★
All Star Rating

Fund
S&P 500

Industry Diversification

Durables	5%
Energy	22%
Finance	1%
Industrial	8%
Non-Durables	0%
Retail	0%
Health	3%
Services	7%
Technology	39%
Utilities	13%
Precious Metals	2%
Other	0%

Safety Rating (0-10)	6.3	Sales Load (max.)	None
Up & Down Market Ranks	A – D	Redemption Fee (max.)	4.2%
Annual Expenses (total)	1.83%	Annual 12b-1 Fee	1.00%

Merrill Lynch Muni Insured "A" $2.02 billion

Insured investment-grade municipals • Portfolio Manager: Ken Jacob
800 Scudders Mill Road, Plainsboro NJ 08536 • 800-637-3863
Founded in 1977 • Ticker symbol: MLMBX • Telephone Switching: See prospectus
Minimum Initial Investment: $1,000 • Minimum IRA Investment: None

Portfolio

Yield	5.2%
Average Quality	AAA
Average Maturity	22 years
Average Duration	11 years
Average Coupon	6.0%
Correlation with U.S. T-Bond (R^2)	52%

★
All Star Rating

Bond Index
Fund

Quality

AAA	94%
AA	0%
A	3%
BBB	0%
BB & Below	0%
No Rating	3%

Sectors

General Oblig.	11%
Utility	40%
Health	14%
Housing	3%
Education	13%
Transportation	15%
Other	4%

Safety Rating (0-10)	8.9	Sales Load (max.)	4.2%
Up & Down Market Ranks	B – C	Redemption Fee (max.)	None
Annual Expenses (total)	0.42%	Annual 12b-1 Fee	None

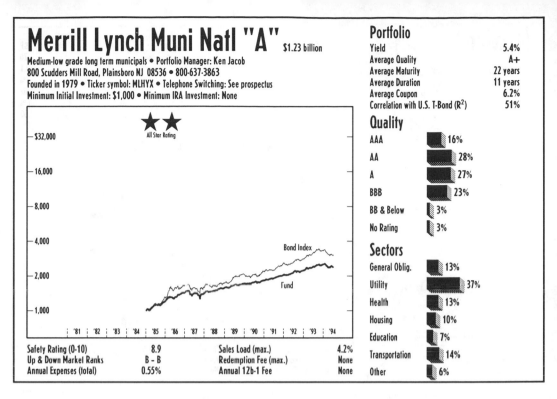

Merrill Lynch Muni Natl "A" $1.23 billion

Medium-low grade long term municipals • Portfolio Manager: Ken Jacob
800 Scudders Mill Road, Plainsboro NJ 08536 • 800-637-3863
Founded in 1979 • Ticker symbol: MLHYX • Telephone Switching: See prospectus
Minimum Initial Investment: $1,000 • Minimum IRA Investment: None

Portfolio

Yield	5.4%
Average Quality	A+
Average Maturity	22 years
Average Duration	11 years
Average Coupon	6.2%
Correlation with U.S. T-Bond (R^2)	51%

Quality

AAA	16%
AA	28%
A	27%
BBB	23%
BB & Below	3%
No Rating	3%

Sectors

General Oblig.	13%
Utility	37%
Health	13%
Housing	10%
Education	7%
Transportation	14%
Other	6%

★★ All Star Rating

Safety Rating (0-10)	8.9	Sales Load (max.)	4.2%
Up & Down Market Ranks	B – B	Redemption Fee (max.)	None
Annual Expenses (total)	0.55%	Annual 12b-1 Fee	None

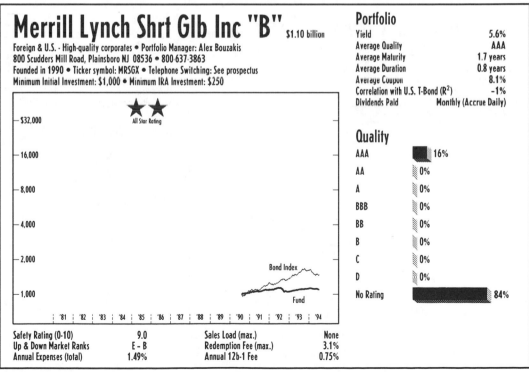

Merrill Lynch Shrt Glb Inc "B" $1.10 billion

Foreign & U.S. - High-quality corporates • Portfolio Manager: Alex Bouzakis
800 Scudders Mill Road, Plainsboro NJ 08536 • 800-637-3863
Founded in 1990 • Ticker symbol: MRSGX • Telephone Switching: See prospectus
Minimum Initial Investment: $1,000 • Minimum IRA Investment: $250

Portfolio

Yield	5.6%
Average Quality	AAA
Average Maturity	1.7 years
Average Duration	0.8 years
Average Coupon	8.1%
Correlation with U.S. T-Bond (R^2)	–1%
Dividends Paid	Monthly (Accrue Daily)

Quality

AAA	16%
AA	0%
A	0%
BBB	0%
BB	0%
B	0%
C	0%
D	0%
No Rating	84%

★★ All Star Rating

Safety Rating (0-10)	9.0	Sales Load (max.)	None
Up & Down Market Ranks	E – B	Redemption Fee (max.)	3.1%
Annual Expenses (total)	1.49%	Annual 12b-1 Fee	0.75%

Mexico $1.19 billion

Foreign - Mexican stocks ● Portfolio Manager: Jose Luis Gomez-Pimienta
399 Park Avenue, New York NY 10022 ● 800-224-4134
Founded in 1981 ● Ticker symbol: MXF ● Telephone Switching: Via broker
Minimum Initial Investment: $0 ● Minimum IRA Investment: None

Portfolio	Fund	S&P
Avg. P/E Ratio	19	20
Avg. Price/Book	2.5	3.1
Avg. 5-Year Earning Growth	N/A	5.2%
Median Mkt. Capitalization	$175 mil.	$3.60 bil.
Correlation v. S&P 500 (R^2)	15%	100%
Market Volatility (Beta)	1.58	1.00
Superiority Rating (Alpha)	+6%	0%

Industry Diversification

Durables	0%
Energy	0%
Finance	13%
Industrial	46%
Non-Durables	12%
Retail	20%
Health	0%
Services	2%
Technology	0%
Utilities	7%
Precious Metals	0%
Other	0%

Safety Rating (0-10)	2.5	Sales Load (max.)	None
Up & Down Market Ranks	B – E	Redemption Fee (max.)	None
Annual Expenses (total)	0.97%	Annual 12b-1 Fee	None

MFS - Investors Trust "A"(MIT) $1.61 billion

High-quality stocks ● Portfolio Managers: A. De Rham/J. Laupheimer/K. Parke
500 Boylston Street, Boston MA 02116 ● 800-225-2606
Founded in 1924 ● Ticker symbol: MITTX ● Telephone Switching: Unlimited; free
Minimum Initial Investment: $1,000 ● Minimum IRA Investment: None

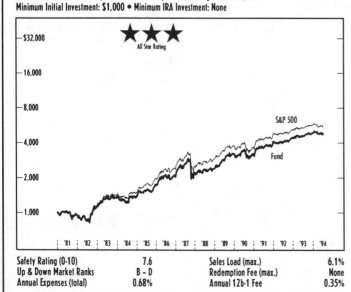

Portfolio	Fund	S&P
Avg. P/E Ratio	19	20
Avg. Price/Book	3.3	3.1
Avg. 5-Year Earning Growth	10.3%	5.2%
Median Mkt. Capitalization	$7.32 bil.	$3.60 bil.
Correlation v. S&P 500 (R^2)	90%	100%
Market Volatility (Beta)	0.87	1.00
Superiority Rating (Alpha)	–1%	0%

Industry Diversification

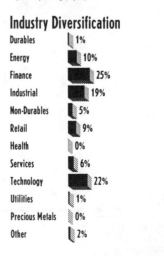

Durables	1%
Energy	10%
Finance	25%
Industrial	19%
Non-Durables	5%
Retail	9%
Health	0%
Services	6%
Technology	22%
Utilities	1%
Precious Metals	0%
Other	2%

Safety Rating (0-10)	7.6	Sales Load (max.)	6.1%
Up & Down Market Ranks	B – D	Redemption Fee (max.)	None
Annual Expenses (total)	0.68%	Annual 12b-1 Fee	0.35%

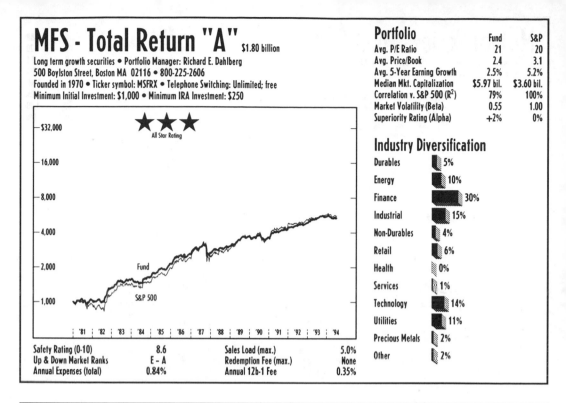

MFS - Total Return "A" $1.80 billion

Long term growth securities • Portfolio Manager: Richard E. Dahlberg
500 Boylston Street, Boston MA 02116 • 800-225-2606
Founded in 1970 • Ticker symbol: MSFRX • Telephone Switching: Unlimited; free
Minimum Initial Investment: $1,000 • Minimum IRA Investment: $250

★★★
All Star Rating

	Fund	S&P
Portfolio		
Avg. P/E Ratio	21	20
Avg. Price/Book	2.4	3.1
Avg. 5-Year Earning Growth	2.5%	5.2%
Median Mkt. Capitalization	$5.97 bil.	$3.60 bil.
Correlation v. S&P 500 (R^2)	79%	100%
Market Volatility (Beta)	0.55	1.00
Superiority Rating (Alpha)	+2%	0%

Industry Diversification

Durables	5%
Energy	10%
Finance	30%
Industrial	15%
Non-Durables	4%
Retail	6%
Health	0%
Services	1%
Technology	14%
Utilities	11%
Precious Metals	2%
Other	2%

Safety Rating (0-10)	8.6	Sales Load (max.)	5.0%
Up & Down Market Ranks	E – A	Redemption Fee (max.)	None
Annual Expenses (total)	0.84%	Annual 12b-1 Fee	0.35%

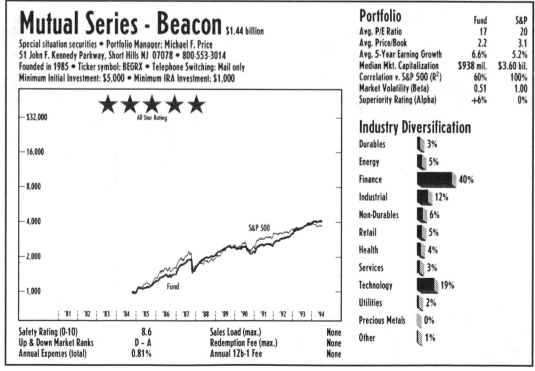

Mutual Series - Beacon $1.44 billion

Special situation securities • Portfolio Manager: Michael F. Price
51 John F. Kennedy Parkway, Short Hills NJ 07078 • 800-553-3014
Founded in 1985 • Ticker symbol: BEGRX • Telephone Switching: Mail only
Minimum Initial Investment: $5,000 • Minimum IRA Investment: $1,000

★★★★★
All Star Rating

	Fund	S&P
Portfolio		
Avg. P/E Ratio	17	20
Avg. Price/Book	2.2	3.1
Avg. 5-Year Earning Growth	6.6%	5.2%
Median Mkt. Capitalization	$938 mil.	$3.60 bil.
Correlation v. S&P 500 (R^2)	60%	100%
Market Volatility (Beta)	0.51	1.00
Superiority Rating (Alpha)	+6%	0%

Industry Diversification

Durables	3%
Energy	5%
Finance	40%
Industrial	12%
Non-Durables	6%
Retail	5%
Health	4%
Services	3%
Technology	19%
Utilities	2%
Precious Metals	0%
Other	1%

Safety Rating (0-10)	8.6	Sales Load (max.)	None
Up & Down Market Ranks	D – A	Redemption Fee (max.)	None
Annual Expenses (total)	0.81%	Annual 12b-1 Fee	None

Mutual Series - Qualified $1.56 billion

Special situation securities • Portfolio Manager: Michael F. Price
51 John F. Kennedy Parkway, Short Hills NJ 07078 • 800-553-3014
Founded in 1980 • Ticker symbol: MQIFX • Telephone Switching: Mail only
Minimum Initial Investment: $1,000 • Minimum IRA Investment: $1,000

Portfolio

	Fund	S&P
Avg. P/E Ratio	18	20
Avg. Price/Book	2.1	3.1
Avg. 5-Year Earning Growth	4.4%	5.2%
Median Mkt. Capitalization	$814 mil.	$3.60 bil.
Correlation v. S&P 500 (R²)	66%	100%
Market Volatility (Beta)	0.58	1.00
Superiority Rating (Alpha)	+6%	0%

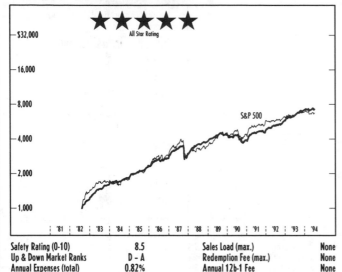

★★★★★
All Star Rating

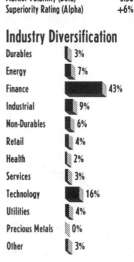

Industry Diversification

Durables	3%
Energy	7%
Finance	43%
Industrial	9%
Non-Durables	6%
Retail	4%
Health	2%
Services	3%
Technology	16%
Utilities	4%
Precious Metals	0%
Other	3%

Safety Rating (0-10)	8.5	Sales Load (max.)	None
Up & Down Market Ranks	D – A	Redemption Fee (max.)	None
Annual Expenses (total)	0.82%	Annual 12b-1 Fee	None

Mutual Series - Shares $3.56 billion

Special situation securities • Portfolio Manager: Michael F. Price
51 John F. Kennedy Parkway, Short Hills NJ 07078 • 800-553-3014
Founded in 1949 • Ticker symbol: MUTHX • Telephone Switching: Mail only
Minimum Initial Investment: $5,000 • Minimum IRA Investment: $2,000

Portfolio

	Fund	S&P
Avg. P/E Ratio	19	20
Avg. Price/Book	2.2	3.1
Avg. 5-Year Earning Growth	0.3%	5.2%
Median Mkt. Capitalization	$1.17 bil.	$3.60 bil.
Correlation v. S&P 500 (R²)	68%	100%
Market Volatility (Beta)	0.61	1.00
Superiority Rating (Alpha)	+6%	0%

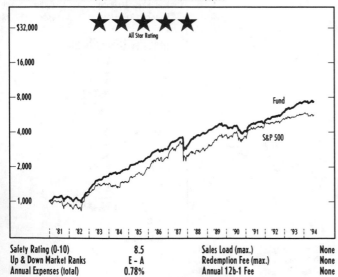

★★★★★
All Star Rating

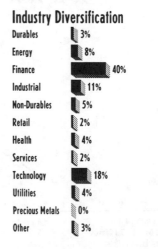

Industry Diversification

Durables	3%
Energy	8%
Finance	40%
Industrial	11%
Non-Durables	5%
Retail	2%
Health	4%
Services	2%
Technology	18%
Utilities	4%
Precious Metals	0%
Other	3%

Safety Rating (0-10)	8.5	Sales Load (max.)	None
Up & Down Market Ranks	E – A	Redemption Fee (max.)	None
Annual Expenses (total)	0.78%	Annual 12b-1 Fee	None

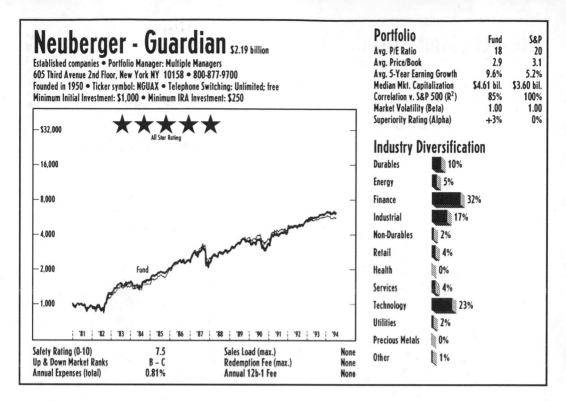

Neuberger - Guardian $2.19 billion

Established companies • Portfolio Manager: Multiple Managers
605 Third Avenue 2nd Floor, New York NY 10158 • 800-877-9700
Founded in 1950 • Ticker symbol: NGUAX • Telephone Switching: Unlimited; free
Minimum Initial Investment: $1,000 • Minimum IRA Investment: $250

★★★★★
All Star Rating

Portfolio

	Fund	S&P
Avg. P/E Ratio	18	20
Avg. Price/Book	2.9	3.1
Avg. 5-Year Earning Growth	9.6%	5.2%
Median Mkt. Capitalization	$4.61 bil.	$3.60 bil.
Correlation v. S&P 500 (R^2)	85%	100%
Market Volatility (Beta)	1.00	1.00
Superiority Rating (Alpha)	+3%	0%

Industry Diversification

Durables	10%
Energy	5%
Finance	32%
Industrial	17%
Non-Durables	2%
Retail	4%
Health	0%
Services	4%
Technology	23%
Utilities	2%
Precious Metals	0%
Other	1%

Safety Rating (0-10)	7.5	Sales Load (max.)	None
Up & Down Market Ranks	B – C	Redemption Fee (max.)	None
Annual Expenses (total)	0.81%	Annual 12b-1 Fee	None

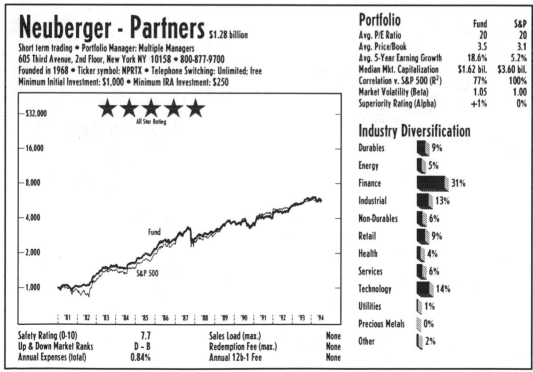

Neuberger - Partners $1.28 billion

Short term trading • Portfolio Manager: Multiple Managers
605 Third Avenue, 2nd Floor, New York NY 10158 • 800-877-9700
Founded in 1968 • Ticker symbol: NPRTX • Telephone Switching: Unlimited; free
Minimum Initial Investment: $1,000 • Minimum IRA Investment: $250

★★★★★
All Star Rating

Portfolio

	Fund	S&P
Avg. P/E Ratio	20	20
Avg. Price/Book	3.5	3.1
Avg. 5-Year Earning Growth	18.6%	5.2%
Median Mkt. Capitalization	$1.62 bil.	$3.60 bil.
Correlation v. S&P 500 (R^2)	77%	100%
Market Volatility (Beta)	1.05	1.00
Superiority Rating (Alpha)	+1%	0%

Industry Diversification

Durables	9%
Energy	5%
Finance	31%
Industrial	13%
Non-Durables	6%
Retail	9%
Health	4%
Services	6%
Technology	14%
Utilities	1%
Precious Metals	0%
Other	2%

Safety Rating (0-10)	7.7	Sales Load (max.)	None
Up & Down Market Ranks	D – B	Redemption Fee (max.)	None
Annual Expenses (total)	0.84%	Annual 12b-1 Fee	None

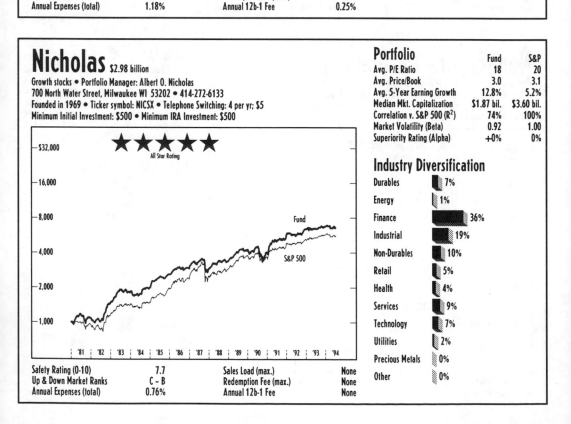

New England Growth "A" $1.12 billion

Established growth stocks • Portfolio Manager: G. Kenneth Heebner
399 Boylston Street, Boston MA 02116 • 800-343-7104
Founded in 1968 • Ticker symbol: NEFGX • Telephone Switching: Unlimited; free
This fund is currently not accepting new accounts.

All Star Rating ★★★

Portfolio	Fund	S&P
Avg. P/E Ratio	13	20
Avg. Price/Book	2.6	3.1
Avg. 5-Year Earning Growth	14.3%	5.2%
Median Mkt. Capitalization	$9.60 bil.	$3.60 bil.
Correlation v. S&P 500 (R^2)	65%	100%
Market Volatility (Beta)	1.10	1.00
Superiority Rating (Alpha)	–2%	0%

Industry Diversification

Durables	6%
Energy	0%
Finance	25%
Industrial	23%
Non-Durables	0%
Retail	7%
Health	0%
Services	13%
Technology	26%
Utilities	0%
Precious Metals	0%
Other	0%

Safety Rating (0-10)	6.6	Sales Load (max.)	7.0%
Up & Down Market Ranks	A – D	Redemption Fee (max.)	None
Annual Expenses (total)	1.18%	Annual 12b-1 Fee	0.25%

Nicholas $2.98 billion

Growth stocks • Portfolio Manager: Albert O. Nicholas
700 North Water Street, Milwaukee WI 53202 • 414-272-6133
Founded in 1969 • Ticker symbol: NICSX • Telephone Switching: 4 per yr; $5
Minimum Initial Investment: $500 • Minimum IRA Investment: $500

All Star Rating ★★★★★

Portfolio	Fund	S&P
Avg. P/E Ratio	18	20
Avg. Price/Book	3.0	3.1
Avg. 5-Year Earning Growth	12.8%	5.2%
Median Mkt. Capitalization	$1.87 bil.	$3.60 bil.
Correlation v. S&P 500 (R^2)	74%	100%
Market Volatility (Beta)	0.92	1.00
Superiority Rating (Alpha)	+0%	0%

Industry Diversification

Durables	7%
Energy	1%
Finance	36%
Industrial	19%
Non-Durables	10%
Retail	5%
Health	4%
Services	9%
Technology	7%
Utilities	2%
Precious Metals	0%
Other	0%

Safety Rating (0-10)	7.7	Sales Load (max.)	None
Up & Down Market Ranks	C – B	Redemption Fee (max.)	None
Annual Expenses (total)	0.76%	Annual 12b-1 Fee	None

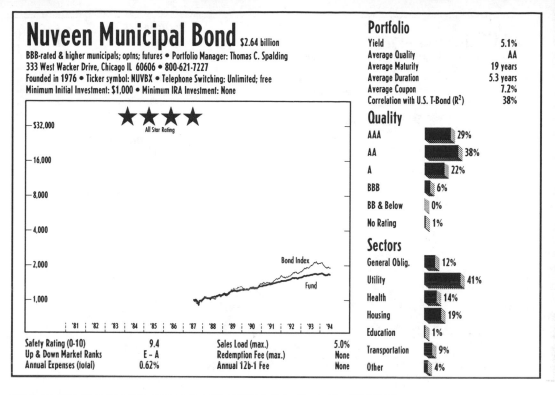

Nuveen Municipal Bond $2.64 billion

BBB-rated & higher municipals; optns; futures • Portfolio Manager: Thomas C. Spalding
333 West Wacker Drive, Chicago IL 60606 • 800-621-7227
Founded in 1976 • Ticker symbol: NUVBX • Telephone Switching: Unlimited; free
Minimum Initial Investment: $1,000 • Minimum IRA Investment: None

★★★★
All Star Rating

Bond Index
Fund

Safety Rating (0-10)	9.4	Sales Load (max.)	5.0%
Up & Down Market Ranks	E – A	Redemption Fee (max.)	None
Annual Expenses (total)	0.62%	Annual 12b-1 Fee	None

Portfolio

Yield	5.1%
Average Quality	AA
Average Maturity	19 years
Average Duration	5.3 years
Average Coupon	7.2%
Correlation with U.S. T-Bond (R^2)	38%

Quality

AAA	29%
AA	38%
A	22%
BBB	6%
BB & Below	0%
No Rating	1%

Sectors

General Oblig.	12%
Utility	41%
Health	14%
Housing	19%
Education	1%
Transportation	9%
Other	4%

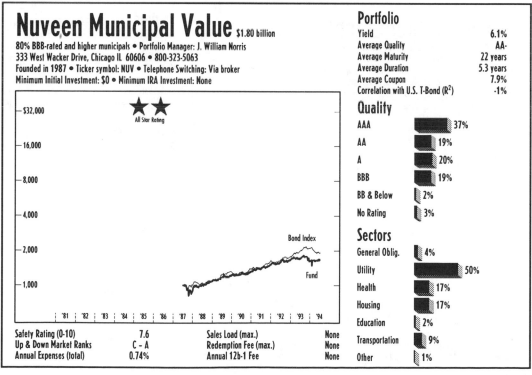

Nuveen Municipal Value $1.80 billion

80% BBB-rated and higher municipals • Portfolio Manager: J. William Norris
333 West Wacker Drive, Chicago IL 60606 • 800-323-5063
Founded in 1987 • Ticker symbol: NUV • Telephone Switching: Via broker
Minimum Initial Investment: $0 • Minimum IRA Investment: None

★★
All Star Rating

Bond Index
Fund

Safety Rating (0-10)	7.6	Sales Load (max.)	None
Up & Down Market Ranks	C – A	Redemption Fee (max.)	None
Annual Expenses (total)	0.74%	Annual 12b-1 Fee	None

Portfolio

Yield	6.1%
Average Quality	AA-
Average Maturity	22 years
Average Duration	5.3 years
Average Coupon	7.9%
Correlation with U.S. T-Bond (R^2)	-1%

Quality

AAA	37%
AA	19%
A	20%
BBB	19%
BB & Below	2%
No Rating	3%

Sectors

General Oblig.	4%
Utility	50%
Health	17%
Housing	17%
Education	2%
Transportation	9%
Other	1%

Oakmark $1.36 billion

Underval stks; qlty of mgmt & mgmt stk partic • Portfolio Manager: Robert J. Sanborn
2 North LaSalle Street, Chicago IL 60602 • 800-625-6275
Founded in 1991 • Ticker symbol: OAKMX • Telephone Switching: Unlimited; $5
Minimum Initial Investment: $2,500 • Minimum IRA Investment: $1,000

Portfolio

	Fund	S&P
Avg. P/E Ratio	19	20
Avg. Price/Book	2.5	3.1
Avg. 5-Year Earning Growth	20.5%	5.2%
Median Mkt. Capitalization	$511 mil.	$3.60 bil.
Correlation v. S&P 500 (R²)	50%	100%
Market Volatility (Beta)	0.85	1.00
Superiority Rating (Alpha)	+6%	0%

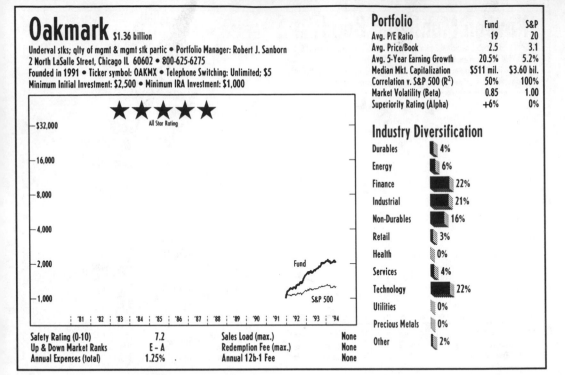

★★★★★
All Star Rating

Fund

S&P 500

Safety Rating (0-10)	7.2	Sales Load (max.)	None
Up & Down Market Ranks	E – A	Redemption Fee (max.)	None
Annual Expenses (total)	1.25%	Annual 12b-1 Fee	None

Industry Diversification

- Durables 4%
- Energy 6%
- Finance 22%
- Industrial 21%
- Non-Durables 16%
- Retail 3%
- Health 0%
- Services 4%
- Technology 22%
- Utilities 0%
- Precious Metals 0%
- Other 2%

Oakmark International $1.45 billion

Foreign - diversified undervalued securities • Portfolio Manager: David G. Herro
2 North LaSalle Street, Chicago IL 60602 • 800-625-6275
Founded in 1992 • Ticker symbol: OAKIX • Telephone Switching: Unlimited; $5
Minimum Initial Investment: $2,500 • Minimum IRA Investment: $1,000

Portfolio

	Fund	S&P
Avg. P/E Ratio	19	20
Avg. Price/Book	2.2	3.1
Avg. 5-Year Earning Growth	9.7%	5.2%
Median Mkt. Capitalization	$2.15 bil.	$3.60 bil.
Correlation v. S&P 500 (R²)	6%	100%
Market Volatility (Beta)	0.41	1.00
Superiority Rating (Alpha)	+6%	0%

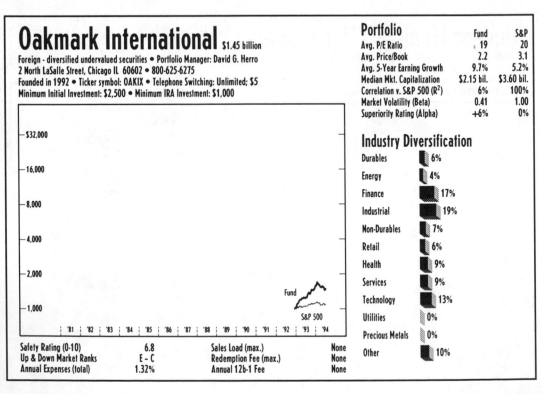

Fund

S&P 500

Safety Rating (0-10)	6.8	Sales Load (max.)	None
Up & Down Market Ranks	E – C	Redemption Fee (max.)	None
Annual Expenses (total)	1.32%	Annual 12b-1 Fee	None

Industry Diversification

- Durables 6%
- Energy 4%
- Finance 17%
- Industrial 19%
- Non-Durables 7%
- Retail 6%
- Health 9%
- Services 9%
- Technology 13%
- Utilities 0%
- Precious Metals 0%
- Other 10%

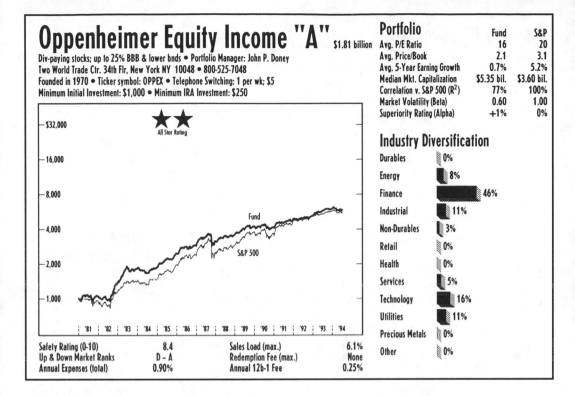

Oppenheimer Equity Income "A" $1.81 billion

Div-paying stocks; up to 25% BBB & lower bnds • Portfolio Manager: John P. Doney
Two World Trade Ctr. 34th Flr, New York NY 10048 • 800-525-7048
Founded in 1970 • Ticker symbol: OPPEX • Telephone Switching: 1 per wk; $5
Minimum Initial Investment: $1,000 • Minimum IRA Investment: $250

★★
All Star Rating

Portfolio

	Fund	S&P
Avg. P/E Ratio	16	20
Avg. Price/Book	2.1	3.1
Avg. 5-Year Earning Growth	0.7%	5.2%
Median Mkt. Capitalization	$5.35 bil.	$3.60 bil.
Correlation v. S&P 500 (R²)	77%	100%
Market Volatility (Beta)	0.60	1.00
Superiority Rating (Alpha)	+1%	0%

Industry Diversification

Durables	0%
Energy	8%
Finance	46%
Industrial	11%
Non-Durables	3%
Retail	0%
Health	0%
Services	5%
Technology	16%
Utilities	11%
Precious Metals	0%
Other	0%

Safety Rating (0-10)	8.4	Sales Load (max.)	6.1%
Up & Down Market Ranks	D – A	Redemption Fee (max.)	None
Annual Expenses (total)	0.90%	Annual 12b-1 Fee	0.25%

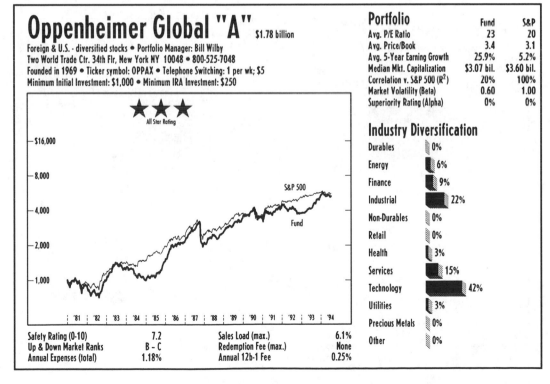

Oppenheimer Global "A" $1.78 billion

Foreign & U.S. - diversified stocks • Portfolio Manager: Bill Wilby
Two World Trade Ctr. 34th Flr, New York NY 10048 • 800-525-7048
Founded in 1969 • Ticker symbol: OPPAX • Telephone Switching: 1 per wk; $5
Minimum Initial Investment: $1,000 • Minimum IRA Investment: $250

★★★
All Star Rating

Portfolio

	Fund	S&P
Avg. P/E Ratio	23	20
Avg. Price/Book	3.4	3.1
Avg. 5-Year Earning Growth	25.9%	5.2%
Median Mkt. Capitalization	$3.07 bil.	$3.60 bil.
Correlation v. S&P 500 (R²)	20%	100%
Market Volatility (Beta)	0.60	1.00
Superiority Rating (Alpha)	0%	0%

Industry Diversification

Durables	0%
Energy	6%
Finance	9%
Industrial	22%
Non-Durables	0%
Retail	0%
Health	3%
Services	15%
Technology	42%
Utilities	3%
Precious Metals	0%
Other	0%

Safety Rating (0-10)	7.2	Sales Load (max.)	6.1%
Up & Down Market Ranks	B – C	Redemption Fee (max.)	None
Annual Expenses (total)	1.18%	Annual 12b-1 Fee	0.25%

Oppenheimer High Yield "A" $1.02 billion

B-rated and lower 10-15 year corporates • Portfolio Manager: Ralph W. Stellmacher
Two World Trade Ctr. 34th Flr, New York NY 10048 • 800-525-7048
Founded in 1978 • Ticker symbol: OPPHX • Telephone Switching: 1 per wk; $5
Minimum Initial Investment: $1,000 • Minimum IRA Investment: $250

Portfolio

Yield	8.7%
Average Quality	B
Average Maturity	N/A
Average Duration	3.8 years
Average Coupon	10.0%
Correlation with U.S. T-Bond (R^2)	1%
Dividends Paid	Monthly

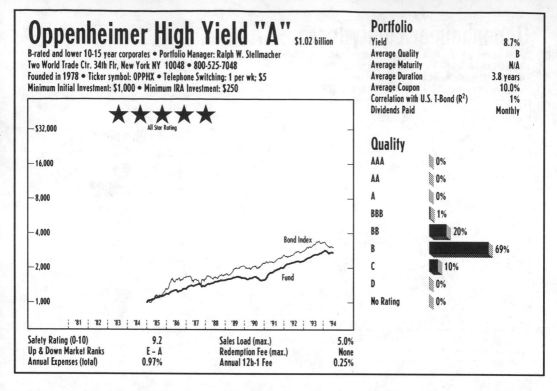

Quality

AAA	0%
AA	0%
A	0%
BBB	1%
BB	20%
B	69%
C	10%
D	0%
No Rating	0%

Safety Rating (0-10)	9.2	Sales Load (max.)	5.0%
Up & Down Market Ranks	E – A	Redemption Fee (max.)	None
Annual Expenses (total)	0.97%	Annual 12b-1 Fee	0.25%

Oppenheimer Strategic Incm "A" $3.14 billion

Foreign & U.S. - governments, corporates • Portfolio Managers: D. Negri/A. Steinmetz
Two World Trade Ctr. 34th Flr, New York NY 10048 • 800-525-7048
Founded in 1989 • Ticker symbol: OPSIX • Telephone Switching: 1 per wk; $5
Minimum Initial Investment: $1,000 • Minimum IRA Investment: $250

Portfolio

Yield	8.7%
Average Quality	B+
Average Maturity	4.0 years
Average Duration	3.3 years
Average Coupon	8.8%
Correlation with U.S. T-Bond (R^2)	27%
Dividends Paid	Monthly (Accrue Daily)

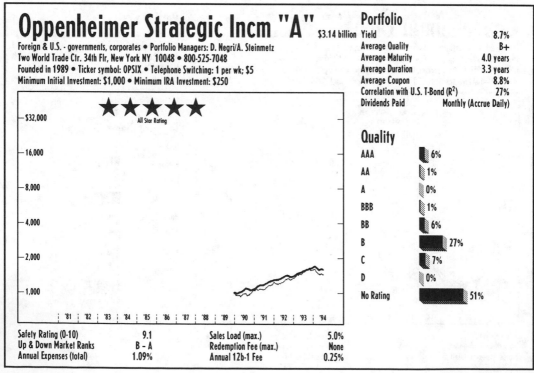

Quality

AAA	6%
AA	1%
A	0%
BBB	1%
BB	6%
B	27%
C	7%
D	0%
No Rating	51%

Safety Rating (0-10)	9.1	Sales Load (max.)	5.0%
Up & Down Market Ranks	B – A	Redemption Fee (max.)	None
Annual Expenses (total)	1.09%	Annual 12b-1 Fee	0.25%

Oppenheimer Total Return "A" $1.26 billion

Diversified securities • Portfolio Manager: John L. Wallace
Two World Trade Ctr. 34th Flr, New York NY 10004 • 800-525-7048
Founded in 1944 • Ticker symbol: OPTRX • Telephone Switching: 1 per wk; $5
Minimum Initial Investment: $1,000 • Minimum IRA Investment: $250

Portfolio

	Fund	S&P
Avg. P/E Ratio	24	20
Avg. Price/Book	3.1	3.1
Avg. 5-Year Earning Growth	16.4%	5.2%
Median Mkt. Capitalization	$1.19 bil.	$3.60 bil.
Correlation v. S&P 500 (R^2)	68%	100%
Market Volatility (Beta)	0.96	1.00
Superiority Rating (Alpha)	+2%	0%

Industry Diversification

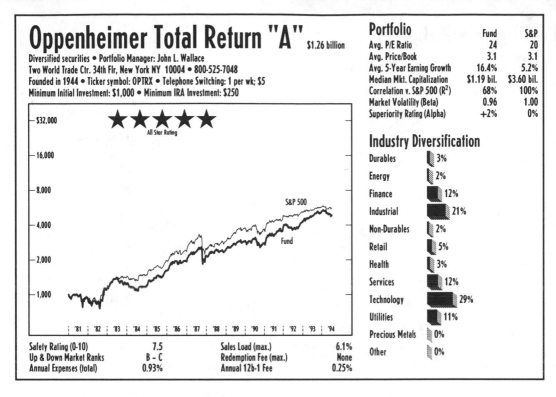

Durables	3%
Energy	2%
Finance	12%
Industrial	21%
Non-Durables	2%
Retail	5%
Health	3%
Services	12%
Technology	29%
Utilities	11%
Precious Metals	0%
Other	0%

Safety Rating (0-10)	7.5	Sales Load (max.)	6.1%
Up & Down Market Ranks	B – C	Redemption Fee (max.)	None
Annual Expenses (total)	0.93%	Annual 12b-1 Fee	0.25%

Overland Variable Rate Gvt "A" $1.80 billion

65% govt & agency adj rate mtg secs; 20-30yrs • Portfolio Managers: Single/Glessman
525 Market Street 12th Floor, San Francisco CA 94105 • 800-552-9612
Founded in 1990 • Ticker symbol: OEVGX • Telephone Switching: Unlimited; free
Minimum Initial Investment: $1,000 • Minimum IRA Investment: $1,000

Portfolio

Yield	3.8%
Average Quality	AAA
Average Maturity	24 years
Average Duration	1.3 years
Average Coupon	0.4%
Correlation with U.S. T-Bond (R^2)	17%
Dividends Paid	Monthly (Accrue Daily)

Quality

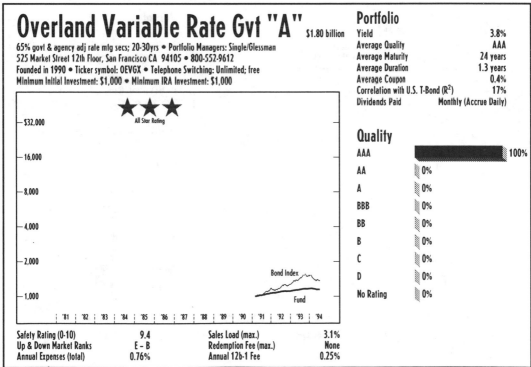

AAA	100%
AA	0%
A	0%
BBB	0%
BB	0%
B	0%
C	0%
D	0%
No Rating	0%

Safety Rating (0-10)	9.4	Sales Load (max.)	3.1%
Up & Down Market Ranks	E – B	Redemption Fee (max.)	None
Annual Expenses (total)	0.76%	Annual 12b-1 Fee	0.25%

Phoenix Balanced $2.83 billion

Income producing securities • Portfolio Manager: Patricia Bannan
100 Bright Meadow Blvd, Bx 2200, Enfield CT 06083 • 800-243-4361
Founded in 1981 • Ticker symbol: PHBLX • Telephone Switching: Unlimited; free
Minimum Initial Investment: $500 • Minimum IRA Investment: $25

Portfolio

	Fund	S&P
Avg. P/E Ratio	21	20
Avg. Price/Book	3.3	3.1
Avg. 5-Year Earning Growth	8.7%	5.2%
Median Mkt. Capitalization	$8.21 bil.	$3.60 bil.
Correlation v. S&P 500 (R^2)	81%	100%
Market Volatility (Beta)	0.51	1.00
Superiority Rating (Alpha)	+2%	0%

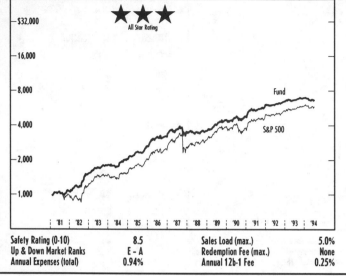

Industry Diversification

Durables	8%
Energy	5%
Finance	4%
Industrial	19%
Non-Durables	9%
Retail	6%
Health	4%
Services	17%
Technology	26%
Utilities	2%
Precious Metals	0%
Other	0%

Safety Rating (0-10)	8.5	Sales Load (max.)	5.0%
Up & Down Market Ranks	E – A	Redemption Fee (max.)	None
Annual Expenses (total)	0.94%	Annual 12b-1 Fee	0.25%

Phoenix Growth $2.22 billion

Diversified growth stocks • Portfolio Manager: Cathy Dudley
100 Bright Meadow Blvd, Bx 2200, Enfield CT 06083 • 800-243-4361
Founded in 1988 • Ticker symbol: PHGRX • Telephone Switching: Unlimited; free
Minimum Initial Investment: $500 • Minimum IRA Investment: $25

Portfolio

	Fund	S&P
Avg. P/E Ratio	19	20
Avg. Price/Book	3.5	3.1
Avg. 5-Year Earning Growth	13.2%	5.2%
Median Mkt. Capitalization	$9.16 bil.	$3.60 bil.
Correlation v. S&P 500 (R^2)	82%	100%
Market Volatility (Beta)	0.72	1.00
Superiority Rating (Alpha)	–1%	0%

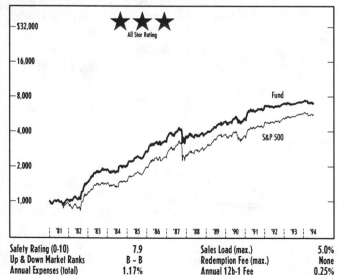

Industry Diversification

Durables	3%
Energy	7%
Finance	6%
Industrial	15%
Non-Durables	8%
Retail	12%
Health	4%
Services	21%
Technology	21%
Utilities	3%
Precious Metals	0%
Other	0%

Safety Rating (0-10)	7.9	Sales Load (max.)	5.0%
Up & Down Market Ranks	B – B	Redemption Fee (max.)	None
Annual Expenses (total)	1.17%	Annual 12b-1 Fee	0.25%

Pimco - Low Duration $2.26 billion

Corporate bonds; 1-3 years portfolio duration • Portfolio Manager: William H. Gross
840 Newport Center Drive, Newport Beach CA 92660 • 800-927-4648
Founded in 1987 • Ticker symbol: PTLDX • Telephone Switching: Unlimited; free
Minimum Initial Investment: $500,000 • Minimum IRA Investment: $500,000

Portfolio

Yield	6.3%
Average Quality	A
Average Maturity	3.1 years
Average Duration	2.0 years
Average Coupon	6.8%
Correlation with U.S. T-Bond (R^2)	25%
Dividends Paid	Monthly (Accrue Daily)

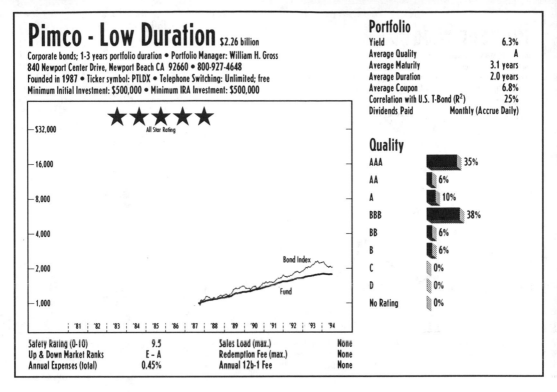

Quality

AAA	35%
AA	6%
A	10%
BBB	38%
BB	6%
B	6%
C	0%
D	0%
No Rating	0%

Safety Rating (0-10)	9.5	Sales Load (max.)	None
Up & Down Market Ranks	E – A	Redemption Fee (max.)	None
Annual Expenses (total)	0.45%	Annual 12b-1 Fee	None

Pimco - Total Return $5.30 billion

Shearson Aggres Bond Indx; gvt, corp, mny mkt • Portfolio Manager: William H. Gross
840 Newport Center Drive, Newport Beach CA 92660 • 800-927-4648
Founded in 1987 • Ticker symbol: PTTRX • Telephone Switching: Unlimited; free
Minimum Initial Investment: $500,000 • Minimum IRA Investment: $500,000

Portfolio

Yield	6.3%
Average Quality	AA-
Average Maturity	10 years
Average Duration	5.0 years
Average Coupon	7.1%
Correlation with U.S. T-Bond (R^2)	67%
Dividends Paid	Monthly (Accrue Daily)

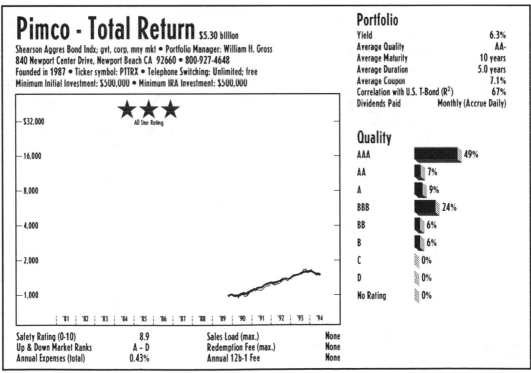

Quality

AAA	49%
AA	7%
A	9%
BBB	24%
BB	6%
B	6%
C	0%
D	0%
No Rating	0%

Safety Rating (0-10)	8.9	Sales Load (max.)	None
Up & Down Market Ranks	A – D	Redemption Fee (max.)	None
Annual Expenses (total)	0.43%	Annual 12b-1 Fee	None

Pioneer Fund $2.04 billion

Diversified stocks • Portfolio Manager: John A. Carey
60 State Street, Boston MA 02109 • 800-225-6292
Founded in 1928 • Ticker symbol: PIODX • Telephone Switching: Unlimited; free
Minimum Initial Investment: $50 • Minimum IRA Investment: $50

Portfolio

	Fund	S&P
Avg. P/E Ratio	22	20
Avg. Price/Book	2.7	3.1
Avg. 5-Year Earning Growth	4.7%	5.2%
Median Mkt. Capitalization	$2.26 bil.	$3.60 bil.
Correlation v. S&P 500 (R^2)	86%	100%
Market Volatility (Beta)	0.81	1.00
Superiority Rating (Alpha)	+0%	0%

★ ★
All Star Rating

Industry Diversification

Durables	10%
Energy	4%
Finance	13%
Industrial	26%
Non-Durables	11%
Retail	8%
Health	0%
Services	4%
Technology	16%
Utilities	7%
Precious Metals	1%
Other	0%

Safety Rating (0-10)	8.0	Sales Load (max.)	6.1%
Up & Down Market Ranks	C – D	Redemption Fee (max.)	None
Annual Expenses (total)	0.95%	Annual 12b-1 Fee	0.25%

Pioneer II $4.39 billion

Diversified stocks • Portfolio Managers: Tripple/Boggan/Kurland
60 State Street, Boston MA 02109 • 800-225-6292
Founded in 1969 • Ticker symbol: PIOTX • Telephone Switching: Unlimited; free
Minimum Initial Investment: $50 • Minimum IRA Investment: $50

Portfolio

	Fund	S&P
Avg. P/E Ratio	17	20
Avg. Price/Book	2.3	3.1
Avg. 5-Year Earning Growth	8.5%	5.2%
Median Mkt. Capitalization	$1.41 bil.	$3.60 bil.
Correlation v. S&P 500 (R^2)	78%	100%
Market Volatility (Beta)	0.81	1.00
Superiority Rating (Alpha)	0%	0%

★ ★
All Star Rating

Industry Diversification

Durables	3%
Energy	1%
Finance	27%
Industrial	20%
Non-Durables	7%
Retail	4%
Health	2%
Services	5%
Technology	19%
Utilities	8%
Precious Metals	1%
Other	3%

Safety Rating (0-10)	7.9	Sales Load (max.)	6.1%
Up & Down Market Ranks	C – D	Redemption Fee (max.)	None
Annual Expenses (total)	0.95%	Annual 12b-1 Fee	0.25%

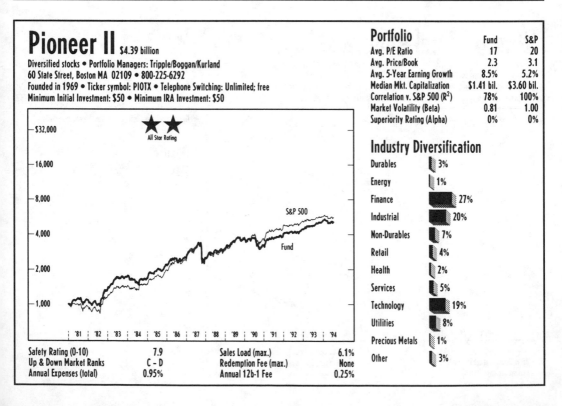

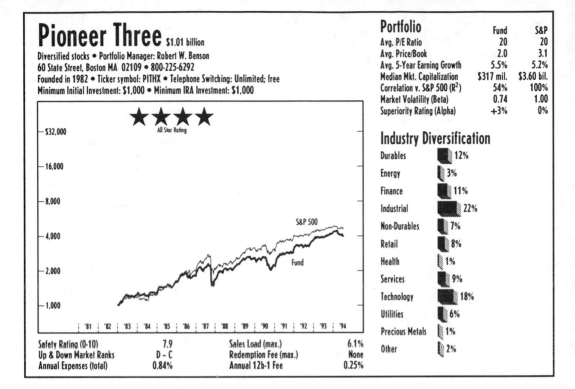

Pioneer Three $1.01 billion

Diversified stocks • Portfolio Manager: Robert W. Benson
60 State Street, Boston MA 02109 • 800-225-6292
Founded in 1982 • Ticker symbol: PITHX • Telephone Switching: Unlimited; free
Minimum Initial Investment: $1,000 • Minimum IRA Investment: $1,000

★★★★
All Star Rating

Portfolio	Fund	S&P
Avg. P/E Ratio	20	20
Avg. Price/Book	2.0	3.1
Avg. 5-Year Earning Growth	5.5%	5.2%
Median Mkt. Capitalization	$317 mil.	$3.60 bil.
Correlation v. S&P 500 (R^2)	54%	100%
Market Volatility (Beta)	0.74	1.00
Superiority Rating (Alpha)	+3%	0%

Industry Diversification

Durables	12%
Energy	3%
Finance	11%
Industrial	22%
Non-Durables	7%
Retail	8%
Health	1%
Services	9%
Technology	18%
Utilities	6%
Precious Metals	1%
Other	2%

Safety Rating (0-10)	7.9	Sales Load (max.)	6.1%
Up & Down Market Ranks	D – C	Redemption Fee (max.)	None
Annual Expenses (total)	0.84%	Annual 12b-1 Fee	0.25%

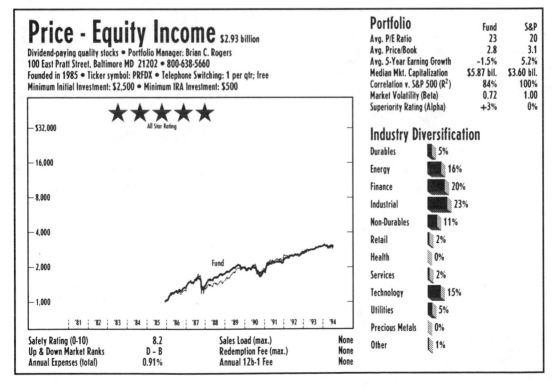

Price - Equity Income $2.93 billion

Dividend-paying quality stocks • Portfolio Manager: Brian C. Rogers
100 East Pratt Street, Baltimore MD 21202 • 800-638-5660
Founded in 1985 • Ticker symbol: PRFDX • Telephone Switching: 1 per qtr; free
Minimum Initial Investment: $2,500 • Minimum IRA Investment: $500

★★★★★
All Star Rating

Portfolio	Fund	S&P
Avg. P/E Ratio	23	20
Avg. Price/Book	2.8	3.1
Avg. 5-Year Earning Growth	-1.5%	5.2%
Median Mkt. Capitalization	$5.87 bil.	$3.60 bil.
Correlation v. S&P 500 (R^2)	84%	100%
Market Volatility (Beta)	0.72	1.00
Superiority Rating (Alpha)	+3%	0%

Industry Diversification

Durables	5%
Energy	16%
Finance	20%
Industrial	23%
Non-Durables	11%
Retail	2%
Health	0%
Services	2%
Technology	15%
Utilities	5%
Precious Metals	0%
Other	1%

Safety Rating (0-10)	8.2	Sales Load (max.)	None
Up & Down Market Ranks	D – B	Redemption Fee (max.)	None
Annual Expenses (total)	0.91%	Annual 12b-1 Fee	None

Price - Growth & Income $1.19 billion

High-yield growth securities • Portfolio Manager: Stephen W. Boesel
100 East Pratt Street, Baltimore MD 21202 • 800-638-5660
Founded in 1982 • Ticker symbol: PRGIX • Telephone Switching: 1 per qtr; free
Minimum Initial Investment: $2,500 • Minimum IRA Investment: $500

Portfolio

	Fund	S&P
Avg. P/E Ratio	22	20
Avg. Price/Book	3.0	3.1
Avg. 5-Year Earning Growth	0.8%	5.2%
Median Mkt. Capitalization	$3.73 bil.	$3.60 bil.
Correlation v. S&P 500 (R^2)	79%	100%
Market Volatility (Beta)	0.82	1.00
Superiority Rating (Alpha)	+1%	0%

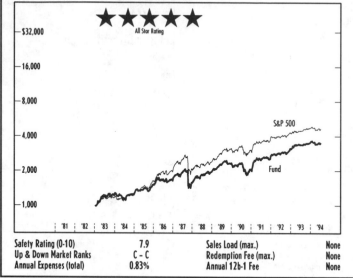

Industry Diversification

Durables	5%
Energy	9%
Finance	21%
Industrial	25%
Non-Durables	11%
Retail	4%
Health	0%
Services	1%
Technology	14%
Utilities	6%
Precious Metals	1%
Other	3%

Safety Rating (0-10)	7.9	Sales Load (max.)	None
Up & Down Market Ranks	C - C	Redemption Fee (max.)	None
Annual Expenses (total)	0.83%	Annual 12b-1 Fee	None

Price - Growth Stock $1.99 billion

Established growth stocks • Portfolio Manager: M. David Testa
100 East Pratt Street, Baltimore MD 21202 • 800-638-5660
Founded in 1950 • Ticker symbol: PRGFX • Telephone Switching: 1 per qtr; free
Minimum Initial Investment: $2,500 • Minimum IRA Investment: $500

Portfolio

	Fund	S&P
Avg. P/E Ratio	21	20
Avg. Price/Book	3.8	3.1
Avg. 5-Year Earning Growth	14.2%	5.2%
Median Mkt. Capitalization	$1.43 bil.	$3.60 bil.
Correlation v. S&P 500 (R^2)	76%	100%
Market Volatility (Beta)	0.90	1.00
Superiority Rating (Alpha)	0%	0%

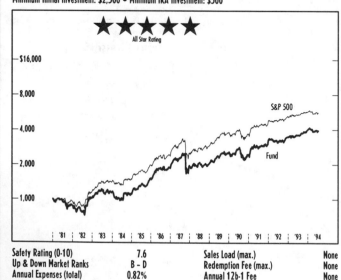

Industry Diversification

Durables	6%
Energy	2%
Finance	21%
Industrial	18%
Non-Durables	4%
Retail	6%
Health	2%
Services	9%
Technology	30%
Utilities	2%
Precious Metals	0%
Other	0%

Safety Rating (0-10)	7.6	Sales Load (max.)	None
Up & Down Market Ranks	B - D	Redemption Fee (max.)	None
Annual Expenses (total)	0.82%	Annual 12b-1 Fee	None

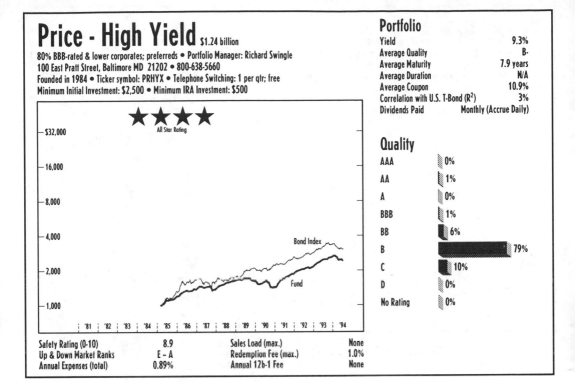

Price - High Yield $1.24 billion

80% BBB-rated & lower corporates; preferreds • Portfolio Manager: Richard Swingle
100 East Pratt Street, Baltimore MD 21202 • 800-638-5660
Founded in 1984 • Ticker symbol: PRHYX • Telephone Switching: 1 per qtr; free
Minimum Initial Investment: $2,500 • Minimum IRA Investment: $500

★★★★
All Star Rating

Portfolio

Yield	9.3%
Average Quality	B-
Average Maturity	7.9 years
Average Duration	N/A
Average Coupon	10.9%
Correlation with U.S. T-Bond (R^2)	3%
Dividends Paid	Monthly (Accrue Daily)

Quality

AAA	0%
AA	1%
A	0%
BBB	1%
BB	6%
B	79%
C	10%
D	0%
No Rating	0%

Safety Rating (0-10)	8.9	Sales Load (max.)	None
Up & Down Market Ranks	E – A	Redemption Fee (max.)	1.0%
Annual Expenses (total)	0.89%	Annual 12b-1 Fee	None

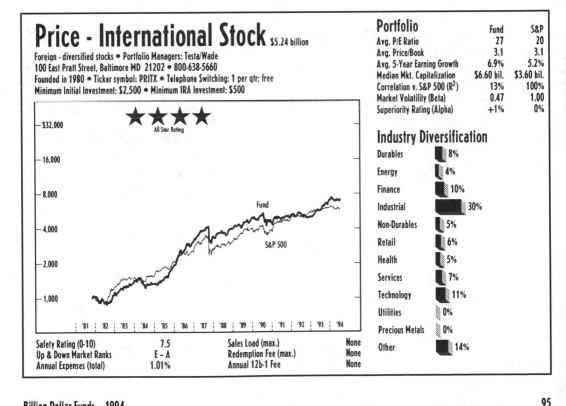

Price - International Stock $5.24 billion

Foreign - diversified stocks • Portfolio Managers: Testa/Wade
100 East Pratt Street, Baltimore MD 21202 • 800-638-5660
Founded in 1980 • Ticker symbol: PRITX • Telephone Switching: 1 per qtr; free
Minimum Initial Investment: $2,500 • Minimum IRA Investment: $500

★★★★
All Star Rating

Portfolio

	Fund	S&P
Avg. P/E Ratio	27	20
Avg. Price/Book	3.1	3.1
Avg. 5-Year Earning Growth	6.9%	5.2%
Median Mkt. Capitalization	$6.60 bil.	$3.60 bil.
Correlation v. S&P 500 (R^2)	13%	100%
Market Volatility (Beta)	0.47	1.00
Superiority Rating (Alpha)	+1%	0%

Industry Diversification

Durables	8%
Energy	4%
Finance	10%
Industrial	30%
Non-Durables	5%
Retail	6%
Health	5%
Services	7%
Technology	11%
Utilities	0%
Precious Metals	0%
Other	14%

Safety Rating (0-10)	7.5	Sales Load (max.)	None
Up & Down Market Ranks	E – A	Redemption Fee (max.)	None
Annual Expenses (total)	1.01%	Annual 12b-1 Fee	None

Price - New Asia $2.02 billion

Foreign - Asia & Pac-Basin; excluding Japan • Portfolio Manager: Martin G. Wade
100 East Pratt Street, Baltimore MD 21298 • 800-638-5660
Founded in 1990 • Ticker symbol: PRASX • Telephone Switching: 1 per qtr; free
Minimum Initial Investment: $2,500 • Minimum IRA Investment: $500

★★★★
All Star Rating

	Fund	S&P
Portfolio		
Avg. P/E Ratio	27	20
Avg. Price/Book	3.9	3.1
Avg. 5-Year Earning Growth	16.1%	5.2%
Median Mkt. Capitalization	$2.20 bil.	$3.60 bil.
Correlation v. S&P 500 (R^2)	0%	100%
Market Volatility (Beta)	0.31	1.00
Superiority Rating (Alpha)	+6%	0%

Industry Diversification

Durables	8%
Energy	0%
Finance	17%
Industrial	30%
Non-Durables	3%
Retail	2%
Health	0%
Services	10%
Technology	3%
Utilities	0%
Precious Metals	4%
Other	23%

Safety Rating (0-10)	6.5	Sales Load (max.)	None
Up & Down Market Ranks	E – E	Redemption Fee (max.)	None
Annual Expenses (total)	1.29%	Annual 12b-1 Fee	None

Price - New Horizons $1.59 billion

Small; growth stocks • Portfolio Manager: John H. Laporte
100 East Pratt Street, Baltimore MD 21202 • 800-638-5660
Founded in 1960 • Ticker symbol: PRNHX • Telephone Switching: 1 per qtr; free
Minimum Initial Investment: $2,500 • Minimum IRA Investment: $500

★★★★★
All Star Rating

	Fund	S&P
Portfolio		
Avg. P/E Ratio	29	20
Avg. Price/Book	4.9	3.1
Avg. 5-Year Earning Growth	35.3%	5.2%
Median Mkt. Capitalization	$335 mil.	$3.60 bil.
Correlation v. S&P 500 (R^2)	59%	100%
Market Volatility (Beta)	1.31	1.00
Superiority Rating (Alpha)	+0%	0%

Industry Diversification

Durables	7%
Energy	2%
Finance	10%
Industrial	8%
Non-Durables	6%
Retail	7%
Health	7%
Services	30%
Technology	22%
Utilities	1%
Precious Metals	0%
Other	0%

Safety Rating (0-10)	6.5	Sales Load (max.)	None
Up & Down Market Ranks	A – E	Redemption Fee (max.)	None
Annual Expenses (total)	0.80%	Annual 12b-1 Fee	None

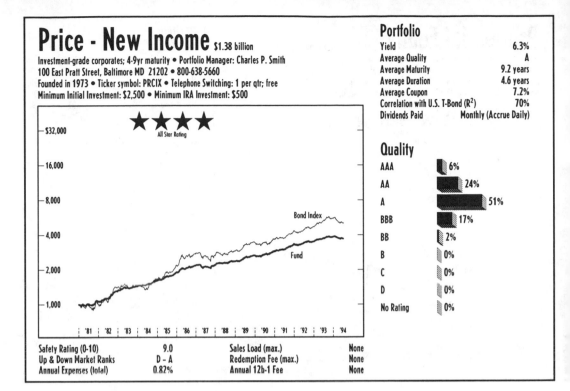

Price - New Income $1.38 billion

Investment-grade corporates; 4-9yr maturity • Portfolio Manager: Charles P. Smith
100 East Pratt Street, Baltimore MD 21202 • 800-638-5660
Founded in 1973 • Ticker symbol: PRCIX • Telephone Switching: 1 per qtr; free
Minimum Initial Investment: $2,500 • Minimum IRA Investment: $500

★ ★ ★ ★
All Star Rating

Bond Index

Fund

Safety Rating (0-10)	9.0	Sales Load (max.)	None
Up & Down Market Ranks	D – A	Redemption Fee (max.)	None
Annual Expenses (total)	0.82%	Annual 12b-1 Fee	None

Portfolio

Yield	6.3%
Average Quality	A
Average Maturity	9.2 years
Average Duration	4.6 years
Average Coupon	7.2%
Correlation with U.S. T-Bond (R^2)	70%
Dividends Paid	Monthly (Accrue Daily)

Quality

AAA	6%
AA	24%
A	51%
BBB	17%
BB	2%
B	0%
C	0%
D	0%
No Rating	0%

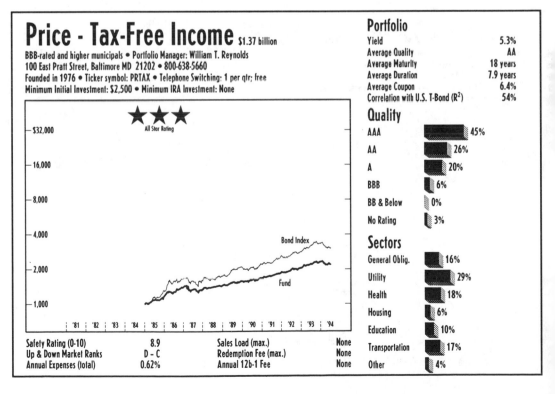

Price - Tax-Free Income $1.37 billion

BBB-rated and higher municipals • Portfolio Manager: William T. Reynolds
100 East Pratt Street, Baltimore MD 21202 • 800-638-5660
Founded in 1976 • Ticker symbol: PRTAX • Telephone Switching: 1 per qtr; free
Minimum Initial Investment: $2,500 • Minimum IRA Investment: None

★ ★ ★
All Star Rating

Bond Index

Fund

Safety Rating (0-10)	8.9	Sales Load (max.)	None
Up & Down Market Ranks	D – C	Redemption Fee (max.)	None
Annual Expenses (total)	0.62%	Annual 12b-1 Fee	None

Portfolio

Yield	5.3%
Average Quality	AA
Average Maturity	18 years
Average Duration	7.9 years
Average Coupon	6.4%
Correlation with U.S. T-Bond (R^2)	54%

Quality

AAA	45%
AA	26%
A	20%
BBB	6%
BB & Below	0%
No Rating	3%

Sectors

General Oblig.	16%
Utility	29%
Health	18%
Housing	6%
Education	10%
Transportation	17%
Other	4%

Prudential Equity "B" $1.89 billion

Established financially sound companies • Portfolio Manager: Tom Jackson
One Seaport Plaza, New York NY 10292 • 800-225-1852
Founded in 1982 • Ticker symbol: PBQFX • Telephone Switching: Unlimited; free
Minimum Initial Investment: $1,000 • Minimum IRA Investment: None

Portfolio

	Fund	S&P
Avg. P/E Ratio	20	20
Avg. Price/Book	1.8	3.1
Avg. 5-Year Earning Growth	-6.2%	5.2%
Median Mkt. Capitalization	$3.80 bil.	$3.60 bil.
Correlation v. S&P 500 (R²)	77%	100%
Market Volatility (Beta)	0.92	1.00
Superiority Rating (Alpha)	+2%	0%

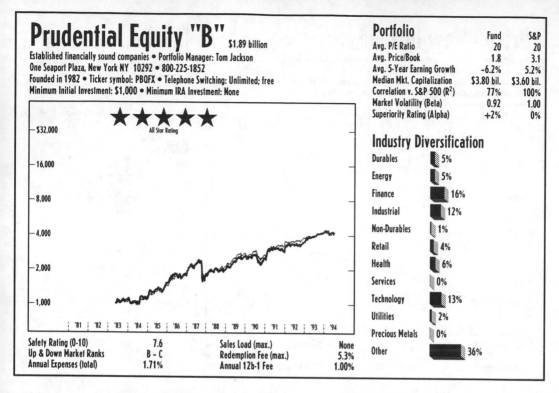

★★★★★
All Star Rating

Industry Diversification

Durables	5%
Energy	5%
Finance	16%
Industrial	12%
Non-Durables	1%
Retail	4%
Health	6%
Services	0%
Technology	13%
Utilities	2%
Precious Metals	0%
Other	36%

Safety Rating (0-10)	7.6	Sales Load (max.)	None
Up & Down Market Ranks	B - C	Redemption Fee (max.)	5.3%
Annual Expenses (total)	1.71%	Annual 12b-1 Fee	1.00%

Prudential Government Plus "B" $1.93 billion

U.S. Government securities • Portfolio Manager: Marty Lawlor
One Seaport Plaza, New York NY 10292 • 800-225-1852
Founded in 1985 • Ticker symbol: PBGPX • Telephone Switching: Unlimited; free
Minimum Initial Investment: $1,000 • Minimum IRA Investment: None

Portfolio

Yield	4.8%
Average Quality	AAA
Average Maturity	8.1 years
Average Duration	6.0 years
Average Coupon	9.2%
Correlation with U.S. T-Bond (R²)	70%
Dividends Paid	Monthly (Accrue Daily)

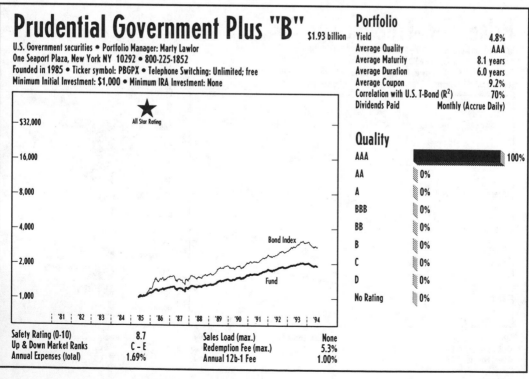

★
All Star Rating

Bond Index

Fund

Quality

AAA	100%
AA	0%
A	0%
BBB	0%
BB	0%
B	0%
C	0%
D	0%
No Rating	0%

Safety Rating (0-10)	8.7	Sales Load (max.)	None
Up & Down Market Ranks	C - E	Redemption Fee (max.)	5.3%
Annual Expenses (total)	1.69%	Annual 12b-1 Fee	1.00%

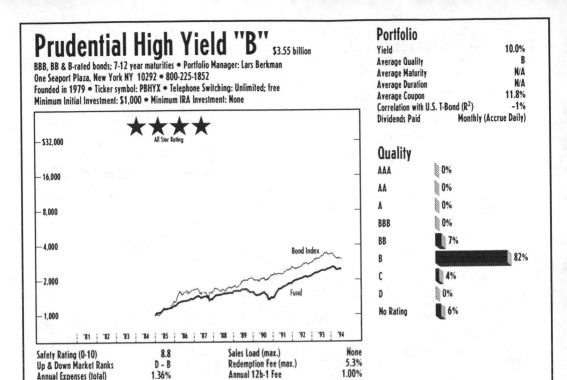

Prudential High Yield "B" $3.55 billion

BBB, BB & B-rated bonds; 7-12 year maturities • Portfolio Manager: Lars Berkman
One Seaport Plaza, New York NY 10292 • 800-225-1852
Founded in 1979 • Ticker symbol: PBHYX • Telephone Switching: Unlimited; free
Minimum Initial Investment: $1,000 • Minimum IRA Investment: None

★★★★
All Star Rating

Safety Rating (0-10)	8.8	Sales Load (max.)	None
Up & Down Market Ranks	D – B	Redemption Fee (max.)	5.3%
Annual Expenses (total)	1.36%	Annual 12b-1 Fee	1.00%

Portfolio

Yield	10.0%
Average Quality	B
Average Maturity	N/A
Average Duration	N/A
Average Coupon	11.8%
Correlation with U.S. T-Bond (R^2)	–1%
Dividends Paid	Monthly (Accrue Daily)

Quality

AAA	0%
AA	0%
A	0%
BBB	0%
BB	7%
B	82%
C	4%
D	0%
No Rating	6%

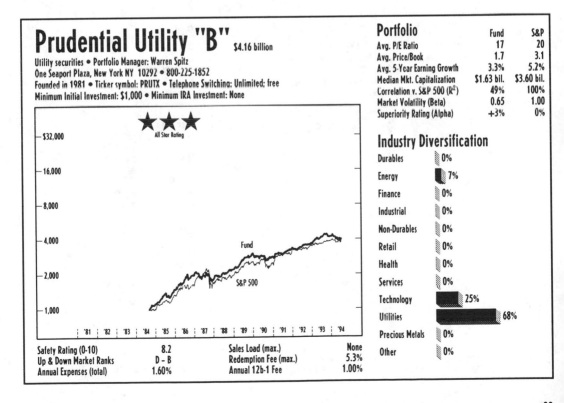

Prudential Utility "B" $4.16 billion

Utility securities • Portfolio Manager: Warren Spitz
One Seaport Plaza, New York NY 10292 • 800-225-1852
Founded in 1981 • Ticker symbol: PRUTX • Telephone Switching: Unlimited; free
Minimum Initial Investment: $1,000 • Minimum IRA Investment: None

★★★
All Star Rating

Safety Rating (0-10)	8.2	Sales Load (max.)	None
Up & Down Market Ranks	D – B	Redemption Fee (max.)	5.3%
Annual Expenses (total)	1.60%	Annual 12b-1 Fee	1.00%

Portfolio

	Fund	S&P
Avg. P/E Ratio	17	20
Avg. Price/Book	1.7	3.1
Avg. 5-Year Earning Growth	3.3%	5.2%
Median Mkt. Capitalization	$1.63 bil.	$3.60 bil.
Correlation v. S&P 500 (R^2)	49%	100%
Market Volatility (Beta)	0.65	1.00
Superiority Rating (Alpha)	+3%	0%

Industry Diversification

Durables	0%
Energy	7%
Finance	0%
Industrial	0%
Non-Durables	0%
Retail	0%
Health	0%
Services	0%
Technology	25%
Utilities	68%
Precious Metals	0%
Other	0%

Putnam American Govt Icm "A" $2.63 billion

A-rated & higher Ginnie Maes; U.S. Govt secs • Portfolio Managers: Kenneth Taubes/Senter
One Post Office Square, Boston MA 02109 • 800-225-1581
Founded in 1985 • Ticker symbol: PAGVX • Telephone Switching: Unlimited; free
Minimum Initial Investment: $500 • Minimum IRA Investment: $250

Portfolio

Yield	7.3%
Average Quality	AAA
Average Maturity	7.1 years
Average Duration	5.0 years
Average Coupon	7.1%
Correlation with U.S. T-Bond (R^2)	77%
Dividends Paid	Monthly

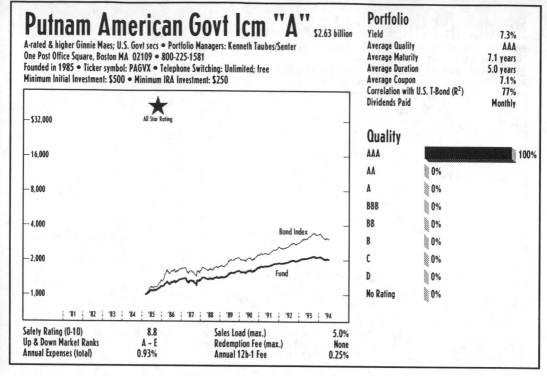

Quality

AAA	100%
AA	0%
A	0%
BBB	0%
BB	0%
B	0%
C	0%
D	0%
No Rating	0%

Safety Rating (0-10)	8.8	Sales Load (max.)	5.0%
Up & Down Market Ranks	A – E	Redemption Fee (max.)	None
Annual Expenses (total)	0.93%	Annual 12b-1 Fee	0.25%

Putnam California Tax-Ex "A" $3.35 billion

BBB-rated and higher California municipals • Portfolio Manager: William H. Reeves
One Post Office Square, Boston MA 02109 • 800-225-1581
Founded in 1983 • Ticker symbol: PCTEX • Telephone Switching: Unlimited; free
Minimum Initial Investment: $500 • Minimum IRA Investment: None

Portfolio

Yield	5.7%
Average Quality	AA
Average Maturity	23 years
Average Duration	8.4 years
Average Coupon	6.9%
Correlation with U.S. T-Bond (R^2)	47%

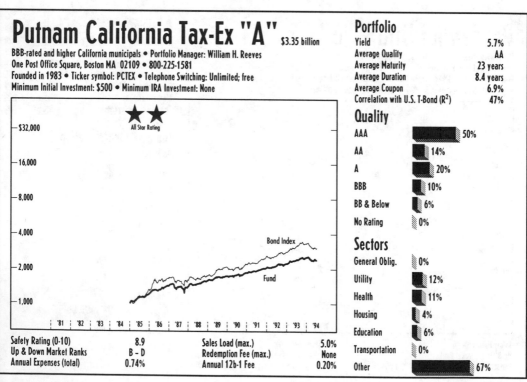

Quality

AAA	50%
AA	14%
A	20%
BBB	10%
BB & Below	6%
No Rating	0%

Sectors

General Oblig.	0%
Utility	12%
Health	11%
Housing	4%
Education	6%
Transportation	0%
Other	67%

Safety Rating (0-10)	8.9	Sales Load (max.)	5.0%
Up & Down Market Ranks	B – D	Redemption Fee (max.)	None
Annual Expenses (total)	0.74%	Annual 12b-1 Fee	0.20%

Putnam Diversified Income "B" $1.49 billion

Governments; high-yield corps, intl bonds • Portfolio Managers: Leichter/Daly/Saef
One Post Office Square, Boston MA 02109 • 800-225-1581
Founded in 1993 • Ticker symbol: PSIBX • Telephone Switching: Unlimited; free
Minimum Initial Investment: $500 • Minimum IRA Investment: $500

Portfolio

Yield	7.5%
Average Quality	AA
Average Maturity	11 years
Average Duration	5.2 years
Average Coupon	8.0%
Correlation with U.S. T-Bond (R^2)	49%
Dividends Paid	Monthly

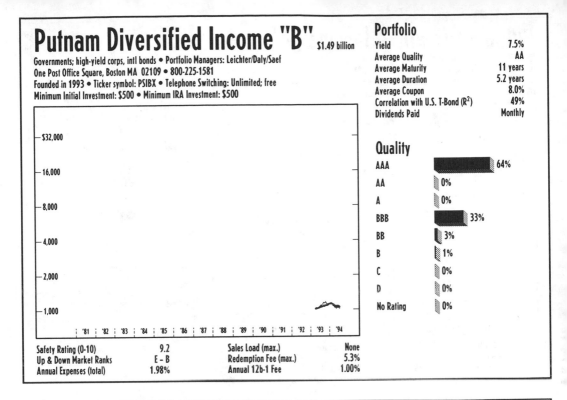

Quality

AAA	64%
AA	0%
A	0%
BBB	33%
BB	3%
B	1%
C	0%
D	0%
No Rating	0%

Safety Rating (0-10)	9.2	Sales Load (max.)	None
Up & Down Market Ranks	E – B	Redemption Fee (max.)	5.3%
Annual Expenses (total)	1.98%	Annual 12b-1 Fee	1.00%

Putnam Global Growth "A" $1.29 billion

Foreign - diversified stocks • Portfolio Managers: Anthony Regan/Zukowski
One Post Office Square, Boston MA 02109 • 800-225-1581
Founded in 1967 • Ticker symbol: PEQUX • Telephone Switching: Unlimited; free
Minimum Initial Investment: $500 • Minimum IRA Investment: $250

Portfolio

	Fund	S&P
Avg. P/E Ratio	24	20
Avg. Price/Book	2.9	3.1
Avg. 5-Year Earning Growth	6.8%	5.2%
Median Mkt. Capitalization	$990 mil.	$3.60 bil.
Correlation v. S&P 500 (R^2)	27%	100%
Market Volatility (Beta)	0.56	1.00
Superiority Rating (Alpha)	+0%	0%

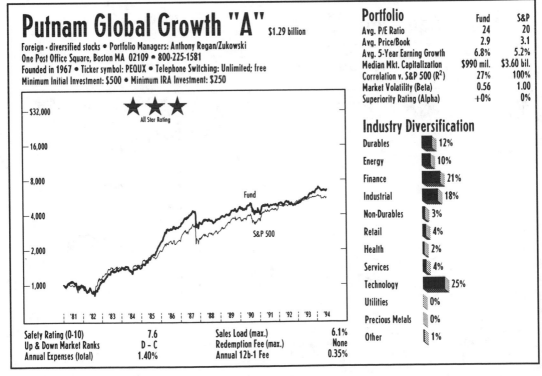

★★★
All Star Rating

Fund
S&P 500

Industry Diversification

Durables	12%
Energy	10%
Finance	21%
Industrial	18%
Non-Durables	3%
Retail	4%
Health	2%
Services	4%
Technology	25%
Utilities	0%
Precious Metals	0%
Other	1%

Safety Rating (0-10)	7.6	Sales Load (max.)	6.1%
Up & Down Market Ranks	D – C	Redemption Fee (max.)	None
Annual Expenses (total)	1.40%	Annual 12b-1 Fee	0.35%

Putnam Growth & Income "A" $5.62 billion

Diversified securities • Portfolio Managers: King/Kreisel/Giblin
One Post Office Square, Boston MA 02109 • 800-225-1581
Founded in 1957 • Ticker symbol: PGRWX • Telephone Switching: Unlimited; free
Minimum Initial Investment: $500 • Minimum IRA Investment: $250

Portfolio

	Fund	S&P
Avg. P/E Ratio	20	20
Avg. Price/Book	3.1	3.1
Avg. 5-Year Earning Growth	3.6%	5.2%
Median Mkt. Capitalization	$1.80 bil.	$3.60 bil.
Correlation v. S&P 500 (R^2)	87%	100%
Market Volatility (Beta)	0.75	1.00
Superiority Rating (Alpha)	+1%	0%

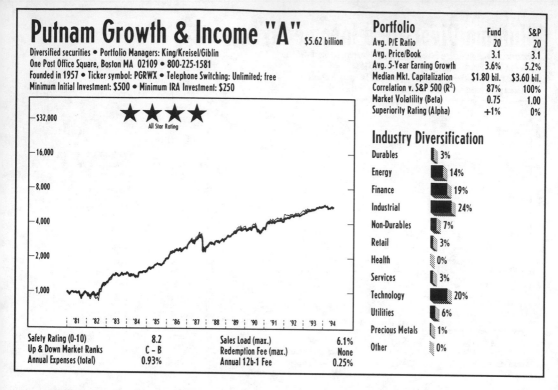

Industry Diversification

Durables	3%
Energy	14%
Finance	19%
Industrial	24%
Non-Durables	7%
Retail	3%
Health	0%
Services	3%
Technology	20%
Utilities	6%
Precious Metals	1%
Other	0%

Safety Rating (0-10)	8.2	Sales Load (max.)	6.1%
Up & Down Market Ranks	C – B	Redemption Fee (max.)	None
Annual Expenses (total)	0.93%	Annual 12b-1 Fee	0.25%

Putnam High Yield "A" $3.01 billion

90% B-rated and lower corporates • Portfolio Managers: Edward H. D'alelio/Ho
One Post Office Square, Boston MA 02109 • 800-225-1581
Founded in 1978 • Ticker symbol: PHIGX • Telephone Switching: Unlimited; free
Minimum Initial Investment: $500 • Minimum IRA Investment: $250

Portfolio

Yield	9.3%
Average Quality	B+
Average Maturity	8.2 years
Average Duration	4.7 years
Average Coupon	10.0%
Correlation with U.S. T-Bond (R^2)	1%
Dividends Paid	Monthly

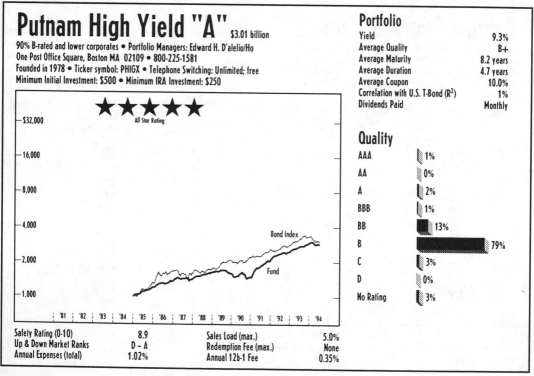

Quality

AAA	1%
AA	0%
A	2%
BBB	1%
BB	13%
B	79%
C	3%
D	0%
No Rating	3%

Safety Rating (0-10)	8.9	Sales Load (max.)	5.0%
Up & Down Market Ranks	D – A	Redemption Fee (max.)	None
Annual Expenses (total)	1.02%	Annual 12b-1 Fee	0.35%

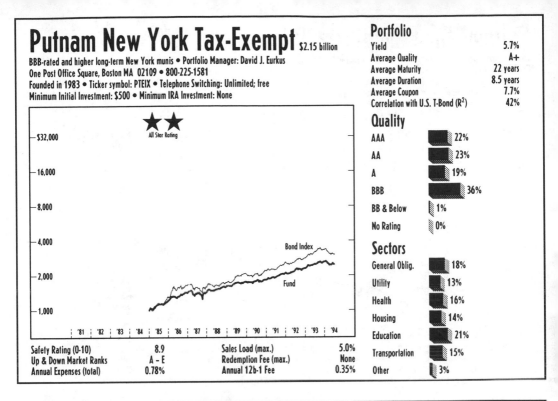

Putnam New York Tax-Exempt $2.15 billion

BBB-rated and higher long-term New York munis • Portfolio Manager: David J. Eurkus
One Post Office Square, Boston MA 02109 • 800-225-1581
Founded in 1983 • Ticker symbol: PTEIX • Telephone Switching: Unlimited; free
Minimum Initial Investment: $500 • Minimum IRA Investment: None

Portfolio

Yield	5.7%
Average Quality	A+
Average Maturity	22 years
Average Duration	8.5 years
Average Coupon	7.7%
Correlation with U.S. T-Bond (R^2)	42%

Quality

AAA	22%
AA	23%
A	19%
BBB	36%
BB & Below	1%
No Rating	0%

Sectors

General Oblig.	18%
Utility	13%
Health	16%
Housing	14%
Education	21%
Transportation	15%
Other	3%

★★ All Star Rating

Safety Rating (0-10)	8.9	Sales Load (max.)	5.0%
Up & Down Market Ranks	A – E	Redemption Fee (max.)	None
Annual Expenses (total)	0.78%	Annual 12b-1 Fee	0.35%

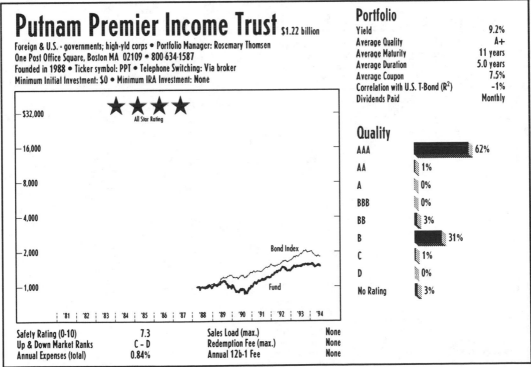

Putnam Premier Income Trust $1.22 billion

Foreign & U.S. - governments; high-yld corps • Portfolio Manager: Rosemary Thomsen
One Post Office Square, Boston MA 02109 • 800-634-1587
Founded in 1988 • Ticker symbol: PPT • Telephone Switching: Via broker
Minimum Initial Investment: $0 • Minimum IRA Investment: None

Portfolio

Yield	9.2%
Average Quality	A+
Average Maturity	11 years
Average Duration	5.0 years
Average Coupon	7.5%
Correlation with U.S. T-Bond (R^2)	–1%
Dividends Paid	Monthly

Quality

AAA	62%
AA	1%
A	0%
BBB	0%
BB	3%
B	31%
C	1%
D	0%
No Rating	3%

★★★★ All Star Rating

Safety Rating (0-10)	7.3	Sales Load (max.)	None
Up & Down Market Ranks	C – D	Redemption Fee (max.)	None
Annual Expenses (total)	0.84%	Annual 12b-1 Fee	None

Putnam Tax-Exempt Icm "A" $2.31 billion

BBB-rated and higher long-term municipals • Portfolio Manager: David J. Eurkus
One Post Office Square, Boston MA 02109 • 800-225-1581
Founded in 1976 • Ticker symbol: PTAEX • Telephone Switching: Unlimited; free
Minimum Initial Investment: $500 • Minimum IRA Investment: None

Portfolio

Yield	6.0%
Average Quality	AA-
Average Maturity	23 years
Average Duration	10 years
Average Coupon	6.7%
Correlation with U.S. T-Bond (R²)	44%

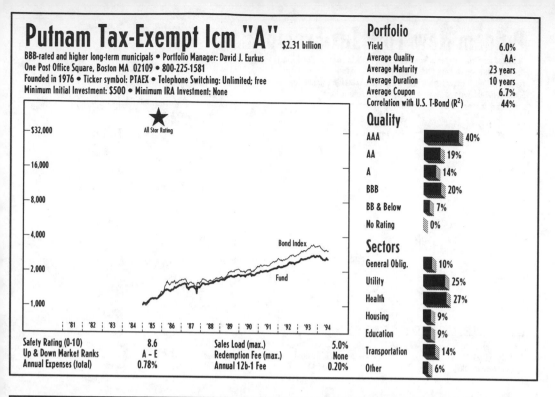

★
All Star Rating

Quality

AAA	40%
AA	19%
A	14%
BBB	20%
BB & Below	7%
No Rating	0%

Sectors

General Oblig.	10%
Utility	25%
Health	27%
Housing	9%
Education	9%
Transportation	14%
Other	6%

Safety Rating (0-10)	8.6	Sales Load (max.)	5.0%
Up & Down Market Ranks	A - E	Redemption Fee (max.)	None
Annual Expenses (total)	0.78%	Annual 12b-1 Fee	0.20%

Putnam Tax-Free High Yield "B" $1.49 billion

BBB-rated and lower long term municipals • Portfolio Manager: Triet N. Nguyen
One Post Office Square, Boston MA 02109 • 800-225-1581
Founded in 1985 • Ticker symbol: PTHYX • Telephone Switching: Unlimited; free
Minimum Initial Investment: $500 • Minimum IRA Investment: None

Portfolio

Yield	6.0%
Average Quality	A-
Average Maturity	24 years
Average Duration	7.6 years
Average Coupon	7.7%
Correlation with U.S. T-Bond (R²)	33%

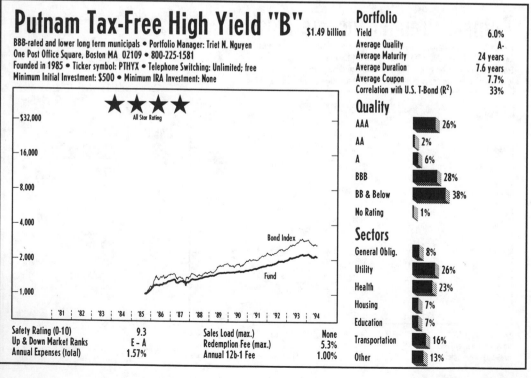

★★★★
All Star Rating

Quality

AAA	26%
AA	2%
A	6%
BBB	28%
BB & Below	38%
No Rating	1%

Sectors

General Oblig.	8%
Utility	26%
Health	23%
Housing	7%
Education	7%
Transportation	16%
Other	13%

Safety Rating (0-10)	9.3	Sales Load (max.)	None
Up & Down Market Ranks	E - A	Redemption Fee (max.)	5.3%
Annual Expenses (total)	1.57%	Annual 12b-1 Fee	1.00%

Putnam U.S. Govt Income "A" $3.50 billion

U.S. Government securities; Ginnie Maes • Portfolio Manager: Michael Martino
One Post Office Square, Boston MA 02109 • 800-225-1581
Founded in 1984 • Ticker symbol: PGSIX • Telephone Switching: Unlimited; free
Minimum Initial Investment: $500 • Minimum IRA Investment: $250

Portfolio

Yield	6.0%
Average Quality	AAA
Average Maturity	8.2 years
Average Duration	4.0 years
Average Coupon	10.3%
Correlation with U.S. T-Bond (R^2)	59%
Dividends Paid	Monthly

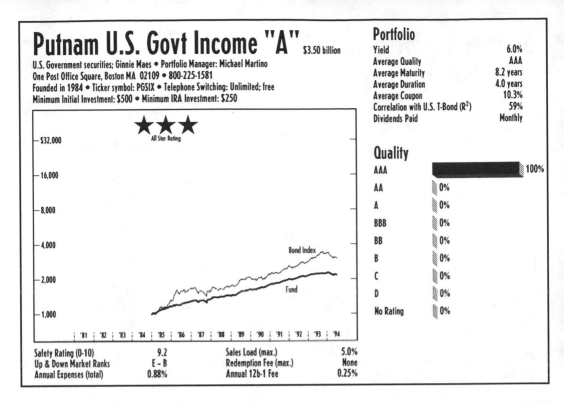

Quality

AAA		100%
AA		0%
A		0%
BBB		0%
BB		0%
B		0%
C		0%
D		0%
No Rating		0%

Safety Rating (0-10)	9.2	Sales Load (max.)	5.0%
Up & Down Market Ranks	E - B	Redemption Fee (max.)	None
Annual Expenses (total)	0.88%	Annual 12b-1 Fee	0.25%

Putnam Voyager "A" $3.03 billion

Small to medium-sized stocks; leveraged • Portfolio Manager: Matthew A. Weatherbie
One Post Office Square, Boston MA 02109 • 800-225-1581
Founded in 1969 • Ticker symbol: PVOYX • Telephone Switching: Unlimited; free
Minimum Initial Investment: $500 • Minimum IRA Investment: $250

Portfolio

	Fund	S&P
Avg. P/E Ratio	26	20
Avg. Price/Book	4.9	3.1
Avg. 5-Year Earning Growth	30.9%	5.2%
Median Mkt. Capitalization	$1.30 bil.	$3.60 bil.
Correlation v. S&P 500 (R^2)	71%	100%
Market Volatility (Beta)	1.33	1.00
Superiority Rating (Alpha)	+1%	0%

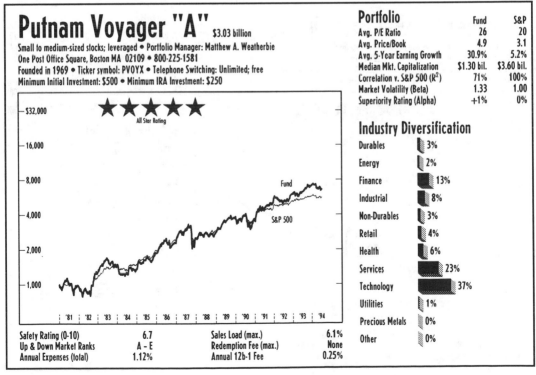

Industry Diversification

Durables		3%
Energy		2%
Finance		13%
Industrial		8%
Non-Durables		3%
Retail		4%
Health		6%
Services		23%
Technology		37%
Utilities		1%
Precious Metals		0%
Other		0%

Safety Rating (0-10)	6.7	Sales Load (max.)	6.1%
Up & Down Market Ranks	A - E	Redemption Fee (max.)	None
Annual Expenses (total)	1.12%	Annual 12b-1 Fee	0.25%

Salomon Brothers $1.12 billion

Diversified securities • Portfolio Manager:
55 Water Street, New York NY 10041 • 800-725-6666
Founded in 1929 • Ticker symbol: SBF • Telephone Switching: Via broker
Minimum Initial Investment: $0 • Minimum IRA Investment: None

Portfolio	Fund	S&P
Avg. P/E Ratio	19	20
Avg. Price/Book	3.2	3.1
Avg. 5-Year Earning Growth	7.1%	5.2%
Median Mkt. Capitalization	$5.01 bil.	$3.60 bil.
Correlation v. S&P 500 (R^2)	38%	100%
Market Volatility (Beta)	0.89	1.00
Superiority Rating (Alpha)	–4%	0%

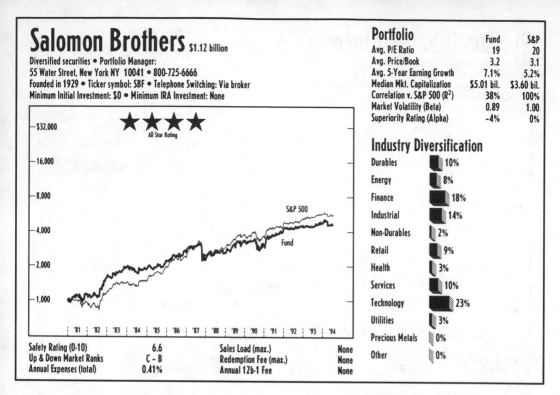

Industry Diversification

Durables	10%
Energy	8%
Finance	18%
Industrial	14%
Non-Durables	2%
Retail	9%
Health	3%
Services	10%
Technology	23%
Utilities	3%
Precious Metals	0%
Other	0%

Safety Rating (0-10)	6.6	Sales Load (max.)	None
Up & Down Market Ranks	C – B	Redemption Fee (max.)	None
Annual Expenses (total)	0.41%	Annual 12b-1 Fee	None

Scudder Capital Growth $1.33 billion

Diversified growth stocks • Portfolio Managers: Aronoff/Cox/Gadsen
160 Federal Street, Boston MA 02110 • 800-225-2470
Founded in 1956 • Ticker symbol: SCDUX • Telephone Switching: 4 per yr; free
Minimum Initial Investment: $1,000 • Minimum IRA Investment: $500

Portfolio	Fund	S&P
Avg. P/E Ratio	22	20
Avg. Price/Book	4.5	3.1
Avg. 5-Year Earning Growth	20.8%	5.2%
Median Mkt. Capitalization	$1.24 bil.	$3.60 bil.
Correlation v. S&P 500 (R^2)	69%	100%
Market Volatility (Beta)	1.21	1.00
Superiority Rating (Alpha)	–2%	0%

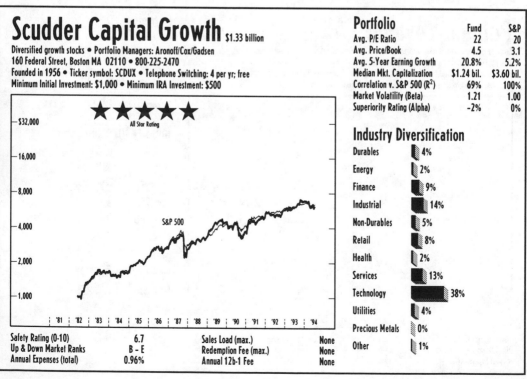

Industry Diversification

Durables	4%
Energy	2%
Finance	9%
Industrial	14%
Non-Durables	5%
Retail	8%
Health	2%
Services	13%
Technology	38%
Utilities	4%
Precious Metals	0%
Other	1%

Safety Rating (0-10)	6.7	Sales Load (max.)	None
Up & Down Market Ranks	B – E	Redemption Fee (max.)	None
Annual Expenses (total)	0.96%	Annual 12b-1 Fee	None

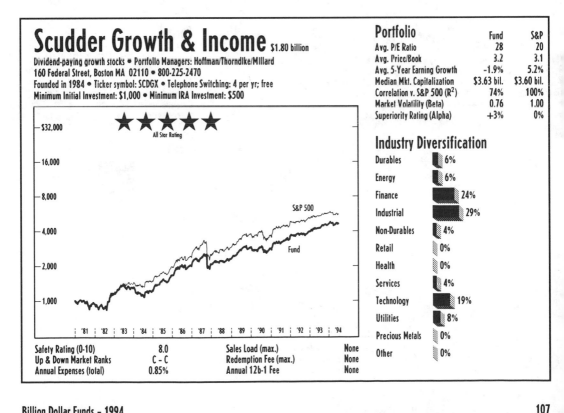

Scudder Global $1.11 billion

Foreign & U.S. - diversif stks; conv; bonds ● Portfolio Managers: Holzer/Bratt
160 Federal Street, Boston MA 02110 ● 800-225-2470
Founded in 1986 ● Ticker symbol: SCOBX ● Telephone Switching: 4 per yr; free
Minimum Initial Investment: $1,000 ● Minimum IRA Investment: $500

Portfolio

	Fund	S&P
Avg. P/E Ratio	23	20
Avg. Price/Book	2.1	3.1
Avg. 5-Year Earning Growth	3.1%	5.2%
Median Mkt. Capitalization	$2.60 bil.	$3.60 bil.
Correlation v. S&P 500 (R^2)	30%	100%
Market Volatility (Beta)	0.52	1.00
Superiority Rating (Alpha)	+2%	0%

★★★★
All Star Rating

S&P 500

Industry Diversification

Durables	8%
Energy	0%
Finance	29%
Industrial	15%
Non-Durables	0%
Retail	0%
Health	5%
Services	5%
Technology	15%
Utilities	19%
Precious Metals	4%
Other	0%

Safety Rating (0-10)	8.0	Sales Load (max.)	None
Up & Down Market Ranks	D – B	Redemption Fee (max.)	None
Annual Expenses (total)	1.48%	Annual 12b-1 Fee	None

Scudder Growth & Income $1.80 billion

Dividend-paying growth stocks ● Portfolio Managers: Hoffman/Thorndike/Millard
160 Federal Street, Boston MA 02110 ● 800-225-2470
Founded in 1984 ● Ticker symbol: SCDGX ● Telephone Switching: 4 per yr; free
Minimum Initial Investment: $1,000 ● Minimum IRA Investment: $500

Portfolio

	Fund	S&P
Avg. P/E Ratio	28	20
Avg. Price/Book	3.2	3.1
Avg. 5-Year Earning Growth	-1.9%	5.2%
Median Mkt. Capitalization	$3.63 bil.	$3.60 bil.
Correlation v. S&P 500 (R^2)	74%	100%
Market Volatility (Beta)	0.76	1.00
Superiority Rating (Alpha)	+3%	0%

★★★★★
All Star Rating

S&P 500

Fund

Industry Diversification

Durables	6%
Energy	6%
Finance	24%
Industrial	29%
Non-Durables	4%
Retail	0%
Health	0%
Services	4%
Technology	19%
Utilities	8%
Precious Metals	0%
Other	0%

Safety Rating (0-10)	8.0	Sales Load (max.)	None
Up & Down Market Ranks	C – C	Redemption Fee (max.)	None
Annual Expenses (total)	0.85%	Annual 12b-1 Fee	None

Scudder International $2.31 billion

Foreign - diversified securities • Portfolio Managers: Franklin/Bratt/Cheng
160 Federal Street, Boston MA 02110 • 800-225-2470
Founded in 1957 • Ticker symbol: SCINX • Telephone Switching: 4 per yr; free
Minimum Initial Investment: $1,000 • Minimum IRA Investment: $500

Portfolio

	Fund	S&P
Avg. P/E Ratio	28	20
Avg. Price/Book	3.1	3.1
Avg. 5-Year Earning Growth	10.8%	5.2%
Median Mkt. Capitalization	$6.10 bil.	$3.60 bil.
Correlation v. S&P 500 (R^2)	12%	100%
Market Volatility (Beta)	0.41	1.00
Superiority Rating (Alpha)	+0%	0%

★★★★
All Star Rating

Industry Diversification

Durables	8%
Energy	0%
Finance	17%
Industrial	0%
Non-Durables	6%
Retail	19%
Health	0%
Services	8%
Technology	7%
Utilities	6%
Precious Metals	0%
Other	29%

Safety Rating (0-10)	7.6
Up & Down Market Ranks	E – B
Annual Expenses (total)	1.26%

Sales Load (max.)	None
Redemption Fee (max.)	None
Annual 12b-1 Fee	None

Scudder Short Term Bond $2.72 billion

A-rated and higher corporates; avg maty 3-yrs • Portfolio Managers: Poor/Gootkind/Dolan
160 Federal Street, Boston MA 02110 • 800-225-2470
Founded in 1984 • Ticker symbol: SCSTX • Telephone Switching: 4 per yr; free
Minimum Initial Investment: $1,000 • Minimum IRA Investment: $500

Portfolio

Yield	7.3%
Average Quality	AA
Average Maturity	3.0 years
Average Duration	2.3 years
Average Coupon	7.4%
Correlation with U.S. T-Bond (R^2)	34%
Dividends Paid	Monthly (Accrue Daily)

★★★★★
All Star Rating

Quality

AAA	42%
AA	26%
A	18%
BBB	15%
BB	0%
B	0%
C	0%
D	0%
No Rating	0%

Safety Rating (0-10)	9.4
Up & Down Market Ranks	E – A
Annual Expenses (total)	0.68%

Sales Load (max.)	None
Redemption Fee (max.)	None
Annual 12b-1 Fee	None

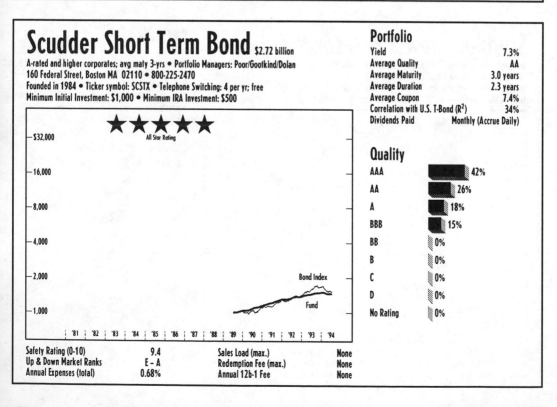

108

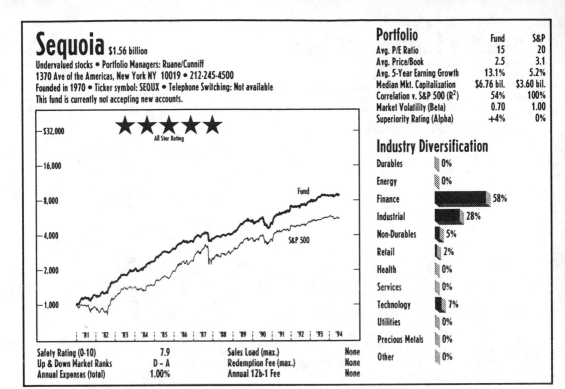

Sequoia $1.56 billion

Undervalued stocks • Portfolio Managers: Ruane/Cunniff
1370 Ave of the Americas, New York NY 10019 • 212-245-4500
Founded in 1970 • Ticker symbol: SEQUX • Telephone Switching: Not available
This fund is currently not accepting new accounts.

★★★★★
All Star Rating

$32,000
16,000
8,000
4,000
2,000
1,000

Fund
S&P 500

'81 '82 '83 '84 '85 '86 '87 '88 '89 '90 '91 '92 '93 '94

Safety Rating (0-10)	7.9	Sales Load (max.)	None
Up & Down Market Ranks	D – A	Redemption Fee (max.)	None
Annual Expenses (total)	1.00%	Annual 12b-1 Fee	None

Portfolio

	Fund	S&P
Avg. P/E Ratio	15	20
Avg. Price/Book	2.5	3.1
Avg. 5-Year Earning Growth	13.1%	5.2%
Median Mkt. Capitalization	$6.76 bil.	$3.60 bil.
Correlation v. S&P 500 (R^2)	54%	100%
Market Volatility (Beta)	0.70	1.00
Superiority Rating (Alpha)	+4%	0%

Industry Diversification

Durables	0%
Energy	0%
Finance	58%
Industrial	28%
Non-Durables	5%
Retail	2%
Health	0%
Services	0%
Technology	7%
Utilities	0%
Precious Metals	0%
Other	0%

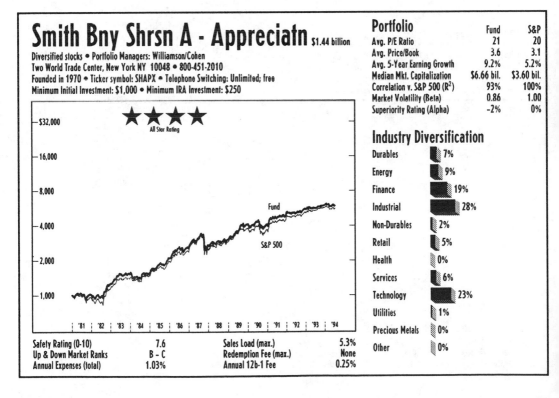

Smith Bny Shrsn A - Appreciatn $1.44 billion

Diversified stocks • Portfolio Managers: Williamson/Cohen
Two World Trade Center, New York NY 10048 • 800-451-2010
Founded in 1970 • Ticker symbol: SHAPX • Telephone Switching: Unlimited; free
Minimum Initial Investment: $1,000 • Minimum IRA Investment: $250

★★★★
All Star Rating

$32,000
16,000
8,000
4,000
2,000
1,000

Fund
S&P 500

'81 '82 '83 '84 '85 '86 '87 '88 '89 '90 '91 '92 '93 '94

Safety Rating (0-10)	7.6	Sales Load (max.)	5.3%
Up & Down Market Ranks	B – C	Redemption Fee (max.)	None
Annual Expenses (total)	1.03%	Annual 12b-1 Fee	0.25%

Portfolio

	Fund	S&P
Avg. P/E Ratio	21	20
Avg. Price/Book	3.6	3.1
Avg. 5-Year Earning Growth	9.2%	5.2%
Median Mkt. Capitalization	$6.66 bil.	$3.60 bil.
Correlation v. S&P 500 (R^2)	93%	100%
Market Volatility (Beta)	0.86	1.00
Superiority Rating (Alpha)	-2%	0%

Industry Diversification

Durables	7%
Energy	9%
Finance	19%
Industrial	28%
Non-Durables	2%
Retail	5%
Health	0%
Services	6%
Technology	23%
Utilities	1%
Precious Metals	0%
Other	0%

Smith Bny Shrsn B - Pr Tot Ret $1.63 billion

Dividend-paying stocks • Portfolio Manager: Multiple Managers
Two World Trade Center, New York NY 10048 • 800-451-2010
Founded in 1985 • Ticker symbol: SOPTX • Telephone Switching: Unlimited; free
Minimum Initial Investment: $1,000 • Minimum IRA Investment: $250

Portfolio

	Fund	S&P
Avg. P/E Ratio	17	20
Avg. Price/Book	2.1	3.1
Avg. 5-Year Earning Growth	9.5%	5.2%
Median Mkt. Capitalization	$2.85 bil.	$3.60 bil.
Correlation v. S&P 500 (R^2)	72%	100%
Market Volatility (Beta)	0.67	1.00
Superiority Rating (Alpha)	+3%	0%

Industry Diversification

Durables	2%
Energy	8%
Finance	44%
Industrial	12%
Non-Durables	7%
Retail	6%
Health	1%
Services	5%
Technology	10%
Utilities	3%
Precious Metals	2%
Other	0%

★★★★ All Star Rating

(Chart: S&P 500, Fund; $32,000 / 16,000 / 8,000 / 4,000 / 2,000 / 1,000; '81 '82 '83 '84 '85 '86 '87 '88 '89 '90 '91 '92 '93 '94)

Safety Rating (0-10)	8.2	Sales Load (max.)	None
Up & Down Market Ranks	A – C	Redemption Fee (max.)	5.3%
Annual Expenses (total)	1.69%	Annual 12b-1 Fee	0.75%

Smith Bny Shrsn B - Tax-Exempt $1.08 billion

Intermediate-long-term municipals • Portfolio Manager: Larry McDermott
Two World Trade Center, New York NY 10048 • 800-451-2010
Founded in 1985 • Ticker symbol: SXMTX • Telephone Switching: Unlimited; free
Minimum Initial Investment: $1,000 • Minimum IRA Investment: None

Portfolio

Yield	5.1%
Average Quality	AA-
Average Maturity	20 years
Average Duration	N/A
Average Coupon	7.3%
Correlation with U.S. T-Bond (R^2)	49%

Quality

AAA	43%
AA	7%
A	18%
BBB	24%
BB & Below	2%
No Rating	5%

Sectors

General Oblig.	13%
Utility	44%
Health	13%
Housing	6%
Education	4%
Transportation	15%
Other	5%

★★ All Star Rating

(Chart: Bond Index, Fund; $32,000 / 16,000 / 8,000 / 4,000 / 2,000 / 1,000; '81 '82 '83 '84 '85 '86 '87 '88 '89 '90 '91 '92 '93 '94)

Safety Rating (0-10)	9.1	Sales Load (max.)	None
Up & Down Market Ranks	D – C	Redemption Fee (max.)	4.7%
Annual Expenses (total)	1.38%	Annual 12b-1 Fee	0.65%

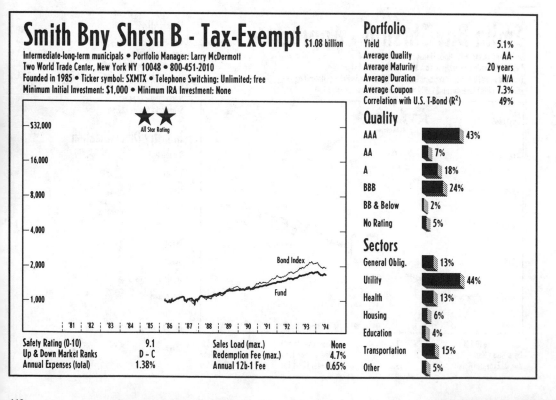

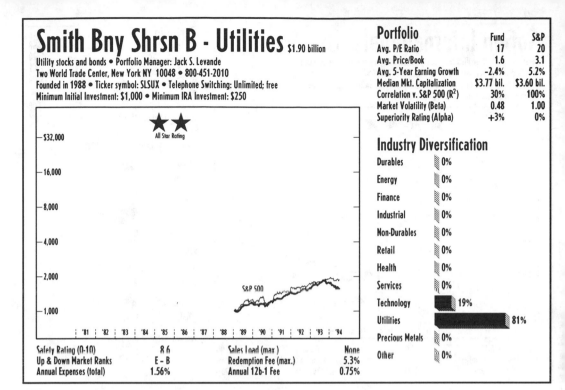

Smith Bny Shrsn B - Utilities $1.90 billion

Utility stocks and bonds • Portfolio Manager: Jack S. Levande
Two World Trade Center, New York NY 10048 • 800-451-2010
Founded in 1988 • Ticker symbol: SLSUX • Telephone Switching: Unlimited; free
Minimum Initial Investment: $1,000 • Minimum IRA Investment: $250

Portfolio

	Fund	S&P
Avg. P/E Ratio	17	20
Avg. Price/Book	1.6	3.1
Avg. 5-Year Earning Growth	-2.4%	5.2%
Median Mkt. Capitalization	$3.77 bil.	$3.60 bil.
Correlation v. S&P 500 (R^2)	30%	100%
Market Volatility (Beta)	0.48	1.00
Superiority Rating (Alpha)	+3%	0%

Industry Diversification

Durables	0%
Energy	0%
Finance	0%
Industrial	0%
Non-Durables	0%
Retail	0%
Health	0%
Services	0%
Technology	19%
Utilities	81%
Precious Metals	0%
Other	0%

★★ All Star Rating

Safety Rating (0-10)	8.6	Sales Load (max.)	None
Up & Down Market Ranks	E – B	Redemption Fee (max.)	5.3%
Annual Expenses (total)	1.56%	Annual 12b-1 Fee	0.75%

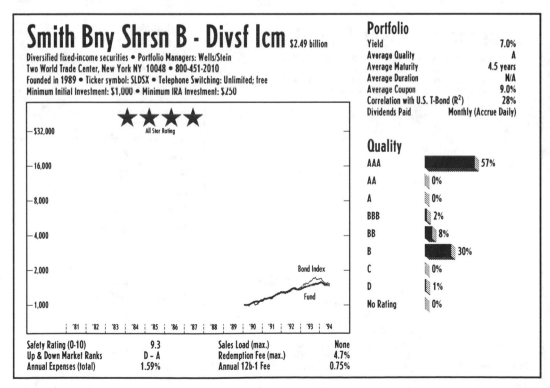

Smith Bny Shrsn B - Divsf Icm $2.49 billion

Diversified fixed-income securities • Portfolio Managers: Wells/Stein
Two World Trade Center, New York NY 10048 • 800-451-2010
Founded in 1989 • Ticker symbol: SLDSX • Telephone Switching: Unlimited; free
Minimum Initial Investment: $1,000 • Minimum IRA Investment: $250

Portfolio

Yield	7.0%
Average Quality	A
Average Maturity	4.5 years
Average Duration	N/A
Average Coupon	9.0%
Correlation with U.S. T-Bond (R^2)	28%
Dividends Paid	Monthly (Accrue Daily)

Quality

AAA	57%
AA	0%
A	0%
BBB	2%
BB	8%
B	30%
C	0%
D	1%
No Rating	0%

★★★★ All Star Rating

Safety Rating (0-10)	9.3	Sales Load (max.)	None
Up & Down Market Ranks	D – A	Redemption Fee (max.)	4.7%
Annual Expenses (total)	1.59%	Annual 12b-1 Fee	0.75%

SoGen International $1.81 billion

Foreign & U.S. - diversified securities • Portfolio Manager: Jean-Marie Eveillard
520 Madison Avenue, New York NY 10022 • 800-628-0252
Founded in 1970 • Ticker symbol: SGENX • Telephone Switching: See prospectus
This fund is currently not accepting new accounts.

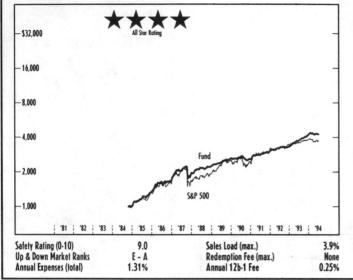

Safety Rating (0-10)	9.0	Sales Load (max.)	3.9%
Up & Down Market Ranks	E – A	Redemption Fee (max.)	None
Annual Expenses (total)	1.31%	Annual 12b-1 Fee	0.25%

Portfolio

	Fund	S&P
Avg. P/E Ratio	29	20
Avg. Price/Book	2.3	3.1
Avg. 5-Year Earning Growth	6.5%	5.2%
Median Mkt. Capitalization	$209 mil.	$3.60 bil.
Correlation v. S&P 500 (R²)	26%	100%
Market Volatility (Beta)	0.26	1.00
Superiority Rating (Alpha)	+6%	0%

Industry Diversification

Durables	18%
Energy	7%
Finance	13%
Industrial	25%
Non-Durables	3%
Retail	6%
Health	0%
Services	5%
Technology	13%
Utilities	1%
Precious Metals	6%
Other	3%

Stagecoach - Asset Allocation $1.08 billion

S&P 500 stks; 20+yr Treas bonds; money market • Portfolio Manager: Janic Derringer
525 Market Street, San Francisco CA 94163 • 800-222-8222
Founded in 1986 • Ticker symbol: SFAAX • Telephone Switching: Unlimited; free
Minimum Initial Investment: $1,000 • Minimum IRA Investment: $250

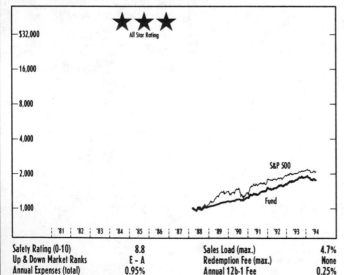

Safety Rating (0-10)	8.8	Sales Load (max.)	4.7%
Up & Down Market Ranks	E – A	Redemption Fee (max.)	None
Annual Expenses (total)	0.95%	Annual 12b-1 Fee	0.25%

Portfolio

	Fund	S&P
Avg. P/E Ratio	21	20
Avg. Price/Book	3.3	3.1
Avg. 5-Year Earning Growth	6.2%	5.2%
Median Mkt. Capitalization	$3.53 bil.	$3.60 bil.
Correlation v. S&P 500 (R²)	57%	100%
Market Volatility (Beta)	0.53	1.00
Superiority Rating (Alpha)	+4%	0%

Industry Diversification

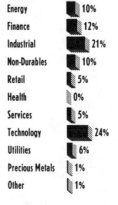

Durables	5%
Energy	10%
Finance	12%
Industrial	21%
Non-Durables	10%
Retail	5%
Health	0%
Services	5%
Technology	24%
Utilities	6%
Precious Metals	1%
Other	1%

Stein Roe Special $1.19 billion

Diversified stocks • Portfolio Managers: Dunn/Peterson
150 South Wacker Drive, Chicago IL 60606 • 800-338-2550
Founded in 1968 • Ticker symbol: SRSPX • Telephone Switching: 4 per yr; free
Minimum Initial Investment: $2,500 • Minimum IRA Investment: $500

Portfolio

	Fund	S&P
Avg. P/E Ratio	26	20
Avg. Price/Book	2.8	3.1
Avg. 5-Year Earning Growth	14.9%	5.2%
Median Mkt. Capitalization	$922 mil.	$3.60 bil.
Correlation v. S&P 500 (R^2)	67%	100%
Market Volatility (Beta)	0.86	1.00
Superiority Rating (Alpha)	+1%	0%

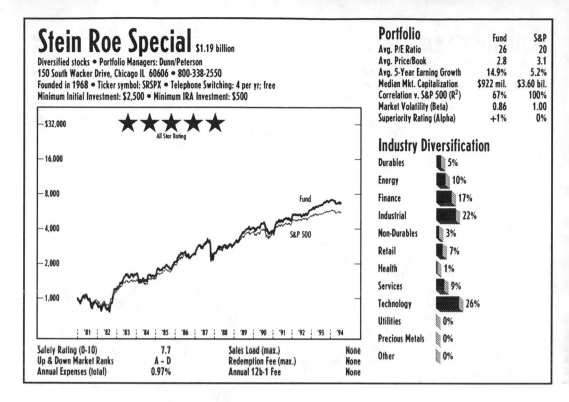

Industry Diversification

Durables	5%
Energy	10%
Finance	17%
Industrial	22%
Non-Durables	3%
Retail	7%
Health	1%
Services	9%
Technology	26%
Utilities	0%
Precious Metals	0%
Other	0%

Safety Rating (0-10)	7.7	Sales Load (max.)	None
Up & Down Market Ranks	A – D	Redemption Fee (max.)	None
Annual Expenses (total)	0.97%	Annual 12b-1 Fee	None

Strong Short Term Bond $1.38 billion

Investment-grade short term corporates • Portfolio Manager: Brad Tank
100 Heritage Reserve, Menomonee Falls WI 53051 • 800-368-3863
Founded in 1987 • Ticker symbol: SSTBX • Telephone Switching: 5 per yr; free
Minimum Initial Investment: $1,000 • Minimum IRA Investment: $250

Portfolio

Yield	7.1%
Average Quality	A+
Average Maturity	2.5 years
Average Duration	2.1 years
Average Coupon	7.9%
Correlation with U.S. T-Bond (R^2)	23%
Dividends Paid	Monthly (Accrue Daily)

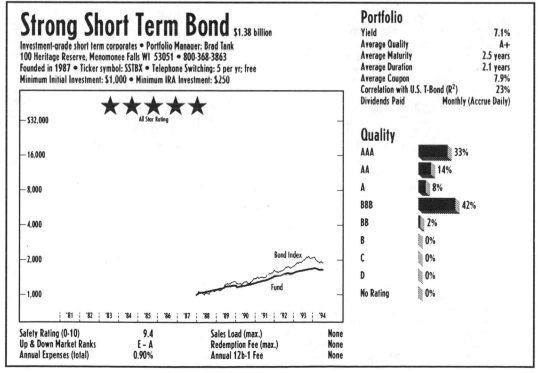

Quality

AAA	33%
AA	14%
A	8%
BBB	42%
BB	2%
B	0%
C	0%
D	0%
No Rating	0%

Safety Rating (0-10)	9.4	Sales Load (max.)	None
Up & Down Market Ranks	E – A	Redemption Fee (max.)	None
Annual Expenses (total)	0.90%	Annual 12b-1 Fee	None

Templeton Foreign $4.29 billion

Foreign - diversified stocks • Portfolio Manager: Mark G. Holowesko
700 Central Avenue, St Petersburg FL 33701 • 800-292-9293
Founded in 1982 • Ticker symbol: TEMFX • Telephone Switching: Unlimited; free
Minimum Initial Investment: $100 • Minimum IRA Investment: $100

Portfolio	Fund	S&P
Avg. P/E Ratio	63	20
Avg. Price/Book	2.0	3.1
Avg. 5-Year Earning Growth	-6.8%	5.2%
Median Mkt. Capitalization	$13.8 bil.	$3.60 bil.
Correlation v. S&P 500 (R^2)	16%	100%
Market Volatility (Beta)	0.40	1.00
Superiority Rating (Alpha)	+4%	0%

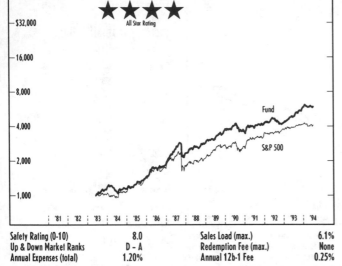

★★★★
All Star Rating

Industry Diversification

Durables	0%
Energy	0%
Finance	0%
Industrial	0%
Non-Durables	0%
Retail	0%
Health	0%
Services	9%
Technology	90%
Utilities	1%
Precious Metals	0%
Other	0%

Safety Rating (0-10)	8.0	Sales Load (max.)	6.1%
Up & Down Market Ranks	D – A	Redemption Fee (max.)	None
Annual Expenses (total)	1.20%	Annual 12b-1 Fee	0.25%

Templeton Growth $5.03 billion

Foreign & U.S. - diversified stocks • Portfolio Manager: Mark G. Holowesko
700 Central Avenue, St Petersburg FL 33701 • 800-292-9293
Founded in 1982 • Ticker symbol: TEPLX • Telephone Switching: Unlimited; free
Minimum Initial Investment: $100 • Minimum IRA Investment: $100

Portfolio	Fund	S&P
Avg. P/E Ratio	20	20
Avg. Price/Book	1.8	3.1
Avg. 5-Year Earning Growth	-2.4%	5.2%
Median Mkt. Capitalization	$2.95 bil.	$3.60 bil.
Correlation v. S&P 500 (R^2)	45%	100%
Market Volatility (Beta)	0.66	1.00
Superiority Rating (Alpha)	+4%	0%

★★★★
All Star Rating

Industry Diversification

Durables	16%
Energy	1%
Finance	37%
Industrial	23%
Non-Durables	3%
Retail	3%
Health	3%
Services	2%
Technology	4%
Utilities	4%
Precious Metals	0%
Other	4%

Safety Rating (0-10)	7.9	Sales Load (max.)	6.1%
Up & Down Market Ranks	D – B	Redemption Fee (max.)	None
Annual Expenses (total)	1.09%	Annual 12b-1 Fee	0.25%

Templeton Smaller Companies $1.37 billion

Foreign & U.S. - diversified stocks • Portfolio Manager: Dan Jacobs
700 Central Avenue, St Petersburg FL 33701 • 800-292-9293
Founded in 1981 • Ticker symbol: TEMGX • Telephone Switching: Unlimited; free
Minimum Initial Investment: $100 • Minimum IRA Investment: $100

Portfolio

	Fund	S&P
Avg. P/E Ratio	23	20
Avg. Price/Book	2.3	3.1
Avg. 5-Year Earning Growth	9.4%	5.2%
Median Mkt. Capitalization	$417 mil.	$3.60 bil.
Correlation v. S&P 500 (R^2)	47%	100%
Market Volatility (Beta)	0.72	1.00
Superiority Rating (Alpha)	+3%	0%

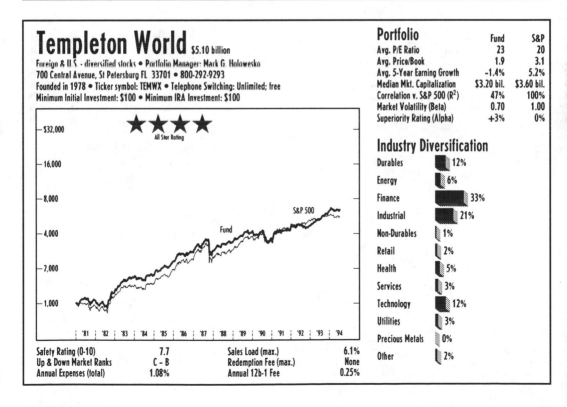

★★★ All Star Rating

Fund
S&P 500

Industry Diversification

Durables	5%
Energy	1%
Finance	30%
Industrial	8%
Non-Durables	6%
Retail	7%
Health	2%
Services	13%
Technology	16%
Utilities	7%
Precious Metals	0%
Other	5%

Safety Rating (0-10)	7.8	Sales Load (max.)	6.1%
Up & Down Market Ranks	D – B	Redemption Fee (max.)	None
Annual Expenses (total)	1.42%	Annual 12b-1 Fee	0.25%

Templeton World $5.10 billion

Foreign & U.S. - diversified stocks • Portfolio Manager: Mark G. Holowesko
700 Central Avenue, St Petersburg FL 33701 • 800-292-9293
Founded in 1978 • Ticker symbol: TEMWX • Telephone Switching: Unlimited; free
Minimum Initial Investment: $100 • Minimum IRA Investment: $100

Portfolio

	Fund	S&P
Avg. P/E Ratio	23	20
Avg. Price/Book	1.9	3.1
Avg. 5-Year Earning Growth	-1.4%	5.2%
Median Mkt. Capitalization	$3.20 bil.	$3.60 bil.
Correlation v. S&P 500 (R^2)	47%	100%
Market Volatility (Beta)	0.70	1.00
Superiority Rating (Alpha)	+3%	0%

★★★★ All Star Rating

S&P 500
Fund

Industry Diversification

Durables	12%
Energy	6%
Finance	33%
Industrial	21%
Non-Durables	1%
Retail	2%
Health	5%
Services	3%
Technology	12%
Utilities	3%
Precious Metals	0%
Other	2%

Safety Rating (0-10)	7.7	Sales Load (max.)	6.1%
Up & Down Market Ranks	C – B	Redemption Fee (max.)	None
Annual Expenses (total)	1.08%	Annual 12b-1 Fee	0.25%

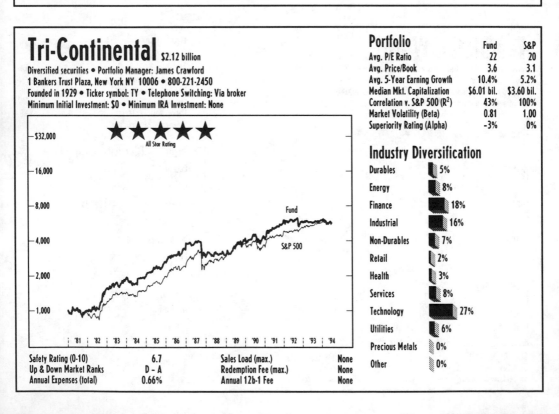

Thomson - Growth "B" $1.06 billion

Diversified growth stocks • Portfolio Manager: Multiple Managers
One Station Place, Stamford CT 06902 • 800-628-1237
Founded in 1984 • Ticker symbol: TGWBX • Telephone Switching: Unlimited; free
Minimum Initial Investment: $1,000 • Minimum IRA Investment: $25

Portfolio

	Fund	S&P
Avg. P/E Ratio	20	20
Avg. Price/Book	4.6	3.1
Avg. 5-Year Earning Growth	24.2%	5.2%
Median Mkt. Capitalization	$12.3 bil.	$3.60 bil.
Correlation v. S&P 500 (R^2)	70%	100%
Market Volatility (Beta)	1.00	1.00
Superiority Rating (Alpha)	–1%	0%

★ ★ ★ ★ ★
All Star Rating

$32,000
16,000
8,000
4,000
2,000
1,000

Fund
S&P 500

'81 '82 '83 '84 '85 '86 '87 '88 '89 '90 '91 '92 '93 '94

Industry Diversification

Durables	6%
Energy	8%
Finance	22%
Industrial	8%
Non-Durables	4%
Retail	11%
Health	5%
Services	5%
Technology	24%
Utilities	3%
Precious Metals	0%
Other	4%

Safety Rating (0-10)	7.2	Sales Load (max.)	None
Up & Down Market Ranks	A – E	Redemption Fee (max.)	1.0%
Annual Expenses (total)	1.90%	Annual 12b-1 Fee	1.00%

Tri-Continental $2.12 billion

Diversified securities • Portfolio Manager: James Crawford
1 Bankers Trust Plaza, New York NY 10006 • 800-221-2450
Founded in 1929 • Ticker symbol: TY • Telephone Switching: Via broker
Minimum Initial Investment: $0 • Minimum IRA Investment: None

Portfolio

	Fund	S&P
Avg. P/E Ratio	22	20
Avg. Price/Book	3.6	3.1
Avg. 5-Year Earning Growth	10.4%	5.2%
Median Mkt. Capitalization	$6.01 bil.	$3.60 bil.
Correlation v. S&P 500 (R^2)	43%	100%
Market Volatility (Beta)	0.81	1.00
Superiority Rating (Alpha)	–3%	0%

★ ★ ★ ★ ★
All Star Rating

$32,000
16,000
8,000
4,000
2,000
1,000

Fund
S&P 500

'81 '82 '83 '84 '85 '86 '87 '88 '89 '90 '91 '92 '93 '94

Industry Diversification

Durables	5%
Energy	8%
Finance	18%
Industrial	16%
Non-Durables	7%
Retail	2%
Health	3%
Services	8%
Technology	27%
Utilities	6%
Precious Metals	0%
Other	0%

Safety Rating (0-10)	6.7	Sales Load (max.)	None
Up & Down Market Ranks	D – A	Redemption Fee (max.)	None
Annual Expenses (total)	0.66%	Annual 12b-1 Fee	None

Twentieth Century Growth $4.41 billion

Large established growth stocks • Portfolio Manager: Team Managed
4500 Main Street, Kansas City MO 64141 • 800-345-2021
Founded in 1958 • Ticker symbol: TWCGX • Telephone Switching: 4 per yr; free
Minimum Initial Investment: $2,500 • Minimum IRA Investment: None

Portfolio

	Fund	S&P
Avg. P/E Ratio	16	20
Avg. Price/Book	3.7	3.1
Avg. 5-Year Earning Growth	20.7%	5.2%
Median Mkt. Capitalization	$6.24 bil.	$3.60 bil.
Correlation v. S&P 500 (R^2)	65%	100%
Market Volatility (Beta)	1.25	1.00
Superiority Rating (Alpha)	–3%	0%

★★★★★
All Star Rating

$16,000
8,000
4,000 — S&P 500
2,000 — Fund
1,000

'81 '82 '83 '84 '85 '86 '87 '88 '89 '90 '91 '92 '93 '94

Industry Diversification

Durables	1%
Energy	2%
Finance	16%
Industrial	6%
Non-Durables	5%
Retail	1%
Health	5%
Services	9%
Technology	53%
Utilities	1%
Precious Metals	1%
Other	0%

Safety Rating (0-10)	6.2	Sales Load (max.)	None
Up & Down Market Ranks	A – E	Redemption Fee (max.)	None
Annual Expenses (total)	1.00%	Annual 12b-1 Fee	None

Twentieth Century Intl Equity $1.22 billion

Foreign - growth securities • Portfolio Managers: Kopinski/Tyson
4500 Main Street, Kansas City MO 64141 • 800-345-2021
Founded in 1991 • Ticker symbol: TWIEX • Telephone Switching: 4 per yr; free
Minimum Initial Investment: $2,500 • Minimum IRA Investment: None

Portfolio

	Fund	S&P
Avg. P/E Ratio	14	20
Avg. Price/Book	1.6	3.1
Avg. 5-Year Earning Growth	4.6%	5.2%
Median Mkt. Capitalization	$955 mil.	$3.60 bil.
Correlation v. S&P 500 (R^2)	8%	100%
Market Volatility (Beta)	0.37	1.00
Superiority Rating (Alpha)	+6%	0%

★★★★
All Star Rating

$32,000
16,000
8,000
4,000
2,000 — Fund
1,000 — S&P 500

'81 '82 '83 '84 '85 '86 '87 '88 '89 '90 '91 '92 '93 '94

Industry Diversification

Durables	0%
Energy	24%
Finance	15%
Industrial	48%
Non-Durables	0%
Retail	0%
Health	0%
Services	9%
Technology	4%
Utilities	0%
Precious Metals	0%
Other	0%

Safety Rating (0-10)	7.5	Sales Load (max.)	None
Up & Down Market Ranks	E – A	Redemption Fee (max.)	None
Annual Expenses (total)	1.90%	Annual 12b-1 Fee	None

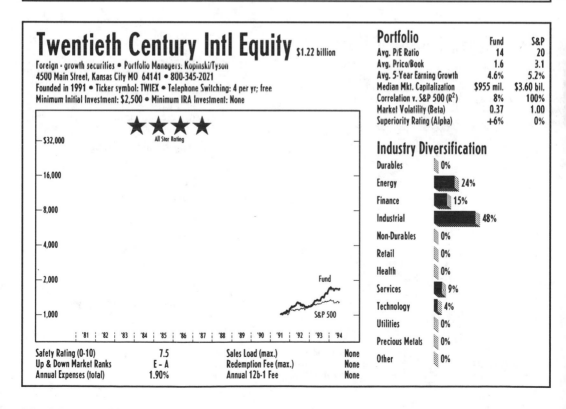

Twentieth Century Select $4.40 billion

Dividend-paying; large growth stocks • Portfolio Manager: Team Managed
4500 Main Street, Kansas City MO 64141 • 800-345-2021
Founded in 1958 • Ticker symbol: TWCIX • Telephone Switching: 4 per yr; free
Minimum Initial Investment: $2,500 • Minimum IRA Investment: None

Portfolio

	Fund	S&P
Avg. P/E Ratio	19	20
Avg. Price/Book	2.9	3.1
Avg. 5-Year Earning Growth	10.8%	5.2%
Median Mkt. Capitalization	$8.12 bil.	$3.60 bil.
Correlation v. S&P 500 (R^2)	77%	100%
Market Volatility (Beta)	0.99	1.00
Superiority Rating (Alpha)	–5%	0%

★★★
All Star Rating

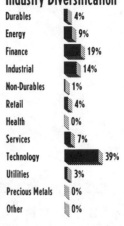

Industry Diversification

Durables	4%
Energy	9%
Finance	19%
Industrial	14%
Non-Durables	1%
Retail	4%
Health	0%
Services	7%
Technology	39%
Utilities	3%
Precious Metals	0%
Other	0%

Safety Rating (0-10)	6.7	Sales Load (max.)	None
Up & Down Market Ranks	A – E	Redemption Fee (max.)	None
Annual Expenses (total)	1.00%	Annual 12b-1 Fee	None

Twentieth Century Ultra $9.26 billion

Medium-small capitalization growth stocks • Portfolio Manager: Team Managed
4500 Main Street, Kansas City MO 64141 • 800-345-2021
Founded in 1981 • Ticker symbol: TWCUX • Telephone Switching: 4 per yr; free
Minimum Initial Investment: $2,500 • Minimum IRA Investment: None

Portfolio

	Fund	S&P
Avg. P/E Ratio	26	20
Avg. Price/Book	6.0	3.1
Avg. 5-Year Earning Growth	51.1%	5.2%
Median Mkt. Capitalization	$1.47 bil.	$3.60 bil.
Correlation v. S&P 500 (R^2)	47%	100%
Market Volatility (Beta)	1.47	1.00
Superiority Rating (Alpha)	+6%	0%

★★★★★
All Star Rating

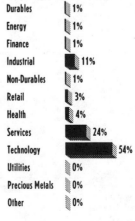

Industry Diversification

Durables	1%
Energy	1%
Finance	1%
Industrial	11%
Non-Durables	1%
Retail	3%
Health	4%
Services	24%
Technology	54%
Utilities	0%
Precious Metals	0%
Other	0%

Safety Rating (0-10)	5.5	Sales Load (max.)	None
Up & Down Market Ranks	A – E	Redemption Fee (max.)	None
Annual Expenses (total)	1.00%	Annual 12b-1 Fee	None

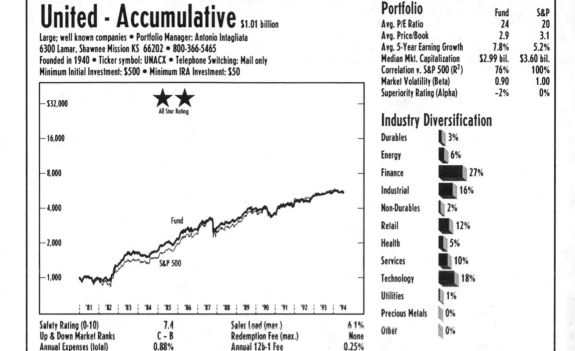

United - Accumulative $1.01 billion

Large; well known companies • Portfolio Manager: Antonio Intagliata
6300 Lamar, Shawnee Mission KS 66202 • 800-366-5465
Founded in 1940 • Ticker symbol: UNACX • Telephone Switching: Mail only
Minimum Initial Investment: $500 • Minimum IRA Investment: $50

★★ All Star Rating

Portfolio	Fund	S&P
Avg. P/E Ratio	24	20
Avg. Price/Book	2.9	3.1
Avg. 5-Year Earning Growth	7.8%	5.2%
Median Mkt. Capitalization	$2.99 bil.	$3.60 bil.
Correlation v. S&P 500 (R^2)	76%	100%
Market Volatility (Beta)	0.90	1.00
Superiority Rating (Alpha)	-2%	0%

Industry Diversification

Durables	3%
Energy	6%
Finance	27%
Industrial	16%
Non-Durables	2%
Retail	12%
Health	5%
Services	10%
Technology	18%
Utilities	1%
Precious Metals	0%
Other	0%

Safety Rating (0-10)	7.4	Sales Load (max.)	6.1%
Up & Down Market Ranks	C – B	Redemption Fee (max.)	None
Annual Expenses (total)	0.88%	Annual 12b-1 Fee	0.25%

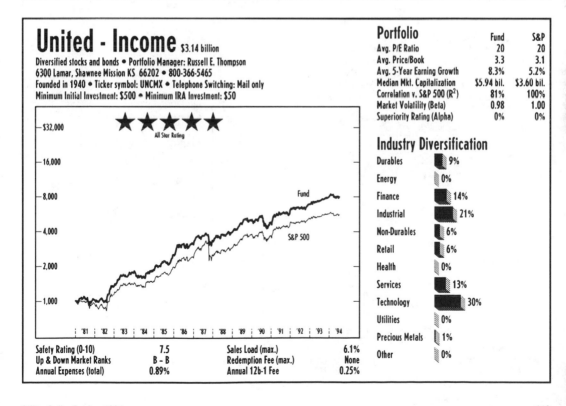

United - Income $3.14 billion

Diversified stocks and bonds • Portfolio Manager: Russell E. Thompson
6300 Lamar, Shawnee Mission KS 66202 • 800-366-5465
Founded in 1940 • Ticker symbol: UNCMX • Telephone Switching: Mail only
Minimum Initial Investment: $500 • Minimum IRA Investment: $50

★★★★★ All Star Rating

Portfolio	Fund	S&P
Avg. P/E Ratio	20	20
Avg. Price/Book	3.3	3.1
Avg. 5-Year Earning Growth	8.3%	5.2%
Median Mkt. Capitalization	$5.94 bil.	$3.60 bil.
Correlation v. S&P 500 (R^2)	81%	100%
Market Volatility (Beta)	0.98	1.00
Superiority Rating (Alpha)	0%	0%

Industry Diversification

Durables	9%
Energy	0%
Finance	14%
Industrial	21%
Non-Durables	6%
Retail	6%
Health	0%
Services	13%
Technology	30%
Utilities	0%
Precious Metals	1%
Other	0%

Safety Rating (0-10)	7.5	Sales Load (max.)	6.1%
Up & Down Market Ranks	B – B	Redemption Fee (max.)	None
Annual Expenses (total)	0.89%	Annual 12b-1 Fee	0.25%

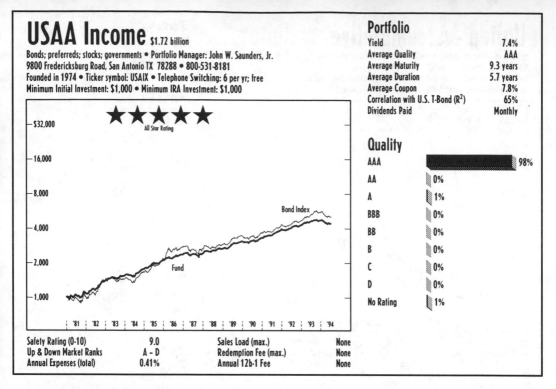

USAA Income $1.72 billion

Bonds; preferreds; stocks; governments • Portfolio Manager: John W. Saunders, Jr.
9800 Fredericksburg Road, San Antonio TX 78288 • 800-531-8181
Founded in 1974 • Ticker symbol: USAIX • Telephone Switching: 6 per yr; free
Minimum Initial Investment: $1,000 • Minimum IRA Investment: $1,000

Portfolio

Yield	7.4%
Average Quality	AAA
Average Maturity	9.3 years
Average Duration	5.7 years
Average Coupon	7.8%
Correlation with U.S. T-Bond (R^2)	65%
Dividends Paid	Monthly

Quality

AAA	98%
AA	0%
A	1%
BBB	0%
BB	0%
B	0%
C	0%
D	0%
No Rating	1%

★★★★★
All Star Rating

Safety Rating (0-10)	9.0	Sales Load (max.)	None
Up & Down Market Ranks	A – D	Redemption Fee (max.)	None
Annual Expenses (total)	0.41%	Annual 12b-1 Fee	None

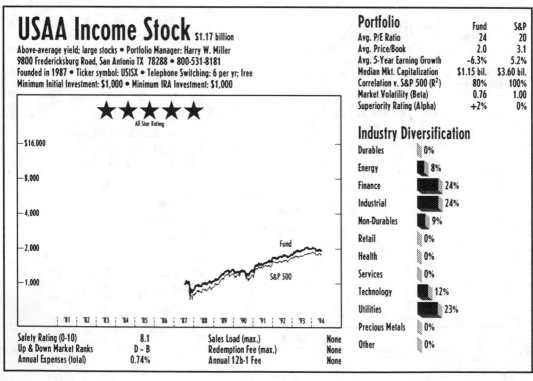

USAA Income Stock $1.17 billion

Above-average yield; large stocks • Portfolio Manager: Harry W. Miller
9800 Fredericksburg Road, San Antonio TX 78288 • 800-531-8181
Founded in 1987 • Ticker symbol: USISX • Telephone Switching: 6 per yr; free
Minimum Initial Investment: $1,000 • Minimum IRA Investment: $1,000

Portfolio

	Fund	S&P
Avg. P/E Ratio	24	20
Avg. Price/Book	2.0	3.1
Avg. 5-Year Earning Growth	-6.3%	5.2%
Median Mkt. Capitalization	$1.15 bil.	$3.60 bil.
Correlation v. S&P 500 (R^2)	80%	100%
Market Volatility (Beta)	0.76	1.00
Superiority Rating (Alpha)	+2%	0%

Industry Diversification

Durables	0%
Energy	8%
Finance	24%
Industrial	24%
Non-Durables	9%
Retail	0%
Health	0%
Services	0%
Technology	12%
Utilities	23%
Precious Metals	0%
Other	0%

★★★★★
All Star Rating

Safety Rating (0-10)	8.1	Sales Load (max.)	None
Up & Down Market Ranks	D – B	Redemption Fee (max.)	None
Annual Expenses (total)	0.74%	Annual 12b-1 Fee	None

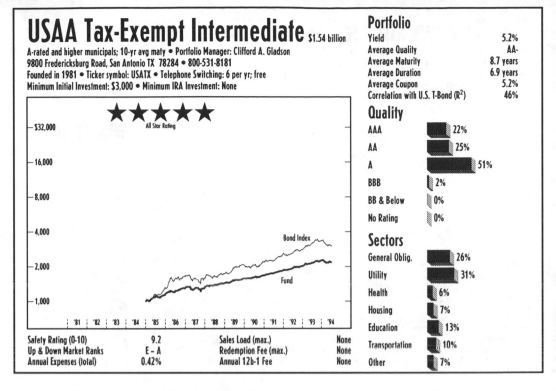

USAA Tax-Exempt Intermediate $1.54 billion

A-rated and higher municipals; 10-yr avg maty • Portfolio Manager: Clifford A. Gladson
9800 Fredericksburg Road, San Antonio TX 78284 • 800-531-8181
Founded in 1981 • Ticker symbol: USATX • Telephone Switching: 6 per yr; free
Minimum Initial Investment: $3,000 • Minimum IRA Investment: None

Portfolio

Yield	5.2%
Average Quality	AA-
Average Maturity	8.7 years
Average Duration	6.9 years
Average Coupon	5.2%
Correlation with U.S. T-Bond (R^2)	46%

Quality

AAA	22%
AA	25%
A	51%
BBB	2%
BB & Below	0%
No Rating	0%

Sectors

General Oblig.	26%
Utility	31%
Health	6%
Housing	7%
Education	13%
Transportation	10%
Other	7%

★★★★★ All Star Rating

Safety Rating (0-10)	9.2	Sales Load (max.)	None
Up & Down Market Ranks	E – A	Redemption Fee (max.)	None
Annual Expenses (total)	0.42%	Annual 12b-1 Fee	None

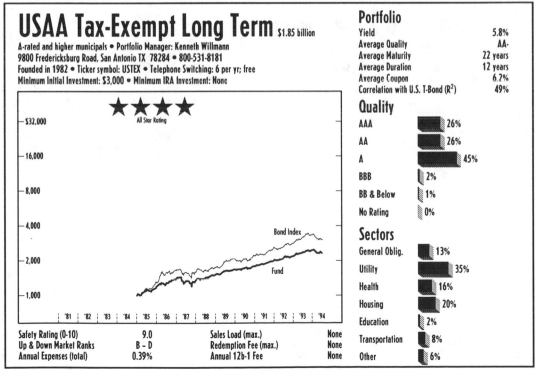

USAA Tax-Exempt Long Term $1.85 billion

A-rated and higher municipals • Portfolio Manager: Kenneth Willmann
9800 Fredericksburg Road, San Antonio TX 78284 • 800-531-8181
Founded in 1982 • Ticker symbol: USTEX • Telephone Switching: 6 per yr; free
Minimum Initial Investment: $3,000 • Minimum IRA Investment: None

Portfolio

Yield	5.8%
Average Quality	AA-
Average Maturity	22 years
Average Duration	12 years
Average Coupon	6.2%
Correlation with U.S. T-Bond (R^2)	49%

Quality

AAA	26%
AA	26%
A	45%
BBB	2%
BB & Below	1%
No Rating	0%

Sectors

General Oblig.	13%
Utility	35%
Health	16%
Housing	20%
Education	2%
Transportation	8%
Other	6%

★★★★ All Star Rating

Safety Rating (0-10)	9.0	Sales Load (max.)	None
Up & Down Market Ranks	B – D	Redemption Fee (max.)	None
Annual Expenses (total)	0.39%	Annual 12b-1 Fee	None

Van Kampen Insured Tax-Fr "A" $1.17 billion

Diversified insured municipals • Portfolio Manager: Joe Piraro
1 Parkview Plaza, Oakbrook Terrace IL 60181 • 800-225-2222
Founded in 1984 • Ticker symbol: VKMTX • Telephone Switching: 2 per month; free
Minimum Initial Investment: $1,000 • Minimum IRA Investment: None

Portfolio

Yield	4.8%
Average Quality	AAA
Average Maturity	19 years
Average Duration	8.3 years
Average Coupon	7.0%
Correlation with U.S. T-Bond (R^2)	44%

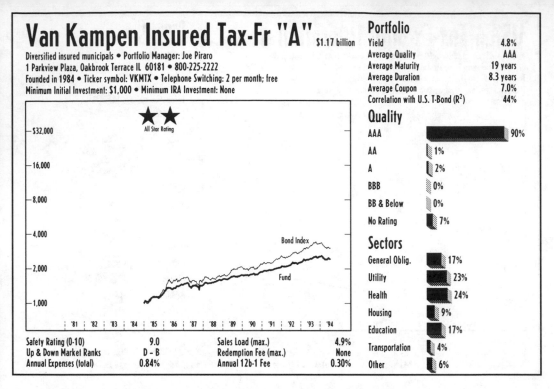

Quality

AAA	90%
AA	1%
A	2%
BBB	0%
BB & Below	0%
No Rating	7%

★★ All Star Rating

Sectors

General Oblig.	17%
Utility	23%
Health	24%
Housing	9%
Education	17%
Transportation	4%
Other	6%

Safety Rating (0-10)	9.0	Sales Load (max.)	4.9%
Up & Down Market Ranks	D – B	Redemption Fee (max.)	None
Annual Expenses (total)	0.84%	Annual 12b-1 Fee	0.30%

Van Kampen U.S. Governmnt "A" $3.27 bil.

U.S. Government securities and agencies • Portfolio Manager: J. Doyle
1 Parkview Plaza, Oakbrook Terrace IL 60181 • 800-225-2222
Founded in 1994 • Ticker symbol: VKMGX • Telephone Switching: 2 per month; free
Minimum Initial Investment: $1,000 • Minimum IRA Investment: $250

Portfolio

Yield	7.5%
Average Quality	AAA
Average Maturity	6.0 years
Average Duration	5.8 years
Average Coupon	10.3%
Correlation with U.S. T-Bond (R^2)	55%
Dividends Paid	Monthly (Accrue Daily)

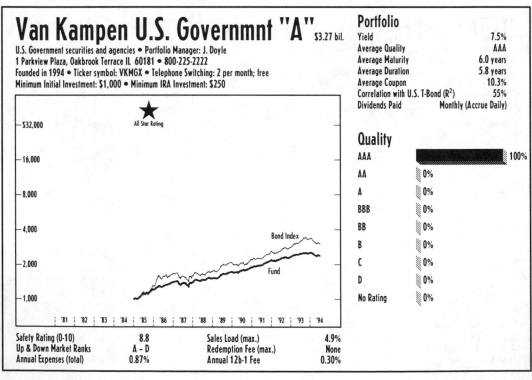

Quality

AAA	100%
AA	0%
A	0%
BBB	0%
BB	0%
B	0%
C	0%
D	0%
No Rating	0%

★ All Star Rating

Safety Rating (0-10)	8.8	Sales Load (max.)	4.9%
Up & Down Market Ranks	A – D	Redemption Fee (max.)	None
Annual Expenses (total)	0.87%	Annual 12b-1 Fee	0.30%

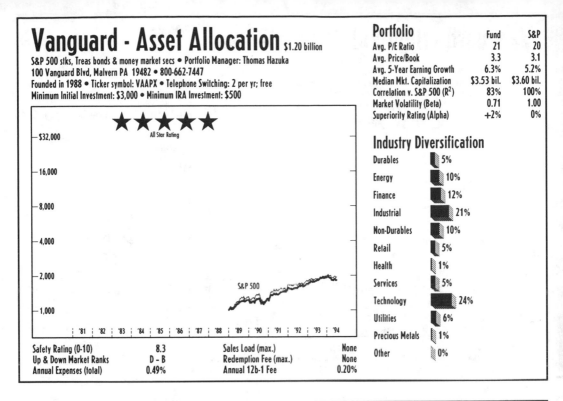

Vanguard - Asset Allocation $1.20 billion

S&P 500 stks, Treas bonds & money market secs • Portfolio Manager: Thomas Hazuka
100 Vanguard Blvd, Malvern PA 19482 • 800-662-7447
Founded in 1988 • Ticker symbol: VAAPX • Telephone Switching: 2 per yr; free
Minimum Initial Investment: $3,000 • Minimum IRA Investment: $500

Portfolio

	Fund	S&P
Avg. P/E Ratio	21	20
Avg. Price/Book	3.3	3.1
Avg. 5-Year Earning Growth	6.3%	5.2%
Median Mkt. Capitalization	$3.53 bil.	$3.60 bil.
Correlation v. S&P 500 (R^2)	83%	100%
Market Volatility (Beta)	0.71	1.00
Superiority Rating (Alpha)	+2%	0%

Industry Diversification

Durables	5%
Energy	10%
Finance	12%
Industrial	21%
Non-Durables	10%
Retail	5%
Health	1%
Services	5%
Technology	24%
Utilities	6%
Precious Metals	1%
Other	0%

Safety Rating (0-10)	8.3	Sales Load (max.)	None
Up & Down Market Ranks	D – B	Redemption Fee (max.)	None
Annual Expenses (total)	0.49%	Annual 12b-1 Fee	0.20%

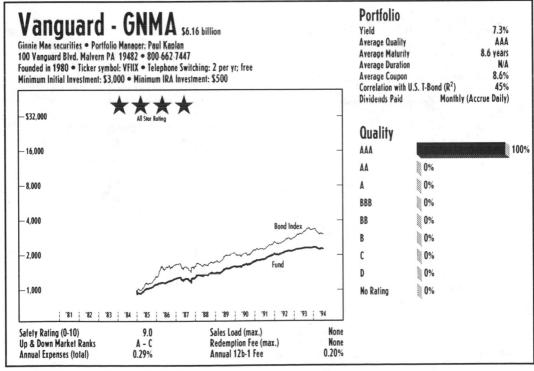

Vanguard - GNMA $6.16 billion

Ginnie Mae securities • Portfolio Manager: Paul Kaplan
100 Vanguard Blvd, Malvern PA 19482 • 800-662-7447
Founded in 1980 • Ticker symbol: VFIIX • Telephone Switching: 2 per yr; free
Minimum Initial Investment: $3,000 • Minimum IRA Investment: $500

Portfolio

Yield	7.3%
Average Quality	AAA
Average Maturity	8.6 years
Average Duration	N/A
Average Coupon	8.6%
Correlation with U.S. T-Bond (R^2)	45%
Dividends Paid	Monthly (Accrue Daily)

Quality

AAA	100%
AA	0%
A	0%
BBB	0%
BB	0%
B	0%
C	0%
D	0%
No Rating	0%

Safety Rating (0-10)	9.0	Sales Load (max.)	None
Up & Down Market Ranks	A – C	Redemption Fee (max.)	None
Annual Expenses (total)	0.29%	Annual 12b-1 Fee	0.20%

Vanguard - High Yld Corporate $2.13 billion

BB average rated corporate bonds • Portfolio Manager: Earl E. McEvoy
100 Vanguard Blvd, Malvern PA 19482 • 800-662-7447
Founded in 1978 • Ticker symbol: VWEHX • Telephone Switching: 2 per yr; free
Minimum Initial Investment: $3,000 • Minimum IRA Investment: $500

Portfolio

Yield	9.9%
Average Quality	BB-
Average Maturity	10 years
Average Duration	5.7 years
Average Coupon	9.8%
Correlation with U.S. T-Bond (R²)	18%
Dividends Paid	Monthly (Accrue Daily)

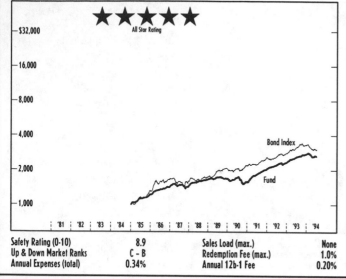

★★★★★
All Star Rating

Quality

AAA	0%
AA	0%
A	0%
BBB	14%
BB	35%
B	51%
C	0%
D	0%
No Rating	0%

Safety Rating (0-10)	8.9	Sales Load (max.)	None
Up & Down Market Ranks	C – B	Redemption Fee (max.)	1.0%
Annual Expenses (total)	0.34%	Annual 12b-1 Fee	0.20%

Vanguard - Index 500 $8.60 billion

Matches S&P 500 Index • Portfolio Manager: George U. Sauter
100 Vanguard Blvd., Malvern PA 19482 • 800-662-7447
Founded in 1976 • Ticker symbol: VFINX • Telephone Switching: Mail only
Minimum Initial Investment: $3,000 • Minimum IRA Investment: $500

Portfolio

	Fund	S&P
Avg. P/E Ratio	20	20
Avg. Price/Book	3.1	3.1
Avg. 5-Year Earning Growth	5.2%	5.2%
Median Mkt. Capitalization	$3.60 bil.	$3.60 bil.
Correlation v. S&P 500 (R²)	98%	100%
Market Volatility (Beta)	0.98	1.00
Superiority Rating (Alpha)	0%	0%

★★★★★
All Star Rating

Industry Diversification

Durables	5%
Energy	10%
Finance	12%
Industrial	21%
Non-Durables	10%
Retail	5%
Health	1%
Services	5%
Technology	24%
Utilities	6%
Precious Metals	1%
Other	0%

Safety Rating (0-10)	7.4	Sales Load (max.)	None
Up & Down Market Ranks	B – D	Redemption Fee (max.)	None
Annual Expenses (total)	0.19%	Annual 12b-1 Fee	0.20%

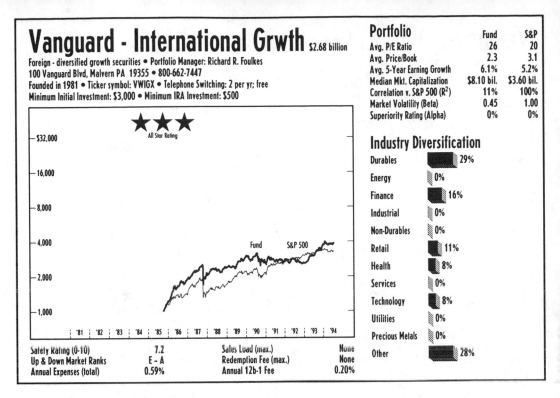

Vanguard - International Grwth $2.68 billion

Foreign - diversified growth securities • Portfolio Manager: Richard R. Foulkes
100 Vanguard Blvd, Malvern PA 19355 • 800-662-7447
Founded in 1981 • Ticker symbol: VWIGX • Telephone Switching: 2 per yr; free
Minimum Initial Investment: $3,000 • Minimum IRA Investment: $500

★★★
All Star Rating

Fund   S&P 500

Portfolio	Fund	S&P
Avg. P/E Ratio	26	20
Avg. Price/Book	2.3	3.1
Avg. 5-Year Earning Growth	6.1%	5.2%
Median Mkt. Capitalization	$8.10 bil.	$3.60 bil.
Correlation v. S&P 500 (R^2)	11%	100%
Market Volatility (Beta)	0.45	1.00
Superiority Rating (Alpha)	0%	0%

Industry Diversification

Durables	29%
Energy	0%
Finance	16%
Industrial	0%
Non-Durables	0%
Retail	11%
Health	8%
Services	0%
Technology	8%
Utilities	0%
Precious Metals	0%
Other	28%

Safety Rating (0-10)	7.2	Sales Load (max.)	None
Up & Down Market Ranks	E - A	Redemption Fee (max.)	None
Annual Expenses (total)	0.59%	Annual 12b-1 Fee	0.20%

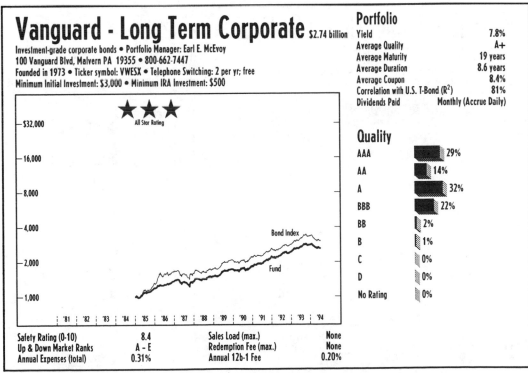

Vanguard - Long Term Corporate $2.74 billion

Investment-grade corporate bonds • Portfolio Manager: Earl E. McEvoy
100 Vanguard Blvd, Malvern PA 19355 • 800-662-7447
Founded in 1973 • Ticker symbol: VWESX • Telephone Switching: 2 per yr; free
Minimum Initial Investment: $3,000 • Minimum IRA Investment: $500

★★★
All Star Rating

Bond Index

Fund

Portfolio

Yield	7.8%
Average Quality	A+
Average Maturity	19 years
Average Duration	8.6 years
Average Coupon	8.4%
Correlation with U.S. T-Bond (R^2)	81%
Dividends Paid	Monthly (Accrue Daily)

Quality

AAA	29%
AA	14%
A	32%
BBB	22%
BB	2%
B	1%
C	0%
D	0%
No Rating	0%

Safety Rating (0-10)	8.4	Sales Load (max.)	None
Up & Down Market Ranks	A - E	Redemption Fee (max.)	None
Annual Expenses (total)	0.31%	Annual 12b-1 Fee	0.20%

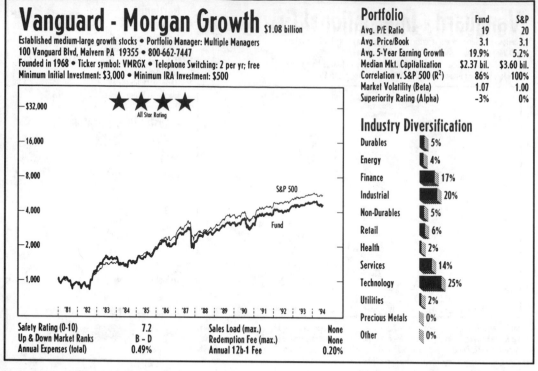

Vanguard - Morgan Growth $1.08 billion

Established medium-large growth stocks • Portfolio Manager: Multiple Managers
100 Vanguard Blvd, Malvern PA 19355 • 800-662-7447
Founded in 1968 • Ticker symbol: VMRGX • Telephone Switching: 2 per yr; free
Minimum Initial Investment: $3,000 • Minimum IRA Investment: $500

★★★★
All Star Rating

Portfolio	Fund	S&P
Avg. P/E Ratio	19	20
Avg. Price/Book	3.1	3.1
Avg. 5-Year Earning Growth	19.9%	5.2%
Median Mkt. Capitalization	$2.37 bil.	$3.60 bil.
Correlation v. S&P 500 (R^2)	86%	100%
Market Volatility (Beta)	1.07	1.00
Superiority Rating (Alpha)	-3%	0%

Industry Diversification

Durables	5%
Energy	4%
Finance	17%
Industrial	20%
Non-Durables	5%
Retail	6%
Health	2%
Services	14%
Technology	25%
Utilities	2%
Precious Metals	0%
Other	0%

Safety Rating (0-10)	7.2	Sales Load (max.)	None
Up & Down Market Ranks	B – D	Redemption Fee (max.)	None
Annual Expenses (total)	0.49%	Annual 12b-1 Fee	0.20%

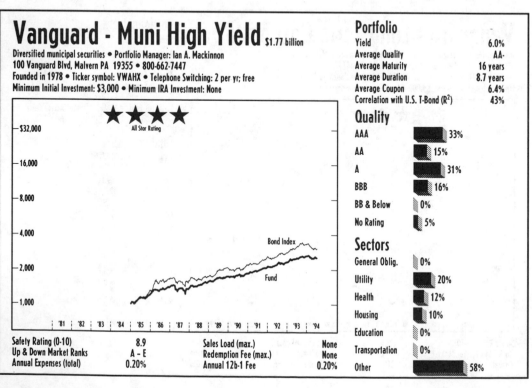

Vanguard - Muni High Yield $1.77 billion

Diversified municipal securities • Portfolio Manager: Ian A. Mackinnon
100 Vanguard Blvd, Malvern PA 19355 • 800-662-7447
Founded in 1978 • Ticker symbol: VWAHX • Telephone Switching: 2 per yr; free
Minimum Initial Investment: $3,000 • Minimum IRA Investment: None

★★★★
All Star Rating

Portfolio	
Yield	6.0%
Average Quality	AA-
Average Maturity	16 years
Average Duration	8.7 years
Average Coupon	6.4%
Correlation with U.S. T-Bond (R^2)	43%

Quality

AAA	33%
AA	15%
A	31%
BBB	16%
BB & Below	0%
No Rating	5%

Sectors

General Oblig.	0%
Utility	20%
Health	12%
Housing	10%
Education	0%
Transportation	0%
Other	58%

Safety Rating (0-10)	8.9	Sales Load (max.)	None
Up & Down Market Ranks	A – E	Redemption Fee (max.)	None
Annual Expenses (total)	0.20%	Annual 12b-1 Fee	0.20%

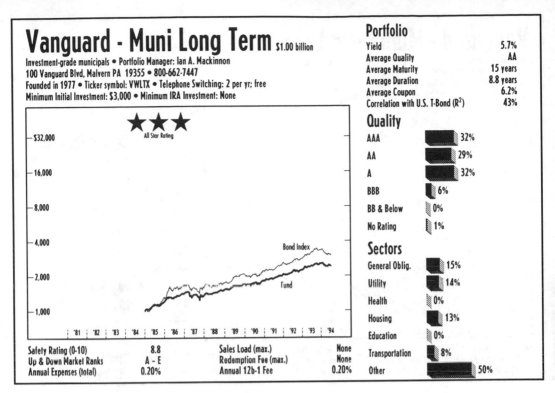

Vanguard - Muni Long Term $1.00 billion

Investment-grade municipals • Portfolio Manager: Ian A. Mackinnon
100 Vanguard Blvd, Malvern PA 19355 • 800-662-7447
Founded in 1977 • Ticker symbol: VWLTX • Telephone Switching: 2 per yr; free
Minimum Initial Investment: $3,000 • Minimum IRA Investment: None

Portfolio

Yield	5.7%
Average Quality	AA
Average Maturity	15 years
Average Duration	8.8 years
Average Coupon	6.2%
Correlation with U.S. T-Bond (R²)	43%

Quality

AAA	32%
AA	29%
A	32%
BBB	6%
BB & Below	0%
No Rating	1%

Sectors

General Oblig.	15%
Utility	14%
Health	0%
Housing	13%
Education	0%
Transportation	8%
Other	50%

★★★ All Star Rating

Safety Rating (0-10)	8.8	Sales Load (max.)	None
Up & Down Market Ranks	A - E	Redemption Fee (max.)	None
Annual Expenses (total)	0.20%	Annual 12b-1 Fee	0.20%

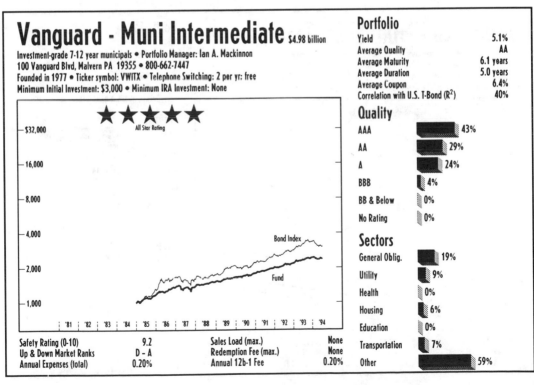

Vanguard - Muni Intermediate $4.98 billion

Investment-grade 7-12 year municipals • Portfolio Manager: Ian A. Mackinnon
100 Vanguard Blvd, Malvern PA 19355 • 800-662-7447
Founded in 1977 • Ticker symbol: VWITX • Telephone Switching: 2 per yr; free
Minimum Initial Investment: $3,000 • Minimum IRA Investment: None

Portfolio

Yield	5.1%
Average Quality	AA
Average Maturity	6.1 years
Average Duration	5.0 years
Average Coupon	6.4%
Correlation with U.S. T-Bond (R²)	40%

Quality

AAA	43%
AA	29%
A	24%
BBB	4%
BB & Below	0%
No Rating	0%

Sectors

General Oblig.	19%
Utility	9%
Health	0%
Housing	6%
Education	0%
Transportation	7%
Other	59%

★★★★★ All Star Rating

Safety Rating (0-10)	9.2	Sales Load (max.)	None
Up & Down Market Ranks	D - A	Redemption Fee (max.)	None
Annual Expenses (total)	0.20%	Annual 12b-1 Fee	0.20%

Vanguard - Muni Insrd Long Trm $1.94 billion

Investment-grade insured municipals • Portfolio Manager: Ian A. Mackinnon
100 Vanguard Blvd, Malvern PA 19355 • 800-662-7447
Founded in 1984 • Ticker symbol: VILPX • Telephone Switching: 2 per yr; free
Minimum Initial Investment: $3,000 • Minimum IRA Investment: None

Portfolio

Yield	5.6%
Average Quality	AAA
Average Maturity	13 years
Average Duration	8.3 years
Average Coupon	6.4%
Correlation with U.S. T-Bond (R^2)	47%

Quality

AAA	95%
AA	5%
A	0%
BBB	0%
BB & Below	0%
No Rating	0%

Sectors

General Oblig.	8%
Utility	32%
Health	12%
Housing	0%
Education	0%
Transportation	10%
Other	38%

★★★ All Star Rating

Safety Rating (0-10)	8.8	Sales Load (max.)	None
Up & Down Market Ranks	A – D	Redemption Fee (max.)	None
Annual Expenses (total)	0.20%	Annual 12b-1 Fee	0.20%

Vanguard - Muni Short Term $1.52 billion

Investment-grade 1-4 year municipals • Portfolio Manager: Ian A. Mackinnon
100 Vanguard Blvd, Malvern PA 19355 • 800-662-7447
Founded in 1977 • Ticker symbol: VWSTX • Telephone Switching: 2 per yr; free
Minimum Initial Investment: $3,000 • Minimum IRA Investment: None

Portfolio

Yield	3.5%
Average Quality	AAA-
Average Maturity	1.2 years
Average Duration	1.1 years
Average Coupon	6.5%
Correlation with U.S. T-Bond (R^2)	15%

Quality

AAA	70%
AA	14%
A	14%
BBB	2%
BB & Below	0%
No Rating	0%

Sectors

General Oblig.	20%
Utility	0%
Health	0%
Housing	3%
Education	0%
Transportation	0%
Other	77%

★★★★ All Star Rating

Safety Rating (0-10)	9.6	Sales Load (max.)	None
Up & Down Market Ranks	E – A	Redemption Fee (max.)	None
Annual Expenses (total)	0.20%	Annual 12b-1 Fee	0.20%

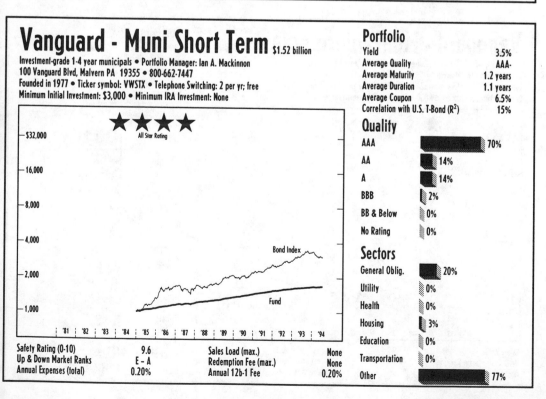

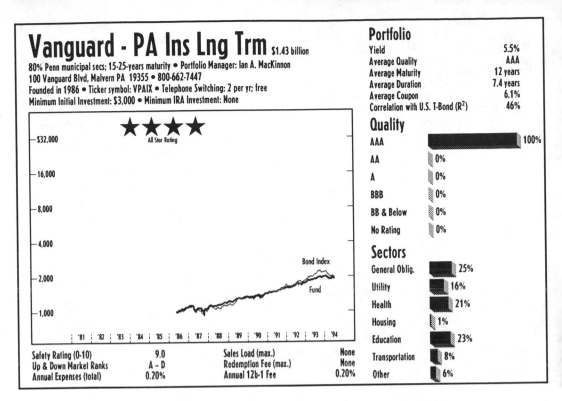

Vanguard - PA Ins Lng Trm $1.43 billion

80% Penn municipal secs; 15-25-years maturity • Portfolio Manager: Ian A. MacKinnon
100 Vanguard Blvd, Malvern PA 19355 • 800-662-7447
Founded in 1986 • Ticker symbol: VPAIX • Telephone Switching: 2 per yr; free
Minimum Initial Investment: $3,000 • Minimum IRA Investment: None

★★★★
All Star Rating

Bond Index

Fund

Safety Rating (0-10)	9.0	Sales Load (max.)	None
Up & Down Market Ranks	A – D	Redemption Fee (max.)	None
Annual Expenses (total)	0.20%	Annual 12b-1 Fee	0.20%

Portfolio
Yield	5.5%
Average Quality	AAA
Average Maturity	12 years
Average Duration	7.4 years
Average Coupon	6.1%
Correlation with U.S. T-Bond (R^2)	46%

Quality
AAA	100%
AA	0%
A	0%
BBB	0%
BB & Below	0%
No Rating	0%

Sectors
General Oblig.	25%
Utility	16%
Health	21%
Housing	1%
Education	23%
Transportation	8%
Other	6%

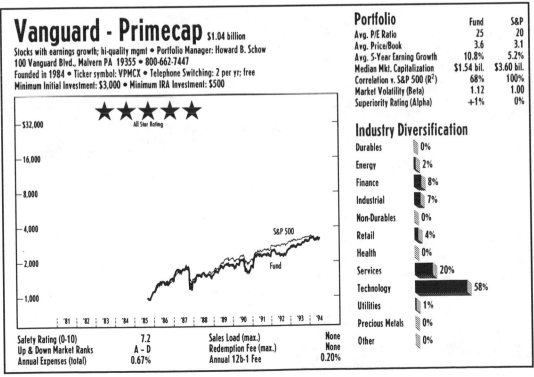

Vanguard - Primecap $1.04 billion

Stocks with earnings growth; hi-quality mgmt • Portfolio Manager: Howard B. Schow
100 Vanguard Blvd., Malvern PA 19355 • 800-662-7447
Founded in 1984 • Ticker symbol: VPMCX • Telephone Switching: 2 per yr; free
Minimum Initial Investment: $3,000 • Minimum IRA Investment: $500

★★★★★
All Star Rating

S&P 500

Fund

Safety Rating (0-10)	7.2	Sales Load (max.)	None
Up & Down Market Ranks	A – D	Redemption Fee (max.)	None
Annual Expenses (total)	0.67%	Annual 12b-1 Fee	0.20%

Portfolio
	Fund	S&P
Avg. P/E Ratio	25	20
Avg. Price/Book	3.6	3.1
Avg. 5-Year Earning Growth	10.8%	5.2%
Median Mkt. Capitalization	$1.54 bil.	$3.60 bil.
Correlation v. S&P 500 (R^2)	68%	100%
Market Volatility (Beta)	1.12	1.00
Superiority Rating (Alpha)	+1%	0%

Industry Diversification
Durables	0%
Energy	2%
Finance	8%
Industrial	7%
Non-Durables	0%
Retail	4%
Health	0%
Services	20%
Technology	58%
Utilities	1%
Precious Metals	0%
Other	0%

Vanguard - Short Term Corp $3.35 billion

BBB-rated and higher 1-3 year corporates • Portfolio Manager: Ian A. Mackinnon
100 Vanguard Blvd, Malvern PA 19355 • 800-662-7447
Founded in 1982 • Ticker symbol: VFSTX • Telephone Switching: 2 per yr; free
Minimum Initial Investment: $3,000 • Minimum IRA Investment: $500

Portfolio

Yield	6.3%
Average Quality	A+
Average Maturity	2.2 years
Average Duration	2.0 years
Average Coupon	6.7%
Correlation with U.S. T-Bond (R^2)	43%
Dividends Paid	Monthly (Accrue Daily)

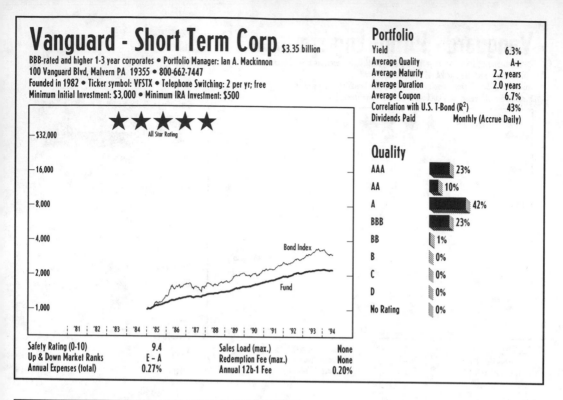

Quality

AAA	23%
AA	10%
A	42%
BBB	23%
BB	1%
B	0%
C	0%
D	0%
No Rating	0%

Safety Rating (0-10)	9.4	Sales Load (max.)	None
Up & Down Market Ranks	E – A	Redemption Fee (max.)	None
Annual Expenses (total)	0.27%	Annual 12b-1 Fee	0.20%

Vanguard - Short Term Federal $1.69 billion

U.S. Government and agency secs, 1-3yr maty • Portfolio Manager: Ian A. MacKinnon
100 Vanguard Blvd, Malvern PA 19355 • 800-662-7447
Founded in 1987 • Ticker symbol: VSGBX • Telephone Switching: 2 per yr; free
Minimum Initial Investment: $3,000 • Minimum IRA Investment: $500

Portfolio

Yield	6.0%
Average Quality	AAA
Average Maturity	2.2 years
Average Duration	2.0 years
Average Coupon	6.9%
Correlation with U.S. T-Bond (R^2)	47%
Dividends Paid	Monthly (Accrue Daily)

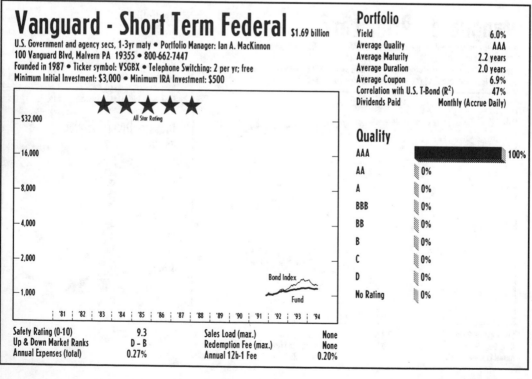

Quality

AAA	100%
AA	0%
A	0%
BBB	0%
BB	0%
B	0%
C	0%
D	0%
No Rating	0%

Safety Rating (0-10)	9.3	Sales Load (max.)	None
Up & Down Market Ranks	D – B	Redemption Fee (max.)	None
Annual Expenses (total)	0.27%	Annual 12b-1 Fee	0.20%

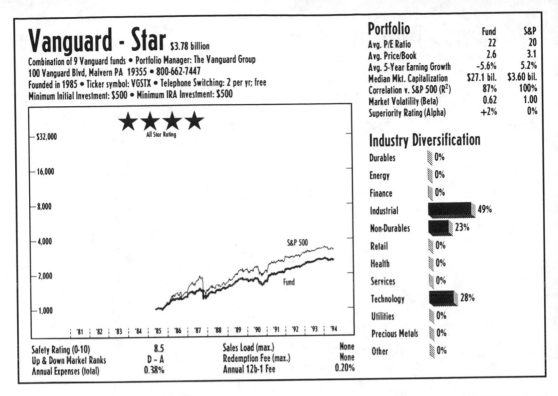

Vanguard - Star $3.78 billion

Combination of 9 Vanguard funds • Portfolio Manager: The Vanguard Group
100 Vanguard Blvd, Malvern PA 19355 • 800-662-7447
Founded in 1985 • Ticker symbol: VGSTX • Telephone Switching: 2 per yr; free
Minimum Initial Investment: $500 • Minimum IRA Investment: $500

★★★★
All Star Rating

Portfolio	Fund	S&P
Avg. P/E Ratio	22	20
Avg. Price/Book	2.6	3.1
Avg. 5-Year Earning Growth	-5.6%	5.2%
Median Mkt. Capitalization	$27.1 bil.	$3.60 bil.
Correlation v. S&P 500 (R^2)	87%	100%
Market Volatility (Beta)	0.62	1.00
Superiority Rating (Alpha)	+2%	0%

Industry Diversification

Durables	0%
Energy	0%
Finance	0%
Industrial	49%
Non-Durables	23%
Retail	0%
Health	0%
Services	0%
Technology	28%
Utilities	0%
Precious Metals	0%
Other	0%

Safety Rating (0-10)	8.5	Sales Load (max.)	None
Up & Down Market Ranks	D – A	Redemption Fee (max.)	None
Annual Expenses (total)	0.38%	Annual 12b-1 Fee	0.20%

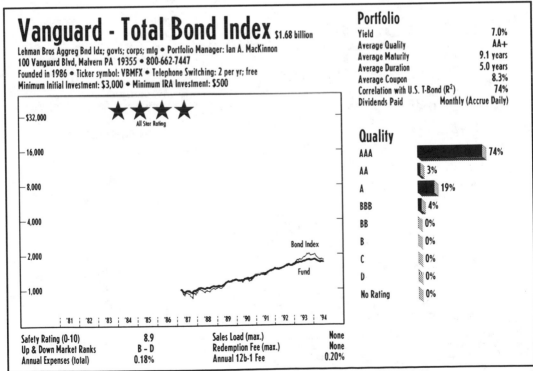

Vanguard - Total Bond Index $1.68 billion

Lehman Bros Aggreg Bnd Idx; govts; corps; mtg • Portfolio Manager: Ian A. MacKinnon
100 Vanguard Blvd, Malvern PA 19355 • 800-662-7447
Founded in 1986 • Ticker symbol: VBMFX • Telephone Switching: 2 per yr; free
Minimum Initial Investment: $3,000 • Minimum IRA Investment: $500

★★★★
All Star Rating

Portfolio

Yield	7.0%
Average Quality	AA+
Average Maturity	9.1 years
Average Duration	5.0 years
Average Coupon	8.3%
Correlation with U.S. T-Bond (R^2)	74%
Dividends Paid	Monthly (Accrue Daily)

Quality

AAA	74%
AA	3%
A	19%
BBB	4%
BB	0%
B	0%
C	0%
D	0%
No Rating	0%

Safety Rating (0-10)	8.9	Sales Load (max.)	None
Up & Down Market Ranks	B – D	Redemption Fee (max.)	None
Annual Expenses (total)	0.18%	Annual 12b-1 Fee	0.20%

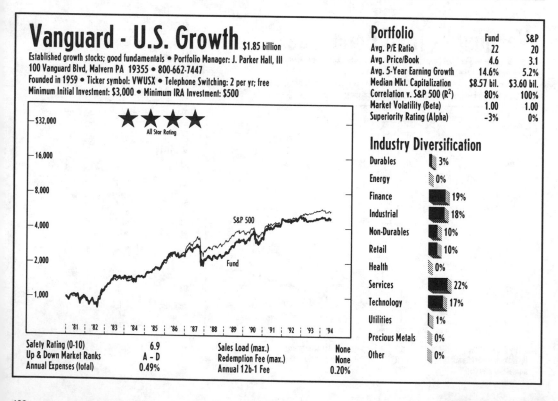

Vanguard - Trustees Eqty Intl $1.10 billion

Foreign - undervalued stocks • Portfolio Manager: Jarrod Wilcox
100 Vanguard Blvd, Malvern PA 19355 • 800-662-7447
Founded in 1983 • Ticker symbol: VTRIX • Telephone Switching: 2 per yr; free
Minimum Initial Investment: $10,000 • Minimum IRA Investment: $500

Portfolio

	Fund	S&P
Avg. P/E Ratio	27	20
Avg. Price/Book	1.8	3.1
Avg. 5-Year Earning Growth	1.0%	5.2%
Median Mkt. Capitalization	$871 mil.	$3.60 bil.
Correlation v. S&P 500 (R^2)	11%	100%
Market Volatility (Beta)	0.40	1.00
Superiority Rating (Alpha)	-1%	0%

★★ All Star Rating

$32,000
16,000
8,000
4,000
2,000
1,000

S&P 500
Fund

'81 '82 '83 '84 '85 '86 '87 '88 '89 '90 '91 '92 '93 '94

Industry Diversification

Durables	5%
Energy	30%
Finance	0%
Industrial	22%
Non-Durables	0%
Retail	0%
Health	0%
Services	12%
Technology	11%
Utilities	0%
Precious Metals	20%
Other	0%

Safety Rating (0-10)	7.5	Sales Load (max.)	None
Up & Down Market Ranks	E - A	Redemption Fee (max.)	None
Annual Expenses (total)	0.40%	Annual 12b-1 Fee	0.20%

Vanguard - U.S. Growth $1.85 billion

Established growth stocks; good fundamentals • Portfolio Manager: J. Parker Hall, III
100 Vanguard Blvd, Malvern PA 19355 • 800-662-7447
Founded in 1959 • Ticker symbol: VWUSX • Telephone Switching: 2 per yr; free
Minimum Initial Investment: $3,000 • Minimum IRA Investment: $500

Portfolio

	Fund	S&P
Avg. P/E Ratio	22	20
Avg. Price/Book	4.6	3.1
Avg. 5-Year Earning Growth	14.6%	5.2%
Median Mkt. Capitalization	$8.57 bil.	$3.60 bil.
Correlation v. S&P 500 (R^2)	80%	100%
Market Volatility (Beta)	1.00	1.00
Superiority Rating (Alpha)	-3%	0%

★★★★ All Star Rating

$32,000
16,000
8,000
4,000
2,000
1,000

S&P 500
Fund

'81 '82 '83 '84 '85 '86 '87 '88 '89 '90 '91 '92 '93 '94

Industry Diversification

Durables	3%
Energy	0%
Finance	19%
Industrial	18%
Non-Durables	10%
Retail	10%
Health	0%
Services	22%
Technology	17%
Utilities	1%
Precious Metals	0%
Other	0%

Safety Rating (0-10)	6.9	Sales Load (max.)	None
Up & Down Market Ranks	A - D	Redemption Fee (max.)	None
Annual Expenses (total)	0.49%	Annual 12b-1 Fee	0.20%

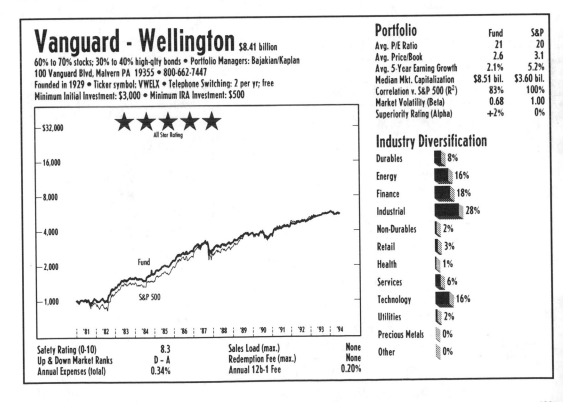

Vanguard - Wellesley Income $6.09 billion

Qlty stks w-above avg div yld; qlty corp & gvt • Portfolio Managers: Ryan/McEvoy
100 Vanguard Blvd, Malvern PA 19355 • 800-662-7447
Founded in 1970 • Ticker symbol: VWINX • Telephone Switching: 2 per yr; free
Minimum Initial Investment: $3,000 • Minimum IRA Investment: $500

★★★★★
All Star Rating

Portfolio	Fund	S&P
Avg. P/E Ratio	23	20
Avg. Price/Book	2.2	3.1
Avg. 5-Year Earning Growth	1.2%	5.2%
Median Mkt. Capitalization	$4.22 bil.	$3.60 bil.
Correlation v. S&P 500 (R^2)	55%	100%
Market Volatility (Beta)	0.43	1.00
Superiority Rating (Alpha)	+5%	0%

Industry Diversification

Durables	5%
Energy	18%
Finance	28%
Industrial	15%
Non-Durables	2%
Retail	0%
Health	0%
Services	0%
Technology	10%
Utilities	22%
Precious Metals	0%
Other	0%

Safety Rating (0-10)	8.9	Sales Load (max.)	None
Up & Down Market Ranks	E – A	Redemption Fee (max.)	None
Annual Expenses (total)	0.33%	Annual 12b-1 Fee	0.20%

Vanguard - Wellington $8.41 billion

60% to 70% stocks; 30% to 40% high-qlty bonds • Portfolio Managers: Bajakian/Kaplan
100 Vanguard Blvd, Malvern PA 19355 • 800-662-7447
Founded in 1929 • Ticker symbol: VWELX • Telephone Switching: 2 per yr; free
Minimum Initial Investment: $3,000 • Minimum IRA Investment: $500

★★★★★
All Star Rating

Portfolio	Fund	S&P
Avg. P/E Ratio	21	20
Avg. Price/Book	2.6	3.1
Avg. 5-Year Earning Growth	2.1%	5.2%
Median Mkt. Capitalization	$8.51 bil.	$3.60 bil.
Correlation v. S&P 500 (R^2)	83%	100%
Market Volatility (Beta)	0.68	1.00
Superiority Rating (Alpha)	+2%	0%

Industry Diversification

Durables	8%
Energy	16%
Finance	18%
Industrial	28%
Non-Durables	2%
Retail	3%
Health	1%
Services	6%
Technology	16%
Utilities	2%
Precious Metals	0%
Other	0%

Safety Rating (0-10)	8.3	Sales Load (max.)	None
Up & Down Market Ranks	D – A	Redemption Fee (max.)	None
Annual Expenses (total)	0.34%	Annual 12b-1 Fee	0.20%

Vanguard - Windsor $11.0 billion

Undervalued stocks • Portfolio Manager: John C. Neff
100 Vanguard Blvd, Malvern PA 19355 • 800-662-7447
Founded in 1958 • Ticker symbol: VWNDX • Telephone Switching: 2 per yr; free
This fund is currently not accepting new accounts.

Portfolio

	Fund	S&P
Avg. P/E Ratio	32	20
Avg. Price/Book	1.7	3.1
Avg. 5-Year Earning Growth	-4.6%	5.2%
Median Mkt. Capitalization	$2.34 bil.	$3.60 bil.
Correlation v. S&P 500 (R^2)	67%	100%
Market Volatility (Beta)	0.91	1.00
Superiority Rating (Alpha)	+3%	0%

★★★★★ All Star Rating

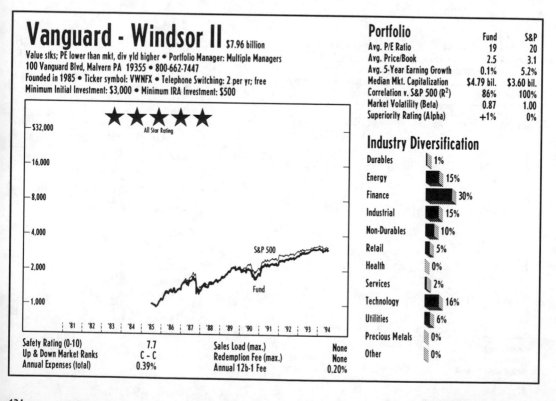

Industry Diversification

Durables	1%
Energy	22%
Finance	45%
Industrial	14%
Non-Durables	2%
Retail	0%
Health	0%
Services	4%
Technology	6%
Utilities	6%
Precious Metals	0%
Other	0%

Safety Rating (0-10)	7.4	Sales Load (max.)	None
Up & Down Market Ranks	B – C	Redemption Fee (max.)	None
Annual Expenses (total)	0.40%	Annual 12b-1 Fee	0.20%

Vanguard - Windsor II $7.96 billion

Value stks; PE lower than mkt, div yld higher • Portfolio Manager: Multiple Managers
100 Vanguard Blvd, Malvern PA 19355 • 800-662-7447
Founded in 1985 • Ticker symbol: VWNFX • Telephone Switching: 2 per yr; free
Minimum Initial Investment: $3,000 • Minimum IRA Investment: $500

Portfolio

	Fund	S&P
Avg. P/E Ratio	19	20
Avg. Price/Book	2.5	3.1
Avg. 5-Year Earning Growth	0.1%	5.2%
Median Mkt. Capitalization	$4.79 bil.	$3.60 bil.
Correlation v. S&P 500 (R^2)	86%	100%
Market Volatility (Beta)	0.87	1.00
Superiority Rating (Alpha)	+1%	0%

★★★★★ All Star Rating

Industry Diversification

Durables	1%
Energy	15%
Finance	30%
Industrial	15%
Non-Durables	10%
Retail	5%
Health	0%
Services	2%
Technology	16%
Utilities	6%
Precious Metals	0%
Other	0%

Safety Rating (0-10)	7.7	Sales Load (max.)	None
Up & Down Market Ranks	C – C	Redemption Fee (max.)	None
Annual Expenses (total)	0.39%	Annual 12b-1 Fee	0.20%

Venture - New York Venture $1.07 billion

Diversified stocks • Portfolio Manager: Shelby M. C. David
124 E. Marcy Street, Santa Fe NM 87504 • 800-279-0279
Founded in 1969 • Ticker symbol: NYVTX • Telephone Switching: 3 per yr; $5
Minimum Initial Investment: $1,000 • Minimum IRA Investment: $250

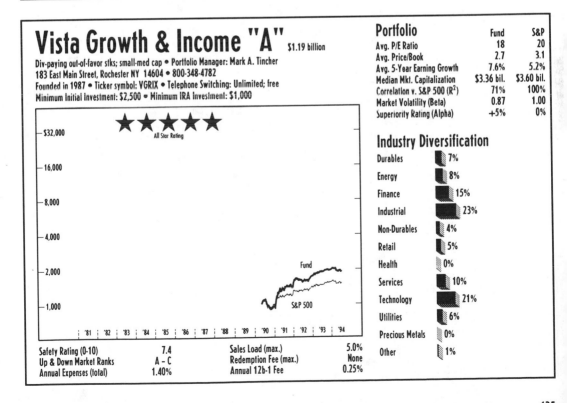

★★★★★
All Star Rating

Portfolio	Fund	S&P
Avg. P/E Ratio	18	20
Avg. Price/Book	3.1	3.1
Avg. 5-Year Earning Growth	20.2%	5.2%
Median Mkt. Capitalization	$64.6 mil.	$3.60 bil.
Correlation v. S&P 500 (R^2)	75%	100%
Market Volatility (Beta)	1.04	1.00
Superiority Rating (Alpha)	+2%	0%

Industry Diversification

Durables	4%
Energy	6%
Finance	37%
Industrial	6%
Non-Durables	0%
Retail	2%
Health	5%
Services	3%
Technology	7%
Utilities	0%
Precious Metals	0%
Other	30%

Safety Rating (0-10)	7.4	Sales Load (max.)	5.0%
Up & Down Market Ranks	A – C	Redemption Fee (max.)	None
Annual Expenses (total)	0.89%	Annual 12b-1 Fee	0.25%

Vista Growth & Income "A" $1.19 billion

Div-paying out-of-favor stks; small-med cap • Portfolio Manager: Mark A. Tincher
183 East Main Street, Rochester NY 14604 • 800-348-4782
Founded in 1987 • Ticker symbol: VGRIX • Telephone Switching: Unlimited; free
Minimum Initial Investment: $2,500 • Minimum IRA Investment: $1,000

★★★★★
All Star Rating

Portfolio	Fund	S&P
Avg. P/E Ratio	18	20
Avg. Price/Book	2.7	3.1
Avg. 5-Year Earning Growth	7.6%	5.2%
Median Mkt. Capitalization	$3.36 bil.	$3.60 bil.
Correlation v. S&P 500 (R^2)	71%	100%
Market Volatility (Beta)	0.87	1.00
Superiority Rating (Alpha)	+5%	0%

Industry Diversification

Durables	7%
Energy	8%
Finance	15%
Industrial	23%
Non-Durables	4%
Retail	5%
Health	0%
Services	10%
Technology	21%
Utilities	6%
Precious Metals	0%
Other	1%

Safety Rating (0-10)	7.4	Sales Load (max.)	5.0%
Up & Down Market Ranks	A – C	Redemption Fee (max.)	None
Annual Expenses (total)	1.40%	Annual 12b-1 Fee	0.25%

All-Star Ratings On Over 2,000 Funds

Five Star Funds
★★★★★

AARP Growth and Income
ABT - Emerging Growth
Acorn Fund
Adams Express (ADX)
Aim - Adjust Rate Govt
Aim - Aggressive Growth
Aim - Constellation
Aim - High Yield "A"
Aim - Tax-Free Intermed
Aim - Value "A"
Alger Growth
Alger Small Capitalizaton
Alliance Growth "B"
American - Bond Fd Amer
American - Fundamentl Inv
American - High Income Tr
American - New Economy
American AAdvantage Institut
American AAdvantage Mileage
American Cap Emrg Gth "A"
American Cap Hi Yield "B"
American Cap TX Muni "A"
Babson Enterprise
Babson Enterprise II
Babson UMB Bond
Babson Value
Bartlett Fixed Income
Benham Cal Tx-Fr Intermed
Berger - One Hundred
Berger - One Hundred One
Bergstrom Capital (BEM)
Bernstein CA Muni Intmed

Bernstein Diversif Muni
Bernstein Intermed Duratn
Bernstein N.Y. Muni Inter
Bernstein Short Dur Plus
Berwyn
Brandywine
Calvert Tax-Free
Castle Convertible (CVF)
Central Securities (CET)
CG Cap Mkts Mtg Backed
CGM Capital Development
CGM Mutual
Clipper
Columbia Balanced
Columbia Growth
Columbia Municipal Bond
Columbia Special
Compass Capitl Equity Icm
Connecticut Mut - Growth
Convert Holdngs Inc(CNVT)
CoreFund Inter Bond "A"
Cowen Standby Reserve
Couns Tandem Cap Shr(CTF)
Delaware Tx-Fr Penn "A"
Delaware Tax-Free USA "A"
Delaware Trend
Delaware Value
Dimensional - Fixed Incme
Dimensional - U.S. Small
Dodge & Cox Balanced
Dodge & Cox Stock
Dreyfus Basic Money Market

Dreyfus Florida Intr Muni
Dreyfus GNMA
Dreyfus Inter Muni Bond
Dreyfus Mass Tax-Exempt
Dreyfus Municipal Bond
Dreyfus New Leaders
Dreyfus Short-Inter Govt
Dreyfus US Treas Sht Trm
Eaton Van Mar - NJ Ltd
Eaton Van Trad - Icm Dost
EBI Income
Eclipse Equity
Ellswrth Cnv Gth&Inc(ECF)
Evergreen Limited Market
Evergreen Money Market
Evergreen Shrt-Inter Muni
Evergreen Value Timing
Feder Income Trust Inst
Feder Short-Intr Gvt Inst
Fidel Inst - Eqty Pt Grth
Fidel Inst - Eqty Ptf Icm
Fidel Adv Grwth Oppor "A"
Fidel Adv High Yield "A"
Fidel Adv Icm & Grth "A"
Fidel Adv Sht Fxd Icm "A"
Fidelity Aggressive Tx-Fr
Fidelity Asset Manager
Fidelity Asset Mgr. Growth
Fidelity Balanced
Fidelity Blue Chip Growth
Fidelity Capital & Income
Fidelity Capital Apprec

Fidelity Cash Reserves
Fidelity Contrafund
Fidelity Convertible Sec
Fidelity Destiny I (cont)
Fidelity Destiny II(cont)
Fidelity Disciplined Eqty
Fidelity Domestic Money Mkt
Fidelity Equity-Income
Fidelity Equity-Income II
Fidelity Fund
Fidelity Growth & Income
Fidelity Growth Company
Fidelity Intermediate Bnd
Fidelity Limitd Term Muni
Fidelity Low-Priced Stock
Fidelity Magellan
Fidelity Mass Tax-Free
Fidelity Mortgage Secur
Fidelity OTC
Fidelity Puritan
Fidelity Retirement Grwth
Fidelity Short Inter Govt
Fidelity Short Term Bond
Fidel Spartan High Income
Fidel Spartan Ltd Maturty
Fidelity Spartan Money Mkt
Fidelity Stock Selector
Fidelity Strategic Oppor
Fidelity Tax-Exempt
Fidelity Trend
Fidelity Value
First Investors Spec Sit

Flex-Funds Muirfield
Fortis Special Stk Portf
Fortress Govt Income Secs
Founders Balanced
Founders Blue Chip
Founders Discovery
Founders Frontier
Founders Growth
Founders Special
FPA - Capital
FPA - Paramount
Franklin AL Tax-Free Icm
Franklin Convertible Secs
Franklin Federal Tax-Free
Franklin High Yld Tx-Free
Franklin Insured Tax-Free
Franklin LA Tax-Free Icm
Franklin Mich Insrd Tx-Ex
Franklin Multi Incm (FMI)
Franklin NY Tax-Free Icm
Franklin VA Tx-Fr Icm
Fundtrust Income
Gabelli Asset
Gabelli Equity Income
Gabelli Growth
Gabelli Small Cap Growth
Gabelli Value
Galaxy Short Term Bond
Galaxy Small Company Eqty
Gemini II - Income (GMIP)
General Amer Invstrs(GAM)
GE S&S Progress
General Securities
Goldman Sachs Capitl Grth
Goldman Sachs Inst Adj Gv
Gradison-McDon Estab Valu
Gradison-McDon Oppt Value
Greenspring
GT Global Amer Grth "A"
Guardian Park Avenue
Guardian Stock
Harbor - Capital Apprec
Harbor - Short Duration
Heartland Value
Heritage Diversified Incm
IAI - Regional
IAI - Value
Idex II Income Plus "A"
IDS Managed Retirement
IDS New Dimensions
IDS Stock
Institutional FedFund
Institutional Liq.Ast.Prime Oblg.
Institutional Muni-Fund
Institutional T-Fund
Institutional TempFund

Invesco - Dynamics
Invesco - Emerg Growth
Invesco - High Yield
Invesco - Industrial Incm
Invesco - Intermed Govt
Janus
Janus Twenty
Janus Venture
John Han Freed Rgl Bk "B"
John Han Sovergn Bond "A"
John Hancock Spl Eqtys"A"
Kaufmann
Kemper "A" - High Yield
Kemper "A" - Muni Bond
Kemper "A" - NY Tax-Free
Keystone Am Omega "A"
Laurel Mgd Income Invstr
Laurel Spcl Growth Invstr
Laurel Tax-Fr Bond Invstr
Laurel Trust Intermed Icm
Legg Mason MD Tax-Fr Icme
Legg Mason PA Tax-Fr Icme
Legg Mason Special Invest
Legg Mason U.S. Gvt Inter
Liberty Equity Income "A"
Liberty High Income "A"
Lindner Dividend
Lord, Abbett Bond Debent
Lutheran Brother High Yld
Lutheran Brotherhood Muni
MainStay - Capital Apprec
MainStay - Convertible
MainStay - Corp Bond
MainStay - Value
Managers Short Inter Bond
Managers Special Equity
Mariner Cash
Mariner Government
MAS Small Cap Value
MAS Value
Merr Lynch Government
Merr Lynch Gr Inv&Ret "B"
Merr Lynch Hi Income "A"
Merr Lynch Institutional
Merr Lynch Phoenix "A"
Merriman - Flexible Bond
MetLife - Cap Apprec "A"
MFS - Emerging Growth "B"
MIM Stock Appreciation
Money Market Trust
Montgomery Small Cap
Mutual Series - Beacon
Mutual Series - Qualfied
Mutual Series - Shares
Neuberger - Guardian
Neuberger - Ltd Maturity

Neuberger - Manhattan
Neuberger - Municipal
Neuberger - Partners
Nicholas
Nicholas Income
Nicholas Limited Edition
Northeast Investors Trust
Norwest Cash Investment
Oakmark
Oberweis Emerging Growth
One Group Inter Tx-Fr Fid
One Group Ltd Vol Bnd Fid
One Group Small Co Gr Fid
Oppenh - Champ Hi-Yld "A"
Oppenh - Discovery "A"
Oppenh - High Yield "A"
Oppenh - Main St In&Gr"A"
Oppenh - Stratgc Incm "A"
Oppenh - Total Return "A"
Pacific Horizon Shares Prime
Paragon - Value Growth
Parkstone Inst Inter Govt
Parkstone Inst Bond
Parkstone Inst Ltd Maty
Parkstone Inst Mich Muni
Parkstone Inst Muni Bond
Parkstone Inst Small Cap
Parnassus
PBHG Growth
PfamCo Small Cap Growth
Phoenix Capital Apprec
Phoenix High Yield "A"
Pilgrim High Yield
Pillar Short Term Invst "A"
Pimco - Low Duration
Pioneer Capital Growth
Pioneer Equity-Income
Piper Jaffray Emerg Grwth
Portico - Bond Immdex
Portico - Short Term Bond
Portico - Special Growth
Preferred Fixed Income
Preferred Short-Term Govt
Price - Balanced
Price - Capital Apprec
Price - Equity Income
Price - Growth & Income
Price - Growth Stock
Price - MD Tax-Free Bond
Price - New America
Price - New Horizons
Priice – NJ Tax-Free Bond
Price - Short Term Bond
Price - Small Cap Value
Price - Spectrum Growth
Price - Spectrum Income

Price - Tax-Free Hi Yield
Princor Emerging Growth
Prudential Equity "A"
Prudential Equity "B"
Prudential Gov Secs Inter
Prudential Growth Opp "A"
Prudential High Yield "A"
Putnam Diversif Incme "A"
Putnam Dividend Inc (PDI)
Putnam High Yield "A"
Putnam High Yld Advtg "A"
Putnam Income "A"
Putnam New Opporntys "A"
Putnam Penn Tax-Ex "A"
Putnam Voyager "A"
Quest For Value Cap (KFV)
Quest For Value Opportnty
Regis - Sirach Specl Eqty
Reich & Tang Equity
Rochester Municipal
Royce - Equity Income
Royce Value Trust (RVT)
Safeco Equity
SBSF Convertible
SBSF Fund
Schafer Value
Schroder - Capitl US Eqty
Schwab US Govt Shrt-Inter
Scudder Capital Growth
Scudder Growth & Income
Scudder Medium Tax-Free
Scudder Short Term Bond
SEI Capital Appreciation
Selected American Shares
Seligman Frontier "A"
Sentry
Sequoia
Sierra Emerging Grwth "A"
SIT - Tax-Free
SIT - US Govt Secs
Skyline Special Equities
Smith Barney Icm Retrn"A"
Smith Bny Sh A - Fund Val
Smith Bny Sh B - High Icm
Sound Shore
Southeastn Asst Mgt Value
State Farm Balanced
State Farm Growth
Stein Roe Income
Stein Roe Intermed Bond
Stein Roe Managed Muni
Stein Roe Prime Equities
Stein Roe Special
Strong Advantage
Strong Common Stock
Strong Discovery

Strong Government Secs
Strong Money Market
Strong Municipal Bond
Strong Municipal MM
Strong Opportunity
Strong Short Term Bond
Third Avenue Value
Thomson - Growth "B"
Thomson - Opportunity "A"
Thomson - Opportunity "B"
Tri-Continental (TY)
20th Century Giftrust
20th Century Growth
20th Century Heritage Inv

20th Century Ultra
United Income
United Muni High Income
United Services Tax-Free
USAA Cornerstone
USAA Income
USAA Income Stock
USAA Money Market
USAA Tax-Exempt Intermed
USAA Tax Exempt MM
Value Line Cash
Vanguard - Asset Allocatn
Vanguard – Federal
Vanguard - High Yld Corp

Vanguard - Index 500
Vanguard - Index Extended
Vanguard - Indx Small Cap
Vanguard Muni Bond MM
Vanguard - Muni Intermed
Vanguard - Muni Limtd Trm
Vanguard - Preferred
Vanguard – Prime
Vanguard - Primecap
Vanguard - Quantitative
Vanguard - Short Trm Corp
Vanguard - Sht Trm Federl
Vanguard - Wellesley Incm
Vanguard - Wellington

Vanguard - Windsor
Vanguard - Windsor II
Venture - Muni Plus
Venture - New York Ventur
Vista Capital Growth "A"
Vista Growth & Income "A"
Warburg Pincus Emerg Grth
Warburg Pincus Fixed Incm
Warburg Pincus NY Muni
Westcore Midco Gwth Instl
Westcore Sht-Tm Gov Instl
William Blair Grth Shares
William Blair Income Shrs
Winthrop Focus Agg Growth
Woodward Opportunity Ret

Four Star Funds
★★★★

AARP Capital Growth
AARP GNMA
Active Assets Money–D.Wittr
Advest Advantage Special
Aetna Select Bond
AHA Balanced
AHA Ltd Mat Fixd Icme
Aim - Charter
Aim - International Eqty
Aim - Limited Mat Treas
Aim - Municipal Bond "A"
Alliance "A"
Ambassador Fid Inter Bond
Amer Adj Rate 1997 (CDJ)
American - Captl Icm Bldr
American - Europacific Gr
American - Growth Fd Amer
American - Invest Co Amer
American - New Perspectve
American - SmallCap Wrld
American Cap Corp Bnd "A"
American Cap Emrg Gth "B"
American Cap Hi Yield "A"
American Cap Muni Bd "A"
American Growth
American Perf Intermed Bd
AmSouth Bond
AmSouth Equity
AmSouth Limited Maturity
Amway
API Trust Growth
Babson Bond Short Term
Babson Growth
Babson Shadow Stock
Babson UMB Stock
Baron Asset
Bartlett Basic Value

Benham Adjust Rate Govt
Benham Equity Growth
Benham GNMA
Benham Income & Growth
Benham Target 1995
Benham Treasury Note
Calamos Growth and Income
Calvert First Govt. MM
Calvert Social Bond "A"
Calvert Tx-Fr Ltd Term"A"
Cash Equivalent Tx-Ex Pt
CG Cap Mkts Inter Fix-Icm
Chile (CH)
Clemente Global Grth(CLM)
C&S Realty Shares
Colonial High Yield "A"
Common Sense Muni Bond
Connecticut Mut - Tot Ret
Daily Cash Accumulation
Daily Tax-Free – Class A
Dean Witter Americn Value
Dean Witter Pacific Grwth
Dean Witter Shrt US Treas
Delaware Delchester "A"
Dodge & Cox Income
Dreyfus Appreciation
Dreyfus Calif Tax-Exempt
Dreyfus General Muni Bond
Dreyfus Institutional MM
Dreyfus New York Tax-Ex
Dreyfus Peoples Index
Dreyfus S&P MidCap Index
Dreyfus Prem MA Muni "A"
Dreyfus Prem PA Muni "A"
Dreyfus Prem TX Muni "A"
Dreyfus Stratgc Growth
Dreyfus Worldwide Dollar

Eaton Van Mar - Fla Ltd
Eaton Van Mar - NY Ltd
Eaton Van Mar - Penn Ltd
Eaton Van Trad - Gvt Oblg
Eaton Van Trad - Muni Bnd
Enterprise Cap Apprec
Enterprise Growth
Enterprise High Yld Bond
Evergreen Amer Retirement
Evergreen Fund
Excelsior Incm Shrs (EIS)
Feder Exchange
Feder High Yield Trust
Feder Interm Govt Inst
Feder Max-Cap
Feder Tax-Free
Feder Trust US Treasury
Feder Stock Trust
Fidel Adv Strtgc Oppor"A"
Fidelity Daily Income
Fidelity Emerging Growth
Fidelity GNMA
Fidelity High Yield Tx-Fr
Fidelity Investment Grade
Fidelity Market Index
Fidelity MI Tax-Fr Hi Yld
Fidelity Municipal Bond
Fidelity Real Estate Inv
Fidelity Select Automotve
Fidelity Select Chemicals
Fidelity Select Finl Svcs
Fidelity Select Food&Agri
Fidelity Select Home Fin
Fidelity Select Leisure
Fidelity Select Multimeda
Fidelity Select Reg Banks
Fidelity Select Retailing

Fidelity Select Telecom
Fidelity Select Transport
Fidelity Spartan GNMA
Fidelity Spartan Muni Incme
Fidelity Spartan Sht Int Mun
Fidelity U.S. Equity Index
Fidelity Spartan US Govt.
Fidelity Spartan US Treasury
Fidelity Utilities Income
Fidelity Worldwide
First Financial (FF)
First Union Fixed Inc "B"
First Union Value "B"
Flag - Interm Income "A"
Flag - Telephone Inc "A"
Fortis High Yield
Fortress Adj Rate US Govt
Founders Worldwide Growth
Franklin Age
Franklin California Growth
Franklin Calif Tax-Free
Franklin CT Tax-Free Icm
Franklin Equity Income
Franklin Income
Franklin NC Tax-Free Icm
Franklin U.S. Government
Gabelli Convertible Secs
Galaxy Equity Value
GAM Pacific Basin
Gateway Index Plus
Gemini II - Capital (GMI)
Gradison-McDon Govt Incme
GT Global Emrg Mkts "A"
GT Global Telecomm "A"
Hanifen Colorado
Harbor - International
Hatteras Incme Secs (HAT)

Hatteras Incme Secs (HAT)
Heritage Captl Apprection
HighMark Income Equity
Horace Mann Growth
Hummer Growth
IAI - Government
IAI - Growth & Income
IAI - Reserve
Idex II Growth "A"
IDS Extra Income
IDS Growth
IDS Mutual
IDS Strategy Equity
Invesco - Financial Svcs
Invesco - Growth
Invesco - Leisure
Invesco - Total Return
Inv Series High Qual Stk
Janus Flexible Income
Janus Worldwide
John Hancock Ltd Govt "A"
John Hancock Strat Icm"A"
John Hancock Tax-Exempt
Kemper "A" - Adj U.S. Gvt
Kemper "A" - Calif Tax-Fr
Kemper "A" - Fla Tax-Free
Kemper "A" - Icm & Cap Pr
Kemper "A" - Shrt-Int Gvt
Kemper "A" - Small Cap Eq
Kemper "A" - TX Tax-Free
Kemper "B" - High Yield
Kemper "B" - Short-Interm. Govt
Kemper Government
Kemper Intermed Govt(KGT)
Kemper Money Market
Keystone Am Capitl Prsv I
Keystone Custodian S-4
Laurel Cap Apprec Invstr
Laurel Trust Stock Shares
Legg Mason Cash Reserve
Legg Mason Total Return
Lexington GNMA
Lexington Growth & Income
Lexington Worldwide Emerg
Liberty Amer Leaders "A"
Liberty Fin - US Govt Sec
Lindner Fund
Loomis Sayles Grwth & Icm
Lord, Abbett Equity 1990
Mackenzie Adj Gvt Secs"A"
Mackenzie Ivy Intl "A"
Managers Capital Apprec
Managers Income Equity
MAS Select Fixed Income
Merr Lynch Basic Val "A"
Merr Lynch CMA Money

Merr Lynch Developing Cap
Merr Lynch Intermed "A"
Merr Lynch Ready Assets
Merr Lynch Retirement
Merr Lynch Technology "A"
Merr Lynch Technology "B"
MFS - Arkansas Muni "A"
MFS - Bond "A"
MFS - Muni High Inc "A"
MFS - Research "A"
MFS - Value "A"
Montgomery Emerg Markets
Morgn Grenfell SmlCp(MGC)
M.S.B.
Mutual Benefit
Nations Sht-Int Gvt Inv "A"
Neuberger - Genesis
Neuberger - Select Sectrs
Neuberger - Ultra Shrt Bd
New England Adj US Gvt"A"
New England Bond Icm "A"
New England Intl Eqty "A"
New England Ltd US Gvt"A"
No Amer Global Growth "C"
No Amer Growth "C"
Northeast Investors Grwth
Nuveen Municipal Bond
Nuveen Tax-Free NY Value
Olympic Equity Income
One Group Discip Val Fid
One Group Income Bond Fid
One Group Income Eq Fid
Oppenh – Govt Secs "A"
Overland Calif Tax-Fr "A"
Pacific Horizon Aggr Grth
Pacifica Asset Preservatn
Pacifica Balanced
Pacifica Equity Value
Paine Webber Cash
Paine Webber Growth "A"
Paine Webber High Icm "A"
Paine Webber High Icm "B"
Paine Webber Reg Fin Gr "A"
Paine Webber Reg Fin Gr "B"
Paine Webber RMA MM
Paine Webber RMA Tx-Fr
Paragon - Gulf South Grth
Parkstone Inst Equity
Parkstone Inst HI Icm Eq
PfamCo Diversified Low PE
PfamCo Managed Bnd &Incm
Phoenix Cal Tax-Exempt
Phoenix Income & Grwth"A"
Pilgrim Regl BnkShrs(PBS)
Pioneer Bond
Pioneer Three

Piper Jaffray Value
Portico - Equity Index
Preferred Growth
Price - Adj Rate US Govt
Price - GNMA
Price - High Yield
Price - Intl Stock
Price - New Asia
Price - New Era
Price - New Income
Price - OTC
Price - Tx-Fr Short Inter
Primary Income
Princor Growth
Prudential Adj Rate "A"
Prudential Command Money
Prudential Eqty Incm "B"
Prudential Globl Util "A"
Prudential Nicholas "A"
Putnam Global Growth "B"
Putnam Grwth & Income "A"
Putnam Muni Income "A"
Putnam OTC Emer Grth "A"
Putnam Premier Incm (PPT)
Putnam Tx-Fr High Yld "B"
Putnam Vista "A"
Quest For Value Gth & Icm
Quest For Value Small Cap
Regis - DSI Discipl Value
Regis - DSI Ltd Maturity
Riverside Value Equity
Rodney Square Growth
Royce - Penn Mutual
Royce - Value
Safeco Growth
Safeco Income
Salomon Bros (SBF)
Salomon Bros - Investors
Salomon Bros - Opportunty
Schwab 1000
Scudder Global
Scudder Global Small Co
Scudder Income
Scudder International
Scudder Managed Cash
Scudder Managed Muni Bnds
Scudder Mass Tax-Free
Scudder New Asia (SAF)
Security Equity
SEI Equity Income
SEI S&P 500 Equity Index
Seligman Common Stock "A"
Seligman High Yld Bond A
Seven Seas Short Trm Govt
Sierra Sht Trm Glbl "A"
SIT - Growth

SIT - Intl Growth
Smith Bny Sh A - Agg Grth
Smith Bny Sh A - Apprec
Smith Bny Sh Daily Div.
Smith Bny Sh B - Dvsf Icm
Smith Bny Sh Government
Smith Bny Sh B - Prem Tot
Society Diversified Stock
Society Limited Term Icm
Society U.S. Govt Income
SoGen International
Southeastrn Thr&Bnk(STBF)
Stagecoach Corp Stock
State Farm Muni
State St Resch Invst "C"
Stein Roe Capital Opporty
Stein Roe Stock
Stein Roe Total Return
Stratton Growth
Strong International
Strong Short Term Muni
Strong Total Return
SunAmerica - High Icm "B"
Templeton American Trust
Templeton Developing Mkts
Templeton Emrg Mkts (EMF)
Templeton Foreign
Templeton Global Opportun
Templeton Growth
Templeton World
Thomson - Equity Incm "A"
Transamer - Emg Grth "B"
T. Rowe Tax-Exempt
20th Century Balanced Inv
20th Century Intl Equity
20th Century Tax-Ex Inter
20th Century US Gvt Sh-Tr
20th Century Vista
United High Income II
United New Concepts
United Retirement Shares
USAA Growth
USAA Tax-Exempt Long Term
USAA Tax-Exempt Shrt Term
UST Master Equity
UST Master Tax-Exempt
Value Line Aggressive Icm
Value Line Convertible
Value Line Fund
Value Line Leveraged Grth
Value Line Tax-Ex Hi Yld
Value Line U.S. Govt
Vanguard - Convertible
Vanguard - Equity Income
Vanguard - Explorer
Vanguard - GNMA

Vanguard - Morgan Growth
Vanguard - Muni High Yld
Vanguard - Muni Shrt Term
Vanguard - NJ Ins Tx-Free
Vanguard - OH Ins Tx-Fr
Vanguard - PA Ins Lng Trm

Vanguard - Star
Vanguard - Total Bond Idx
Vanguard - Trustees U.S.
Vanguard - U.S. Growth
Vanguard - U.S. Treasury
Vanguard - VSP Health

Vista Bond
Warburg Pincus Cap Apprec
Warburg Pincus Intl Eqty
Weiss Peck Greer Gr & Icm
Woodward Intermed Bnd Ret
Woodward Money Market

World - Newport Tiger
Wright Near Term Bond
Wright Quality Core Eqtys
Zweig Appreciation "A"
Zweig Government
Zweig Strategy "A"

Three Star Funds
★★★

AARP Insurd Tax-Free Bond
Advest Advantage Growth
Aetna Select Fund
Aim - Weingarten Equity
Alex Brown Prime
Alliance Corp Bond "A"
Alliance Multi-Mkt Income
Alliance New Europe "A"
Alliance Technology "A"
Alliance World Incme Tr
Allmerica Securities(ALM)
American - Amcap
American - American Mutl
American - Balanced
American - Tax-Exempt Bnd
American - US Govt Secs
American - Washington Mut
American Cap Conv (ACS)
American Cap Enterprs "A"
American Cap Eqty Icm "A"
American Cap Fed Mtg "A"
American Cap Gr & Icm "A"
AmSouth Balanced
Arch Growth & Income Eqty
ASA (ASA)
Asia Pacific (APB)
Atlas National Muni "A"
Babson Bond Long Term
Baird Capital Development
Baker Fentress (BKF)
Bancroft Convertible(BCV)
Bartlett Value Intl
Benham Cal Tx-Fr Long Trm
Benham Government Agency
Benham European Govt Bond
Benham Natl Tax-Free Long
Benham Target 2000
Benham Target 2005
Benham Target 2010
Benham Target 2015
Benham Target 2020
Brazil Fund (BZF)
Brazilian Equity (BZL)
Burnham "A"
Calamos Convertible

Calvert Ariel Growth
Capstone - Govt Income
Cardinal Govt Obligations
Cash Accumulation National
Centennial Government
Centennial Money Market
Century Shares Trust
Circle Income Shrs (CINS)
Colonial Glbl Equity "B"
Colonial Grwth Shares "A"
Colonial Grwth Shares "B"
Colonial MA Tx-Ex "A"
Colonial Tax-Exempt "A"
Colonial US Govt "A"
Composite Income
Composite Northwest 50"A"
Copley
CoreFund Equity Index "A"
Cowen Opportunity "A"
Current Income Shrs (CUR)
Dean Witter Active Asset
Dean Witter Dividend Grth
Dean Witter Liquid Asset
Dean Witter Premier Incme
Dean Witter Strategist
Dean Witter Tax-Exempt
Dean Witter TCW Core Eqty
Dean Witter Value-Added
Delaware DelCap
Delaware Treas Intermed "A"
Dreyfus A Bonds Plus
Dreyfus Fund
Dreyfus Grth & Icm (Conv)
Dreyfus Liquid Assets
Dreyfus Money Market
Dreyfus 100% US Treasury
Dreyfus Prem Capital Grth
Dreyfus Prem Glbl Inv "A"
Dreyfus Prem NY Muni "A"
Dreyfus Stratgc Glb Gr LP
Dreyfus Stratgc Income
Dreyfus Third Century
Dreyfus US Treas Intermed
Eaton Van Mar - Cal Ltd
Eaton Van Mar - High Incm

EBI Equity
EBI Flex
1838 Bond-Deb Trdg (BDF)
Emerging Mexico (MEF)
Evergreen Total Return
Fairmont
FBL Growth
Feder GNMA Trust Inst
Feder Growth Trust
Feder Short Term Muni
Fidel Adv Glb Resource"A"
Fidel Adv Hi Icm Muni "A"
Fidelity CA Tax-Fr Hi Yld
Fidelity Govt Securities
Fidelity Intl Grth & Incm
Fidelity NY Tax-Fr Hi Yld
Fidelity Overseas
Fidelity Pacific Basin
Fidelity Select Biotech
Fidelity Select Brokerage
Fidelity Select Computers
Fidelity Select Construct
Fidelity Select Devel Com
Fidelity Select Electrncs
Fidelity Select Health
Fidelity Select Indst Mat
Fidelity Select Insurance
Fidelity Select Med Deliv
Fidelity Select Software
Fidelity Select Technolog
Fidelity Select Utilities
Fidelity Short Term World
Fidel Spartan Govt Income
Fidel US Govt. Reserve
Fiduciary Capital Growth
First Investors Income
First Philippine (FPF)
Flagship OH Dbl Tx-Ex "A"
Fort Dearborn Income(FTD)
Fortis Capital
Fortis Growth
Fortress Utility
Franklin Adj US Govt Secs
Franklin Premier Return
Franklin Mgd Corp Qualif

Fundtrust Aggressive Grth
Fundtrust Growth
Fundtrust Growth & Income
Galaxy II Small Co Index
Galaxy II US Treas Index
Galaxy Intermediate Bond
GAM International
Germany (GER)
GIT Equity Special Growth
GIT Income Maximum
Goldman Sachs Globl Incm
GT Global Latin Am Gr "A"
GT Global New Pacif Gr"A"
Harbor - Value
Heartland U.S. Govt Secs
Heritage Income Growth
HT Insight Equity
Hyperion Short Duratn Gvt
Hyperion Sht Durtn Gvt II
IAI - Bond
IAI - Emerging Growth
IAI - International
Idex
Idex 3
Idex II Flexible Inc "A"
IDS Blue Chip Advantage
IDS Bond
IDS Equity Plus
IDS High Yield Tax-Exempt
Independ Square Inc(ISIS)
India Growth (IGF)
Inefficient Market (IMF)
Invesco - Health Sciences
Invesco - Pacific Basin
Invesco - Tax-Fr Long Trm
Invesco - Technology
Invesco - Utilities
Janus Growth & Income
Janus Intermediate Govt
John Han Sovergn Invstr "A"
John Hancock Invstrs(JHI)
John Hancock N.Y. Tax-Ex
Kemper "A" - Divsf Income
Kemper "A" - U.S. Govt
Kemper "B" - Divsf Income

Kemper "B" - Total Return
Keystone Am Cap Prs II"B"
Keystone Am Hart Emg Gr "A"
Keystone Custodian B-2
Keystone Custodian K-2
Korea (KF)
Korean Investment (KIF)
Latin America Eqty (LAQ)
Latin Amer Invstmnt (LAM)
Laurel Intmed Govt Invstr
Legg Mason Investmt Grade
Legg Mason Value Trust
Lexington Global
Lexington Money Market
Liberty Fund For US Gv "A"
Liberty Mun Secs "A"
Lincoln Natl Income (LND)
Lord, Abbett Affiliated
Lord, Abbett Fundamtl Val
Lord, Abbett Value Apprec
Lutheran Brother Income
MacKenzie NY Muni "A"
Mackenzie Ivy Gr & Icm"A"
MainStay - Total Return
Malaysia (MF)
Matrix Growth
Mentor Growth
Merr Lynch Adj Rate "A"
Merr Lynch Adj Rate "B"
Merr Lynch Capital "A"
Merr Lynch CMA Govt.
Merr Lynch CMA T-E
Merr Lynch Dragon "A"
Merr Lynch Dragon "B"
Merr Lynch Fed Secs "A"
Merr Lynch Latin Amer "A"
Merr Lynch Latin Amer "B"
Merr Lynch Muni Ltd "A"
Merr Lynch Pacific "A"
Merr Lynch Phoenix "B"
Merriman - Asset Allocatn
MetLife - Eqty Invstmt "A"
MetLife - Equity Incm "A"
MetLife - High Income "A"
MetLife - Mgd Assets "A"
Mexico (MXF)
Mexico Equity & Inc (MXE)
MFS - Calif Muni Bond "A"
MFS - Capital Growth "B"
MFS - Govt Mkts Inc (MGF)
MFS - High Income "A"
MFS - Inv Grth Stock "A"
MFS - Invstrs Tr "A"(MIT)
MFS - Multi-Mkt Inc (MMT)
MFS - Municipal Bond "A"
MFS - Muni Income Tr(MFM)

MFS - N.C. Muni Bond "A"
MFS - Total Return "A"
Monetta
Monitor Inc Equity Trust
Nations Eqty Incm Inv "A"
Nations Value Inv "A"
Nationwide Fund
Nationwide Growth
New England Growth "A"
New England TaxExempt"A"
New England Value "A"
Nomura Pacific Basin
No Amer Asset Alloc "C"
Nuveen Fla Qlty Inc (NUF)
Nuveen Mich Qlty Inc(NUM)
Nuveen PA Qlty Icm (NUP)
One Group Eqty Index Fid
Oppenh - Global "A"
Oppenh - Glbl Gth & Icm A
Oppenh - Invest Grade "A"
Oppenh - Ltd Term Gov "A"
Oppenh – Money Market
Oppenh - NY Tax-Ex "A"
Oppenh - Tax-Free "A"
Oppenh - Value Stock "A"
Overland Asset Alloc "A"
Overland Var Rate Gvt "A"
Pacific Horiz. Shrs. Treas.
Paine Webber Cap App "A"
Paine Webber NY Tx-Fr "A"
Paine Webber RMA US Gv.
Paragon - Value Eqty Incm
Parkstone Inst Balanced
Pasadena Growth "A"
PfamCo Equity Income
Phoenix Balanced
Phoenix Eqty Opportunity
Phoenix Growth
Phoenix Total Return
Pilgrim GNMA
Pillar Eqty Aggr Grth "A"
Pillar Equity Income "A"
Pimco - Total Return
Pioneer Tax-Free Income
Piper Jaffray Sector Perf
Portico - Growth & Income
Preferred International
Preferred Value
Price - Foreign Equity
Price - Intl Bond
Price - Intl Discovery
Price - Japan
Price - Science & Tech
Price - Tax-Free Income
Primary U.S. Government
Princor Bond

Princor Managed
Prudential BlackRk Gvt "A"
Prudential Command Govt.
Prudential Glbl Genes "B"
Prudential Growth Opp "B"
Prudential High Yield "B"
Prudential MoneyMart
Prudential Utility "B"
Putnam Adj U.S. Govt "A"
Putnam Adj U.S. Govt "B"
Putnam Conv Icme & Gr "A"
Putnam Europe Growth "A"
Putnam Global Growth "A"
Putnam Investors "A"
Putnam Master Incm (PMT)
Putnam Tx-Fr Health (PMH)
Putnam U.S. Govt Icm "A"
Putnam Voyager "B"
Quest For Value Fund
Quest For Value Inc (KFVP)
Quest For Value NY Tax-Ex
Regis - C&B Balanced
Regis - C&B Equity
Rightime
Robertson Stephens Emg Gr
Rochester Bond For Growth
Safeco Municipal Bond
Schroder - Intl Equity
Schwab Govt. Money Fund
Schwab Money Market
Scudder Calif Tax-Free
Scudder Cash Investment
Scudder Development
Scudder GNMA
Scudder Intl Bond
Scudder New York Tax-Free
Scudder Ohio Tax-Free
Scudder Short Trm Glb Icm
Scudder Zero Coupon 2000
Seafirst IRA - Asset Aloc
Seafirst IRA - Blue Chip
Selected Special Shares
Selected U.S. Government
Seligman Capital "A"
Seligman Communicatns "A"
Seligman Income "A"
Seligman Qlty Muni (SQF)
Seligman Tx-Ex Mich "A"
Seligman Tx-Ex Minn "A"
Sentinel Bond
Sentinel Common Stock
Sentinel Govt Securities
Short Term Money Mkt. A
Sierra Grwth & Incm "A"
Smith Barney Cash Portf.
Smith Barney Intl "A"

Smith Barney US Govt "A"
Smith Bny Sh Pr Ret 1996
Smith Bny Sh A - NY Muni
Smith Bny Sh A - Telcm Gr
Stagecoach Asset Allocatn
Stagecoach GNMA
State Bond - Diversified
State St Resch Growth "C"
Stein Roe Cash Resrvs.
Stein Roe Govt Income
Strong Income
SunAmerica - US Govt "B"
T. Rowe Price Prime Resv.
Taiwan (TWN)
Templeton Global Inc(GIM)
Templeton Real Estate
Templeton Smaller Cos Gth
Thai Capital (TC)
Thai Fund (TTF)
Thomson - Equity Incm "B"
Thomson - Intl "A"
Thomson - Prec Metals "A"
Transamerica Cash Resv.
20th Century Select
United Intl Growth
United Kingdom (UKM)
Unitd Svcs Income
USAA Balanced
USAA GNMA
USAA International
UST Master Inter Tax-Ex
Value Line Income
Van Kampen Muni Icm "A"
Vanguard - CA Ins Lng Trm
Vanguard - Index Totl Stk
Vanguard - Intl Growth
Vanguard - Long Term Corp
Vanguard - Muni Insrd Lng
Vanguard - Muni Long Term
Vanguard - NY Ins Tax-Fr
Vanguard - VSP Energy
Venture - RPF Growth
Vista Equity
Volumetric
Weiss Peck Greer Govt
Weiss Peck Greer Tudor
Westwood Equity Institnal
William Penn - Penn Sqre
Winthrop Focus Grth & Icm
Woodward Growth Value Ret
Wright Intl Blue Chip
Wright Junior Blue Chip
Wright Selected Blue Chip

Two Star Funds
★★

AAL Capital Growth
AARP High Quality Bond
ACM Mangd Multi-Mkt (MMF)
Active Assets Govt.–D. Witter
Addison Capital
Advest Advantage Income
Aim - Balanced "A"
Aim - Government Secs "A"
Aim - Income "A"
Alex Brown Treasury
Alliance Balanced Shrs"A"
Alliance Capital Reserve
Alliance Counterpoint "A"
Alliance Growth & Icm "A"
Alliance Intl "A"
Alliance Money Reserves
Alliance Muni Icm CA "A"
Alliance ShTr Mlti-Mkt A
Alliance ShTr Mlti-Mkt B
Allmon Trust (GSO)
Ambassador Fid Growth
Ambassador Fid Sm Co Grth
America's All Seasn(FUND)
American - Income Fd Amer
American - Inter Bd Fd Am
American - Tax-Exempt CA
American Cap Bond (ACB)
American Cap Comstock "A"
American Cap Glbl Gov "A"
American Cap Glbl Eq "A"
American Cap Glbl Eq "B"
American Cap Govt Secs A
American Cap Govt Secs B
American Cap Harbor "A"
American Cap Tax-Ex Ins A
American National Growth
American National Income
American National Triflex
American Perf Bond
Analytic Optioned Equity
Arch Govt & Corp Bond
Argentina (AF)
Armstrong Associates
ASM Fund
Atlanta Growth
Atlas Growth & Income "A"
Atlas US Gvt & Mtg Sec"A"
Babson Tax-Free Long Term
Baird Blue Chip
Bascom Hill Balanced
BJB Global Income "A"
Blanchard Global Growth
Blanchard Short Term Glbl

Blue Chip Value (BLU)
Bull & Bear Global Income
Bull & Bear Muni Income
Bull & Bear US Gov Secs
Bull & Bear US Overseas
Calamos Growth
Calvert Ariel Apprec "A"
Calvert Social Mgd Growth
Cambridge Capitl Gwth "B"
Cambridge Govt Income "B"
Capital Preservation
Capstone - Medical Resrch
Cardinal
Cash Equivalent
Cash Equivalent Government
Cash Management Trust
CG Cap Mkts Lrg Cap Value
C&S Realty Income (RIF)
Colonial CA Tax-Ex "A"
Colonial Fund "A"
Colonial Income "A"
Colonial MI Tax-Ex "A"
Colonial Natural Resc "A"
Colonial Natural Resc "B"
Colonial Tax-Exempt "B"
Colonial NY Tx-Ex "A"
Colonial OH Tx-Ex "A"
Colonial Tax-Ex Insrd "A"
Columbia Daily Income
Columbia Fixed Income
Common Sense Growth
Composite Bond & Stock "A"
Composite Growth "A"
Composite Tax-Ex Bond "A"
Convert Holdings Cap(CNV)
Cowen Income & Growth "A"
Dean Witter Develp Growth
Dean Witter Glob Sht Incm
Dean Witter Intermed Icm
Dean Witter Managed Asset
Dean Witter US Government
Dean Witter Utilities
Dean Witter Worldwide Inv
Delaware Decatur Income
Delaware Decatur Tot Ret
Delaware Fund
Dimensional - Continental
Dreyfus Grwth Opportunity
Dreyfus Government (MMI)
Dreyfus Municipal MMF
Dreyfus Stratgc Invst "A"
Dupree Kentucky Tax-Free
Eaton Van Trad - Invstrs

Eaton Van Trad - Stock
Enterprise Govt Secs
Enterprise Growth & Incm
Enterprise Tax-Ex Income
Excel Midas Gold Shares
Feder Stock & Bond "A"
Feder U.S. Govt Bond Inst
Fidel Adv Overseas "A"
Fidelity Canada
Fidelity Europe
Fidelity Select Ind Equip
Fidelity Select Paper
Fidelity Select Prec Metl
Fst Australia Prime (FAX)
First Investors Blue Chip
First Investors Cash
First Investors Global
First Investors High Yld
First Investors Ins Tx-Ex
First Invest NY Ins Tx-Fr
Flagship MI Trpl Tx-Ex"A"
Flex-Funds Growth
Fontaine Capital Apprec
Fortis Asset Allocation
Fortis Fiduciary
Fortis U.S. Government
Founders Govt Securities
FPA - Perennial
Franklin Dyna-Tech
Franklin Growth
Frnkln-Templ - Hard Crncy
Franklin Mgd Rising Divid
Freedom Cash
Freedom Government
Gabelli Equity Trust(GAB)
Galaxy Equity Growth
Galaxy High Quality Bond
GIT Tax-Free National
Global Govt Plus (GOV)
Goldman Sachs Select Eqty
Gradison-McDonald US Govt
GT Global Grth & Incm "A"
GT Global Intl Grth "A"
GT Global Japan Grth "A"
GT Global Strtgc Incm "A"
GT Global Wldwde Grth "A"
H & Q Healthcare Inv(HQH)
Harbor - Growth
Hi Inc Advntg Tr II (YLT)
HighMark Bond
Hilliard-Lyons Government
IAA Trust Growth
IAI - Balanced

IDS Discovery
IDS Federal Income
IDS Global Bond
IDS Global Growth
IDS International
IDS Selective
IDS Strategy Aggressive
IDS Strategy Short Term
INA Investment Secs (IIS)
Istel
Japan
Jefferson-Pilot Captl App
Jefferson-Pilot Inv-Gr Bd
John Han Freed Global "B"
John Han Freed Pac-Bas"A"
John Han Sovergn Ach "B"
John Hancock Growth "A"
John Hancock Inc Sec(JHS)
John Hancock ST Strat "B"
Kemper "A" - Growth
Kemper "A" - International
Kemper "A" - Retirmnt II
Kemper "A" - Retirmnt III
Kemper "A" - Total Return
Kemper "B" - US Mortgage
Keystone Am Eqty Incm "A"
Keystone Am Govt Secs "A"
Keystone Am Hart Grth "A"
Keystone Am PA Tax-Fr "A"
Keystone Custodian B-1
Keystone Custodian B-4
Keystone Custodian K-1
Keystone Custodian S-3
Keystone Precious Metals
Kidder Peabody Cash Res.
Kidder Peabody Premium
Landmark - Balanced
Laurel Cash Mgmt Invst.
Leeb Personal Finance
Liberty All-Star Eqty(USA)
Liberty Intl Equity "A"
Liberty Utility "A"
Loomis Sayles US Gvt Secs
Lord, Abbett Tax-Free Ntl
Lord, Abbett Tax-Free NJ
Lord, Abbett Tax-Free NY
Mackenzie Fixed Icm "A"
Mackenzie Ivy Growth "A"
MainStay - Government
Managers Bond Fund
Managers Short GovIncome
MAS Emerging Growth
Mathers

Merr Lynch Balanced "B"
Merr Lynch Corp Inv Gr"A"
Merr Lynch Corp Inv Gr "B"
Merr Lynch EuroFund "B"
Merr Lynch Glbl Hldg "A"
Merr Lynch Globl Conv "B"
Merr Lynch Glbl Util "A"
Merr Lynch Glbl Util "B"
Merr Lynch Muni Insrd "A"
Merr Lynch Muni Natl "A"
Merr Lynch Sht Glb Icm "B"
Merr Lynch World Incm "B"
Merriman - Capital Apprec
Merriman - Growth & Incme
MetLife - Govt Secs "A"
MetLife - Tax Exempt "A"
MFS - GA Muni Bond "A"
MFS - Govt Securities "A"
MFS - Strategic Icm "A"
MFS - World Equity "B"
MFS - World Govts "A"
MFS - World Total Ret "A"
Midwest - Lesh Fin Util A
MIMLIC Asset Allocation
MIMLIC Investors Fund I
Monitor Growth Trust
Montgomery St. Incm (MTS)
National Industries
Nations VA Inter Inv "A"
Nationwide Money Market
New England Balanced "A"
New Eng Cash Mgmt Trst MM
New England Grth Opp "A"
Nuveen Calif Insrd Value
Nuveen Calif Tx-Fr Value
Nuveen Muni Value (NUV)
Nuveen NJ Qlty Incm (NUJ)
Nuveen Muni Value (NUV)
Nuveen NJ Qlty Incm (NUJ)
One Group Lrg Co Val Fid
Oppenh - Asset Allocation
Oppenh - Equity Incm "A"
Oppenh - Fund "A"
Oppenh - Gold & Specl Min
Oppenh - Special "A"
Overland Muni Income "A"
Pacific Amer Inc Shr(PAI)
Pacific Horizon US Govt.

Pacifica Govt Income
Paine Webber Asset "B"
Paine Webber Blue Chip "A"
Paine Webber Gl Gr&Icm"A"
Paine Webber Glbl Icm "A"
Paine Webber Inv Grade"A"
Paine Webber Natl Tx-Fr A
Patriot Prem Div I (PDF)
Patriot Prem Div II (PDT)
Patriot Selct Div Tr(DIV)
Pax World
Petrolm & Resources (PEO)
PfamCo Intl Equity
Philadelphia
Phoenix Convertible
Phoenix Stock
Pilgrim Magnacap
Pilgrim Sh Mlt-Mkt Icm II
Pillar Equity Growth "A"
Pillar Fixed Income "A"
Pioneer America Income
Pioneer Europe
Pioneer Fund
Pioneer Growth Shares
Pioneer II
Pioneer Income
Piper Jaffray Balanced
Piper Jaffray Pac Eur Gth
PNC Index Equity Inst
PNC Managed Icm Inst
Portico - Balanced
Preferred Asset Allctn
Price - Global Govt Bond
Primary Trend
Princ Presv Div Achievers
Princ Presv S&P 100 Plus
Princor Blue Chip
Princor Capitl Accumulatn
Prudential Flex Cnsrv "B"
Prudential Flex Strgy "B"
Prudential Global "A"
Prudential GNMA "B"
Prudential Gov. Sec. Trust
Prudential IcmVertble "A"
Prudential IcmVertble "B"
Prudential Tax-Free
Prudential Utility "A"
Putnam Calif Tx-Ex "A"

Putnam Corporate Asset Tr
Putnam Daily Dividend Trst A
Putnam Dividend Growth "A"
Putnam Equity Income "A"
Putnam Federal Income "A"
Putnam George "A"
Putnam Grwth & Income "B"
Putnam Health Sciences "A"
Putnam Managed Income "A"
Putnam NY Tax-Exempt "A"
Putnam Util Gr & Icm "A"
Quest For Value CA Tax-Ex
Quest For Value Glbl Eq
Quest For Value Natl TxEx
Quest For Value U.S. Govt
Rightime Blue Chip
Rightime Social Awareness
Safeco Northwest
Salomon Bros - Capital
Schwab Tax-Exempt MF
Scudder Tax-Free MF
Scudder US Treasury Money
Security Corp Bond
Seligman Growth "A"
Seligman Tax-Ex LA "A"
Seligman Tax-Ex MD "A"
Seligman Tax-Ex Mass "A"
Seligman Tax-Ex Ohio "A"
Seligman Tax-Ex Penn "A"
Sentinel Balanced
Sierra Tr Intl Gwth "A"
Sierra US Government "A"
Singapore (SGF)
SIT - Grth & Incm
Smith Barney Icm & Gr "A"
Smith Bny Sh A - Cal Muni
Smith Bny Sh B - Convrtbl
Smith Bny Sh B - Tax-Ex
Smith Bny Sh B - Utilties
Source Capital (SOR)
Stagecoach Grth & Income
Stagecoach U.S. Govt
State Bond - Common Stock
State St Resch Exchange
State St Resch Gvt Icm "A"
Stratton Monthly Dividend
Strong Investment
SunAmerica - Bal Asts "B"

SunAmerica - Fed Secs "B"
SunAmerica - Mid-Cap Gr A
SunAmerica - Sm Co Gr "B"
SunAmerica - TxEx Ins "A"
Swiss Helvetia (SWZ)
Thomson - Growth "A"
Thomson - Intl "B"
Thomson - Tax-Exempt "B"
Thomson - U.S. Govt "B"
Tower Capital Appreciatn
Transamer - Gth & Icm "A"
Transamer - Income (TAI)
T. Rowe Price US Treasury
United Accumulative
United Continental Income
United High Income
United Municipal Bond
United Vanguard
Unitd Svcs All Amer Equty
Unitd Svcs World Gold
Valley Forge
Van Eck - Intl Inv Gold
Van Kampen Grth & Icm "A"
Van Kampen Ins Tx-Fr "A"
Van Kampen Shrt Trm Glb A
Van Kampen Tx-Fr Hi Icm A
Vanguard - Eqty Idx Pacf
Vanguard - Trustees Intl
Vanguard - US Treas Long
Vanguard - VSP Gold
Venture - Income Plus
Venture - RPF Bond
Vestaur Securities (VES)
Voyageur Growth Stock
Warburg Pincus Glob Fx Incm
Warburg Pincus Inter Govt
Weiss Peck Greer Growth
Westcore Basic Val Instl
Westcore Equity Icm Instl
Westcore Long Term Bond
Westcore Modern Value Eq
William Penn - US Gov Sec
Winthrop Focus Growth
World - Vontobel EuroPac
Wright Govt Obligations
Wright Total Return Bond
Zweig Priorty Selectn "A"

One Star Funds

AAL Bond
ABT - Growth & Income
ABT - Utility Income
ACM Government Inc (ACG)
ACM Government Secs (GSF)
ACM Govt Spectrum (SI)
Aim - Growth "A"
Aim - Summit
Aim - Utilities "A"
Alger Income & Growth
Alliance Glb Envrnmt(AEF)
Alliance Globl Sm Cap "A"
Alliance Govt. Reserves
Alliance Insured Muni "A"
Alliance Mortgage Sec "A"
Alliance Mortgage Sec "B"
Alliance Mlt-Mkt Strtgy "B"
Alliance Muni Ins CA "A"
Alliance Municipal Trust
Alliance No Amer Govt "B"
Alliance Quasar "A"
Alliance US Government "A"
Amer Govt Term Trst (AGT)
America's Utility
American - Captl Wrld Bnd
American Cap Enterprs "B"
American Cap Glbl Gov "B"
American Cap Pace "A"
American Cap Pace "B"
American Cap Reserve
American Heritage
American Perf Equity
Anchor Cap Accumulation
Arch US Govt Secs
Austria (OST)
Beacon Hill Mutual
Benham Gold Equities Indx
Blanchard Precious Metals
Bruce
Bull & Bear Gold Investrs
Bull & Bear Special Eqtys
Calvert Income
Calvert Social Equity
Cambridge Growth "B"
Capital Preservation II
Capstone - Fund of the SW
Capstone - U.S. Trend
Cardinal Government
Centennial Tax-Exempt Tr
Central Fd of Canada(CEF)
Centurion Growth
CG Cap Mkts Muni Bond

Charter Blue Chip
CNA Income Shares (CNN)
Colonial CT Tax-Exempt "A"
Colonial Federal Secs "A"
Colonial Small Stock "A"
Colonial Stratgc Icme "A"
Colonial Utilities "A"
Colonial Utilities "B"
Common Sense Government
Common Sense Growth & Icm
Compass Capitl Growth
Composite U.S. Govt "A"
CoreFund Grth Equity "A"
Daily Passport Cash Trust
Dean Witter Calif Tax-Fr
Dean Witter Capital Grwth
Dean Witter Convertible
Dean Witter European
Dean Witter High Yield
Dean Witter Natrl Res Dev
Dean Witter NY Tax-Free
Dean Witter Prec Metals
Dean Witter Sears TF Dly
Dean Witter US Government
Dean Witter Worldwide Icm
Delaware Cash Reserves
Delaware U.S. Govt "A"
Dimensional - Japan
Dimensional - Utd Kngdom
Dreyfus Comstk Cap VI "A"
Dreyfus Edison Elec Index
Dreyfus Prem NC Muni "A"
Duff & Phelps Utilty(DNP)
Eagle Growth Shares
Eaton Van Mar - Cal Muni
Eaton Van Mar - Eqty Incm
Eaton Van Mar - Fla Tx-Fr
Eaton Van Mar - GA Tx-Fr
Eaton Van Mar - KY Tax-Fr
Eaton Van Mar - MD Tax-Fr
Eaton Van Mar - MA Tax-Fr
Eaton Van Mar - MN Tax-Fr
Eaton Van Mar - NC Tax-Fr
Eaton Van Mar - Natl Muni
Eaton Van Mar - NJ Tax-Fr
Eaton Van Mar - NY Tax-Fr
Eaton Van Mar - OH Tax-Fr
Eaton Van Mar - PA Tax-Fr
Eaton Van Mar - Shrt Glbl
Eaton Van Trad - Growth
Eaton Van Trad - Spl Eqty
Eaton Van Trad - Totl Ret

Emerald Equity "A"
Emerging Germany (FRG)
Engex (EGX)
Enterprise Intl Growth
Europe Fund (EF)
European Warrant (EWF)
Excel Value
Fidel Adv Govt Invstmt "A"
Fidelity Select Air Trans
Fidelity Select Amer Gold
Fidelity Select Consmr Pr
Fidelity Select Defense
Fidelity Select Energy
Fidelity Select Engy Svcs
Fidelity Select Envirnmtl
Fidel Spartan CA Hi Yield
Fidel Spartan Lng Trm Gvt
First Australia (IAF)
First Iberian (IBF)
First Investors Govt
First Investors Total Ret
Flag - Emerging Growth
Flag - International
Flag - Quality Growth
Flag - Tot Ret US Tres "A"
FMB Diversf Eqty Consumer
44 Wall Street Equity
France Growth (FRF)
Franklin Equity
Franklin Globl Govt Icm
Franklin Gold
Franklin Money
Franklin Utilities
Frnkln-Templ - Global Cur
Frnkln-Templ - Hi Icm Cur
Fund for Government Invstrs
Fundamental - Calif Muni
Fundamental - N.Y. Muni
Fundamental - U.S. Govt
Future Germany (FGF)
GAM Global
Gintel Erisa
Gintel Fund
GNA - U.S. Govt Secs "B"
Growth Fund of Spain(GSP)
GT Global Europe Grth "A"
GT Global Govt Incm "A"
GT Global Health Care "A"
GT Greater Europe (GTF)
Hampton Utilities Cap(HU)
Hi Inc Advantage Tr (YLD)
IDS Cash Management

IDS Precious Metals
IDS Progressive
IDS Strategy Income
IDS Strategy Worldwide Gr
IDS Tax-Exempt Bond
Indep Cap - Opportunities
Indep Cap - Totl Ret Grth
Indonesia (IF)
Intercapitl Inc Secs(ICB)
Invesco Cash Reserves
Invesco - Energy
Invesco - European
Invesco - Gold
Invesco - Intl Growth
Invesco - U.S. Govt Secs
Inv Series Capit Grth Inv
Investors Research
Irish Investment (IRL)
ISI Managed Muni Shares
ISI Total Return US Treas
Italy (ITA)
Jakarta Growth (JGF)
Japan OTC Equity (JOF)
John Han Freed Av & Tech
John Han Freed Envnmt "A"
John Han Freed Glb Tech"A"
John Han Freed Gold "B"
John Hancock Discovry "B"
Kemper "A" - Blue Chip
Kemper "A" - Envrnmtl Svc
Kemper "A" - Glbl Incomo
Kemper "A" - Shrt Trm Glb
Kemper "A" - Technology
Kemper "B" - Growth
Kemper "B" - Shrt Trm Glb
Keystone Am Australia "A"
Keystone Am FL Tax-Free "A"
Keystone Custodian S-1
Keystone International
Keystone Liquid Trust
Keystone Tax-Exempt
Keystone Tax-Free
Kidder Peab - Eqty Inc "A"
Landmark - Equity
Lexington Goldfund
Lexington Strategic Invst
Lexington Strategic Silvr
Liberty US Government
Liquid Capital
LMH
Lord, Abbett Devloping Gr
Lord, Abbett Global Eqty

Lord, Abbett Global Incme
Lord, Abbett Govt Secs
Lord, Abbett Tax-Free MO
Lord, Abbett Tax-Free WA
Lutheran Brotherhood
Mackenzie American "A"
Mackenzie Canada "A"
Mackenzie North American
MainStay - Global
MainStay - Natrl Res&Gold
Managers Intermed Mtg Sec
Merr Lynch Calif Muni "B"
Merr Lynch EuroFund "A"
Merr Lynch Fd Tomorrw "A"
Merr Lynch Fd Tomorrw "B"
Merr Lynch Glbl Rescs "B"
Merr Lynch Healthcare "A"
Merr Lynch Healthcare "B"
Merr Lynch NY Muni "B"
Merr Lynch Sht Glb Icm "A"
Merr Lynch Spcl Value "A"
Merr Lynch Strtgc Div "B"
MFS - FL Muni Bond "A"
MFS - Gold & Natrl Res "B"
MFS - Govt Mortgage "A"
MFS - Grth Opportntys "A"
MFS Money Market
Midwest - Inter Gvt Icm "A"
MIM Bond Income
MIM Stock Growth
MIM Stock Income
Monitrend Summation
Morgan Keegan Southern
Nationwide Bond
New Alternatives
New America High Inc(HYB)
New England Glbl Govt "A"
New England Govt Secs "A"
New Germany (GF)
New USA
Nicholas II
Norwest Govt Incm Inv "A"
Norwest ValuGrwth Stk "A"
Nuveen OH Qlty Incm (NUO)
Nuveen TX Qlty Incm (NTX)
Old Dominion Investors
One Group Blue Chp Eq Fid

Oppenh - Calif Tax-Ex "A"
Oppenh - Global Bio-Tech
Oppenh - Global Environmt
Oppenh - Target
Oppenh - Time
Overland US Govt Icm "A"
Pacific Horizon Cal Tx-Ex
Paine Webber Atlas "A"
Paine Webber Blue Chip "B"
Paine Webber Cal Tx-Fr "A"
Paine Webber Div Grth "A"
Paine Webber Eur Gr "A"
Paine Webber Glbl Engy "A"
Paine Webber Glbl Engy "B"
Paine Webber Inv Grade "B"
Paine Webber Mun Hi Icm"A"
Paine Webber Mun Hi Icm"B"
Paine Webber US Govt "A"
Paine Webber US Govt "B"
Pasadena Balanced Ret "A"
Pasadena Nifty Fifty "A"
Permanent Portfolio
Perritt Capital Growth
Phoenix International
Phoenix Worldwide Opps
Pilgrim Corp Utilities
Pilgrim Sh Mlt-Mkt Icm I
Pioneer Interest (MUO)
Piper Jaffray Govt Income
Piper Jaffray Instit Govt
Piper Jaffray Money Market
Portugal (PGF)
Price - European Stock
Price - US Treas. Long Term
Princ Presv Govt Portf
Princor Govt Secs Income
Progressive Value
Prospect St High Inc(PHY)
Prudent Speculator
Prudential Calif Muni "B"
Prudential Global "B"
Prudential Global Res "B"
Prudential Govt Plus "B"
Prudential Growth "B"
Prudential Intr Glb Icm "A"
Prudential Muni NY "B"
Prudential Natl Muni "B"

Prudential Sh Trm Glb "A"
Prudential U.S. Govt "B"
Putnam Amer Govt Icm "A"
Putnam Global Govt Icm "A"
Putnam Natural Resc "A"
Putnam Tax-Exempt Icm "A"
Putnam Tax-Free Ins "B"
Quantitative Bostn Fgn "O"
Quantitative Boston Gr&In
Quest Cash Res. Primary
Quest For Value Glbl Incm
Quest For Value Inv Qlty
Rainbow
Rea-Graham Balanced
Reserve Fund –Government
Reserve Fund – Primary
Reserve Interstate
Reynolds Blue Chip Growth
Riverside Fixed Income
ROC Taiwan (ROC)
Rodney Square Intl Equity
Rushmore Amer Gas Index
Scudder Gold
Scudder Mgd. Tax-Free
Scudder New Europe (NEF)
Security Growth & Income
Security Tax Exempt
Security Ultra
SEI Value
Seligman Cash Prime
Seligman Tax-Ex MO "A"
Seligman Tx-Ex Natl "A"
Seligman Tx-Ex NY "A"
Seligman US Govt Secs "A"
Sentinel Growth
Sentinel World
Sierra Growth
Smith Barney Glob Gvt "A"
Smith Barney Utility "A"
Smith Bny Sh A - Glbl Opp
Smith Bny Sh A - Mgd Govt
Smith Bny Sh A - Prec Met
Smith Bny Sh B - Glbl Bnd
Smith Bny Sh B - Gvt Secs
Smith Bny Sh B - Invst Gr
Smith Bny Sh B - Spc Eqty
Spain (SNF)

State St Resch Glb Engy"A"
Steadman American Indstry
Steadman Associated
Steadman Investment
Steadman Oceanographic
SunAmerica - Blue Chp "B"
TCW ConvertibleSecs(CVT)
Templeton Income
Thomson - Income "A"
Thomson - Prec Metals "B"
Thomson - Tax-Exempt "A"
Thomson - U.S. Govt "A"
Transamer - Glbl Rescs"B"
Transamer - Capital Gr"A"
Transamer - Govt Secs
Transamer - Invst Qual"A"
Turkish Investment (TKF)
20th Century Cash Reserve
United Bond
United Cash Management
United Gold & Government
United Govt Securities
United Science and Tech
Unitd Svcs Europn Income
Unitd Svcs Globl Resourcs
Unitd Svcs Gold Shares
Unitd Svcs Growth
Unitd Svcs Real Estate
United Svcs Treasury Cash
US Life Income (UIF)
USAA Aggressive Growth
USAA Gold
UST Master Long Trm TxEx
Value Line Special Situat
Van Eck - Gold Resources
Van Eck - World Income
Van Eck - World Trends
Van Kampen U.S. Govt "A"
Vanguard - Eqty Idx Eurpn
Vista Grth Fd Of Washngtn
Wall Street
Worldwide Value (VLU)
Yamaichi Global
Z-Seven (ZSEV)
Zweig (ZF)
Zweig Govt Securities "A"
Zweig Total Return (ZTR)

146